Archbishop Derek Worlock

'Let the charity of Christ shine out' (*Caritas Christi eluceat*).
National Pastoral Congress, Liverpool, 1980

Archbishop Derek Worlock

His Personal Journey

JOHN FURNIVAL

and

ANN KNOWLES

GEOFFREY
CHAPMAN

Geoffrey Chapman
A Cassell imprint
Wellington House, 125 Strand, London WC2R 0BB
PO Box 605, Herndon, VA 20172

First published 1998

British Library Cataloguing-in-Publication Data
A catalogue record for this book is available from the British Library.

ISBN 0-225-66841-6

Typeset by BookEns Ltd, Royston, Herts.
Printed and bound in Great Britain by Redwood Books, Trowbridge, Wilts.

Contents

Foreword

At first it was unnerving to be working alongside a bishop who had been at the centre of Church life in this land for close on forty years, could tell you why things were done in this way or that, who not only read the small print of any document, but, remarkably, remembered it all. A man clearly blessed with a fine intellect, a gifted administrator and a master with the pen. Such was the impression made on me by Derek Worlock.

Had health problems not stood in the way, first class honours at one of our Universities were awaiting him. It was not to be. Derek was a product of St Edmund's, perhaps one of its more outstanding alumni. Remember St Edmund's was no mediocre academic institution. It was staffed by men of calibre.

How did I cease to be unnerved by this able and experienced bishop? He had, after all, every reason to have confidence in his own experience, intelligence, and judgement, and much less in mine. It was because of his loyalty and support, given generously to me personally.

There were many occasions when our Conference of Bishops needed his gifts to resolve difficult problems or to plan a way ahead in respect of some important issues. His response was always freely given, the result effective. Late night poring over papers, drafting and re-drafting statements were no problem to him. He was an insomniac. He never enjoyed robust health, and yet bouts of ill-health never stopped him from carrying out his engagements. The call of the diary inhibits a bishop – and presumably not only bishops – from ringing up at the last minute to say 'Sorry, I'm too unwell to come'. Derek would never do so.

There was another side to Derek Worlock's character, and a surprising one given the ability with which he had been endowed. He seemed to have a need to seek reassurance from others about himself and about what he had achieved. Achievement was important to him, not only because he was generally right in his assessment and judgement of a situation, but also because he needed the encouragement of recognition. People who knew only the public person, or who had never got to know him personally, were often too quick to conclude that this was a man of ambition and intent on success. It was not so. His seeming want for reassurance — a fault no doubt — was a powerful force within him. But other needs then made themselves heard. Derek was always a priest. He treasured and loved his priesthood. Any biography of him that failed to do justice to this central aspect of his character would not only be less than adequate, but quite inaccurate. I believe that this book is indeed the biography of a priest, who became a bishop. A rather dour exterior masked an affectionate nature. He sought to give affection, though sometimes in an uncertain way, and, as with many people, hoped it would be returned. His sometimes serious look did not always lead one to recognize the wit of an able raconteur. Sitting together at evening time, the day's work done — though probably not for him — he would regale the company with amusing stories of his years as secretary at Archbishop's House, with jocular accounts of episodes long forgotten by the rest of us. Yes, he was good company.

Derek's mind, a finely tuned instrument, as I have already indicated, was practical rather than speculative. The questions to which he sought the answers were 'What was to be done?' He was more at home with the Church's social teaching than with speculative dogmatic theology. Nonetheless, he also saw how the Second Vatican Council's constitutions when developed might, in practice, be implemented. Practical applications of norms rather than the fundamental reasons for them, seemed to me, at any rate, to have been his main preoccupation.

As to his achievements, they form the content of this book. He was an outstanding private secretary to three successive Archbishops of Westminster. He coped adroitly with many delicate and sensitive situations, and often had to do so during lengthy periods when the Archbishop of the day was in failing health. His administrative gifts bore fruit in many ways. I would single out two. One is the development of the structures of our own Bishops' Conference of England and Wales. The other is in contributing to the design of the Ecumenical Instruments which for the first time brought the Catholic Church in these islands into a formal ecumenical partnership with other Christian Churches in the successor bodies to the British Council of Churches. These are just two of the ways in which, often behind the scenes, his contribution has had a significant and lasting impact.

It was, of course, at Liverpool that Derek was able to make his mark. Save for a few years as Bishop of Portsmouth, he had been working under others, often supplying them with essential material for their tasks. At Liverpool he was master. Liverpool had grave social problems, a dwindling population, high unemployment. Helping to tackle poverty rightly made exacting demands on his episcopal ministry. Derek's concern was real. Indeed, it was characteristic of him to make his own the agonies endured by others.

His close co-operation with David Sheppard, the Anglican bishop, was well and widely known. This relationship was practical ecumenism at its best. Less well known, because not so obvious to the media, was the spiritual ecumenism between Derek and David characterized by their sharing the Word of God and prayer. If you did not realize that, then you had not understood the true meaning of the witness these two gave the rest of us.

I have not spoken about Derek's relationship with his priests. I think that most bishops would want this relationship to be the chief criterion whereby the success or otherwise of their ministry is judged. On the other hand other preoccupations, especially the immediate and the urgent, all conspire to take a bishop away from his primary task of caring for his priests. Derek was certainly concerned for his priests and there are many examples of his kindness shown to those in personal need. Sometimes his priests did not seem to be totally at ease with him. Whatever one might say about this, there is no doubt that his priests respected their Archbishop and recognized in him a hardworking and able pastor.

Derek, like most of us, was a complex character. Dwell on the bits you find less appealing, or respond negatively because you objected to his policies, then you will inevitably make a wrong judgement. It has happened already. What is beyond question is that here was a man who devoted his life to serving God and the Church to the best of his considerable ability. No one ever thinks that they have been totally successful or even adequately so. Indeed, none of us are. God's judgements are more merciful, I believe. So rest in peace, Derek, and enjoy your reward for a job well done.

Cardinal Basil Hume
Archbishop of Westminster
3 September 1997

Preface

> There are many who, as Christians and not leaders, attain to
> God, travelling maybe an easier road, and the more speedily
> perhaps, the lighter the load they carry. But I, besides being a
> Christian, and for this having to render an account of my life,
> am a leader also, and for this shall render to God an account of
> my ministry.
>
> (St Augustine, Sermon 46)

Derek Worlock sometimes described himself as 'a travelling man'. He
travelled a hard road at times but always with a purpose, and in his
suitcase he carried many gifts, including a firm faith and a sure hope.
He also had vision, ability and the skills of a good story-teller.

The fact that his family had more than an ordinary interest in
history, and could give an account of events and experiences, has
made our task as biographers easier but still formidable. In his long
journey through life Derek Worlock knew many twists and turns,
joys and sorrows, successes and failures along the road. We have tried
to reflect this and to accompany him on the way.

The Archbishop's unique work for the Catholic Church, his concern for social justice and his contribution to the promotion of
Christian Unity over a period of fifty years, have given him a lasting
place in the grateful memory of his adopted city of Liverpool, and of
those he tried to serve as a priest and bishop. His life as a leader in
the Christian community went hand in hand with a continuous
reflection, so evident in his sermons and writings, about his vocation and about the Church and the society he knew. The attributes of
a good priest and a keen journalist combined powerfully to produce
a rich and important legacy from which we can all profit in some
way. It was this which prompted us to write this book. We hope the
reader will make the journey too.

In writing about Archbishop Worlock we have been encouraged by many of the people who worked with him, and knew him well, and who were concerned that an honest and accurate picture should be presented. As far as human limitations allow, we have attempted to do justice to all aspects of his life and to give the details as accurately as possible, based on the family documents still available, on others' recollections and observations, and on published material.

His family background is important and his parents' influence upon him was profound. His father, Harford Thornhill Worlock, was a student of history, a humorist, and an astute politician with a talent for careful reporting. His mother, Dora Worlock (née Hoblyn), played a courageous part in the emancipation of women before and after the First World War. She had a practical, compassionate approach to her faith, with a deep concern for family values. The qualities which their son possessed are proof positive of the laws of heredity. Yet even after studying a wealth of material left by both his parents and himself, there are certain aspects to Derek Worlock's character which remain a mystery, such as his deep-rooted insecurity. From his parents he learnt an appreciation of the fragile, sacred nature of human life and the reality of human needs. This he brought into the service of the people in his care and to his understanding of the priesthood.

There were other reasons for writing this book. First, to present an account of such an outstanding and important figure in the twentieth-century Catholic Church seemed to us a duty as well as a labour of love. Archbishop Worlock often emphasized the need for accountability on the part of those who exercised ministry and leadership in the Church. He was always anxious that the record should be put straight, that accuracy and attention to detail – the small print he was so adept at reading – should be a part of all that is said and done in the name of Christ. At times this was an obsession with him and some have seen this as an example of the insecurity which led to an over-meticulous approach to things. Whether out of integrity or out of a tendency to mistrust, he believed in leaving nothing to chance and taking nothing for granted. For him nothing in life was mere chance or unimportant. Everything was in some way connected with the consistent, often mysterious, providential plan of God. He subscribed to the view that 'the devil is in the detail'.

Had he lived longer, he might have been persuaded to write his memoirs. Then there would have been less need for the speculation which any biographer or commentator inevitably falls back on from time to time. One close friend ventured to suggest that he never wanted to write his autobiography because he would have been forced to confront the less than happy moments of his childhood, as well as reliving life's many disappointments. His relationship with his twin sister, Patricia, was at times strained. However, during his last illness they kept in touch regularly by telephone. The unfounded, ill-timed criticisms which were made of him in the press shortly after his death, though they could no longer touch him, were hurtful to his family and friends. At the same time, we have in no way tried to write about him as if he were a saint. Human failings and short-comings were evident in him as in everyone, though he tended to take personally the slightest criticism and was easily offended.

Health worries plagued him all his life. Cancer of the lung, and later a brain tumour, coeliac disease contracted after a visit to South America, arthritis of the neck and sinusitis problems from youth, all took their toll. Some have suggested he was a hypochondriac, but we will leave others to judge. What is certainly true is that he was concerned about his health for most of his life and took the unusual step of having frequent health check-ups before problems occurred. It must therefore have been devastating for him to have his worst fears confirmed when cancer was diagnosed in the summer of 1992.

A written apologia of his own life, given the experience, style and thoroughness which were characteristic of him, would have made a good read. For this reason we have tried to write this book as much with the freedom of the journalist as with the discipline of the historian, recognizing that no one's life can be adequately expressed by someone else, or contained in a book, or understood properly from a chronological list of events. Naturally, we have drawn from Derek Worlock's own autobiographical references in his published works such as *Give Me Your Hand* (1977), and *Better Together* (1988), the latter being the result of collaboration with his colleague and great friend, Bishop David Sheppard. With these sources of information and contributions from many willing and patient interviewees, we hope we have produced an accurate portrait and above all a fair and honest account of Derek Worlock's personal journey.

We hope, too, that this book will bring into greater focus the achievement of a man who more than anyone else, apart from his parents, helped to shape Derek Worlock's attitudes and priorities, Cardinal Bernard Griffin, Archbishop of Westminster, whose secretary, close helper, 'eyes and ears' he was for a period of nearly ten years. After Cardinal Griffin's premature death at the age of 57, Derek Worlock always stated that Bernard Griffin was not sufficiently understood and his contribution to the life of the Catholic Church, at home and abroad, in the post-war years was very much under-estimated. He hoped that particular record would be put straight, but unfortunately he was never able to complete his own biography of the Cardinal.

What is written here is a personal account. The book does not claim to be a comprehensive coverage or pretend to be a complete study of the life of the Archbishop and the times in which he lived. The full history of the Catholic Church and the Christian Churches in general since 1945 has yet to be written. The post-war period has been too traumatic, too unsettled and beset by rapid change to allow an ordered, objective history to emerge. Nevertheless, in paying tribute to Archbishop Derek Worlock we can reflect some aspects of the wider scene of which he was a part and salute an extraordinary apostle of the Church, whose legacy in respect of social and ecclesiastical renewal is something which will one day form far more than a footnote in the history of the Church. Well beyond Liverpool – where he ended his days – he was recognized as one of the most consistent and enthusiastic of the English bishops in implementing the teachings and reforms of the Second Vatican Council. That event radically changed his life and attitudes. With Cardinal Basil Hume in the work for the Bishops' Conference, the International Synod of Bishops, and Churches Together in England, he formed an outstanding partnership that encouraged and led the Catholic Community onward. With Bishop David Sheppard in Liverpool he formed a friendship and understanding which have left an enduring inheritance of greater understanding between Christians.

Choices have had to be made about what to include, and what to omit. We have attempted to focus on Derek Worlock the man more than the office-holder, though there can be no real separation of the two and to reflect upon the personal aspects of his life's work is by definition to reflect upon the Church and the priesthood. In what we have written we have tried to incorporate the various facets of his life as portrayed in the countless tributes paid to him after his death in February 1996. The surgeon who treated him spoke of his having borne all the aspects of his disease with 'a supernatural outlook' and great fortitude. The religious correspondent of the *Liverpool Daily*

Post, Ann Todd, referred to him as 'an honorary scouser'; a caller on a phone-in programme on the local radio station, Radio Merseyside, described him as 'the people's Archbishop'. The Archbishop of Canterbury, George Carey, said: 'His life and ministry reached far beyond the boundaries of the Roman Catholic community and touched with grace all the Christian Churches of our land', whilst the former Leader of Liverpool City Council, Mr Harry Rimmer, observed that 'His legacy will be treasured and celebrated by generations to come'. He was thought of, in the dioceses where he served, in Portsmouth and Liverpool, as the right person for the times, able to articulate the mood of the moment and by his example and vision to take people a stage further in their pilgrimage of faith. He was a much-loved and trusted friend to countless people.

However, there were those who found his methods and his ideas very difficult to accept. He was capable of both attracting and alienating. He could generate great loyalty and great antagonism but rarely indifference. Our hope is that out of all the comments made about him, the salient one explored in this biography will be that which the then Prime Minister John Major expressed in a personal letter of appreciation: 'He was a good man in every way – and that is something rare.'

Acknowledgements

We are indebted to many people who have helped us in our research, given us the space and inspiration to write and encouraged us along the way. To single out individuals is often risky and unjust. However, we owe a lot to Derek Worlock's late sister, Patricia Hayward, for her excellent and helpful memories of early childhood in London and Winchester. She passed away in February 1997, almost a year after her brother's death. We acknowledge the contribution of those who kindly agreed to be interviewed for the book and remain grateful to them and to all who have assisted us in any way. We thank Cardinal Hume and Bishop Sheppard who have generously 'topped and tailed' this work for us. The symbolism of that would not have been lost on Archbishop Worlock.

The photographs in the book were provided by courtesy of Tom Murphy of Catholic Pictorial Ltd, except for page 5 (top), provided by courtesy of CAFOD, and pages 1, 2 and 3.

CHAPTER ONE

Family Origins

One autumn day in 1929, soon after his family had moved to Winchester, Derek Worlock, then just over nine years old, walked the short distance from his parents' house, across the Cathedral Close, past the shops and offices to St Peter's Catholic Church in Jewry Street. He had made up his mind to tell the clergy that he wanted to be a priest.

On reaching the presbytery he saw someone in the garden, dressed in working clothes and wearing a sun-hat, kneeling down tending the flower beds. 'Can you tell me, please, where I could find the parish priest?' he asked. The man looked round, got to his feet and wiped the sweat from his brow. Looking down at the boy he took off his hat and made a deep bow, saying 'At your service, Sir'. All his life he would remember that first encounter with Father John Henry King, who later became Bishop of Portsmouth. Thirty-six years after their first meeting that autumn day, John Henry King would be succeeded as bishop by one who as a small boy had stood before him in the garden.

Not everybody sees the hopes and dreams of their childhood years remain unchanged and survive into adult life, but Derek Worlock did. His ambition to become a priest never faltered or diminished until it was fulfilled in remarkable and unexpected ways and the determination he displayed from the beginning remained a feature of his long, often arduous ministry in the Church.

It was at number 7F Grove End Road, London – a city still scarred from the First World War – at 8.20 in the evening of Wednesday 4 February 1920, that Derek John Harford Worlock was born. His sister, Patricia, arrived in the world just twenty-five minutes later, and the health of both babies gave cause for concern, as they were six weeks premature. A brief note in *Better Together* puts it succinctly: 'I was born with my sister during the post-war baby boom which followed the Armistice and the return of the nation's menfolk from France.'

His parents, Dora and Harford Worlock, decided to arrange for the baptism of the babies to take place at home one week later, on Thursday 12 February. The ominous-looking words *in periculum mortis* – not uncommon in those days – were appended to the baptismal certificate by the priest who baptized them, Father Clement Parsons, who at that time was one of three priests resident at Our Lady's Catholic Church, St John's Wood. Derek came to believe that the day of his baptism was the most important day of his life and consequently he considered Father Parsons to have done him the greatest service anyone could do. So, in addition to the love of his parents, Derek Worlock had the grace of God and the protection of the Church around him from his earliest days.

A vocation to the priesthood was not too surprising. In his family there were many precedents for a career in the Church. The first recorded details of the family tree go back six generations to a military event of historical importance. On the battlefield of Dettingen, ten miles north-west of Aschaffenburg in Germany, there was among the courageous soldiers of the British Army and its Hanoverian, Hessian and Dutch allies an Army chaplain, Reverend John Baylies. The Battle of Dettingen was fought all day long on 29 June 1743. As part of the Austrian War of Succession, it resulted in a notable victory for the British over the French and, amid scenes of triumph, the historic nature of the event was sealed by the presence of the English King, George II – the last reigning English monarch to take an active part in battle.

John Baylies later became Vicar of Snitterfield in Warwickshire, the county where his family settled for generations, and died in 1753, ten years after his service at Dettingen. His name is the first recorded in the genealogy which a kindly relative, Phoebe Timmins, a cousin of Derek's father, painstakingly copied out and sent to Harford Worlock, who preserved it among his papers. The record shows that the Reverend John Baylies was one of many in a long line of Anglican clergymen among Derek Worlock's forebears.

Genealogies are not the most exciting things and usually conceal more than they reveal, but they can sometimes be important sources of history. John Baylies' grandson Philemon Williams married into the Cromwell family. His wife, Anne Cromwell, so the family firmly believed, was 'of the same stock as The Protector'. The connection with Oliver Cromwell would prove to be a factor of some significance later on. Anne Cromwell, whose own people came from

Bromsgrove in Worcestershire, moved, after her marriage, to live at Kinerton, and Warwickshire remained the chosen county of residence for the Williams family. Some years later, Anne and Philemon Williams moved to Buckinghamshire and their daughter, Mary Anne, married Thomas Turner of New Bond Street, London. From that union came a daughter, Sophia, who married Walter Thornhill, also of New Bond Street, London, and from this marriage came six children, of whom a daughter, Sophie, married Thomas Worlock (Derek's grandfather). Thomas Worlock's occupation is given, on his son's birth certificate, as 'Gentleman' – he was a civil servant.

Thomas Worlock's brother-in-law Alan Thornhill became an Anglican priest, and four of his five sons went on to receive Holy Orders in the Church of England. Thomas Worlock and Sophia Thornhill's four sons, Ronald, Gerald, Frederick and Harford (Derek's father), pursued other, more lucrative professions. Changing his allegiance from the Anglican Church to the Catholic Church in 1913, and in so doing breaking a long and honoured tradition within the family, Harford married Dora Dennis Hoblyn in 1914. She too became a Catholic a year before their marriage so that the three children born to them – Peter, Derek and Patricia – were the first 'cradle Catholics' in the Worlock family since the Reformation.

The decision to become Catholics was not taken lightly. It involved a great deal of soul-searching for both Harford and Dora. The family history shows a strong affiliation to the Protestant tradition and a patriotism which saw loyalty to the Church – as by law established – and allegiance to the Crown as going hand in hand. This approach played a central role in shaping priorities. The English Protestant, upper middle-class background, which many people discerned in Derek Worlock, enabled his father and himself to have a wide view of the Church and an understanding of the wider Church scene and its history. The break from Anglicanism represented considerable personal sacrifice, encouraged by the belief that it was perfectly possible to be loyal to the Pope of Rome and to one's country at the same time, though the difficulty Harford's family found in accepting this had repercussions for his own future. Harford's mother, Sophie, and his aunt, Constance (known as Con or Connie), also became Catholics in later life, after the death of his father. Otherwise, the High Church tradition prevailed.

3

A pride in English history also prevailed in the family, and among the family papers which Harford Worlock kept was a copy of a letter that had become something of an heirloom. It was a letter written to Thomas Turner (Derek's great-great-grandfather), containing a graphic eye-witness account of the Battle of Waterloo of 1815. The letter, penned three weeks after the climax of Wellington's famous victory, was written by Thomas Turner's cousin, an English lawyer, James Humphreys. It leaves no room for doubt about the partisan feelings of the writer, whose admiration for Wellington and great pride in the English victory were matched only by his disdain for Bonaparte and the French troops. Humphreys described how the historic battle 'raised Wellington and my brave countrymen above all parallel in history and showed them conspicuous to an astonished Europe'. Paying tribute to the Scottish regiments which bolstered the English offensive, he described how, as Bonaparte's approach was announced, the allied soldiers' resolve and courage was spurred on by the rallying cry of Wellington himself: 'Your General will conquer or perish with you.'

The account relates how, 'after some minutes' aweful silence, Wellington drew his sword and the army marched at a steady pace to meet the enemy', and in a final flourish Humphreys records that 'They carried death into the French ranks on all sides'. Patriotism, not entirely devoid of 'jingoism', ran in the family. Derek and his sister remembered how as children at home they always stood up when the National Anthem was played on the wireless.

Derek Worlock's maternal grandfather, Charles Dennis Hoblyn, was from Newlyn in Cornwall. Whilst remaining proud of their Cornish roots, the Hoblyns moved to London and became prominent in the Stock Exchange. Charles Hoblyn founded a firm of London stockbrokers called Hoblyn and King, which he established as a successful family partnership. The money for this came initially not from his own family but from his wife's. Elizabeth or 'Lizzie' Hoblyn, whose family name was Taylor, came from a Quaker tradition and her wealth had come through a family connection with the Cadbury's chocolate empire. Like her husband's family, Lizzie's people were from Cornwall.

Several members of the family joined the Hoblyn and King partnership. It is not clear in which part of London the family home was situated. Dora, Derek's mother, was the middle one of nine children and tells us in her journal that she was born 'in a large corner house in a London square'. She was the fourth of five daughters and was born on Boxing Day 1881 into a well-ordered, well-off and contented family, typical of the large, strict Victorian families of those days. Her brothers were Reggie, Walter, Harry and Tim, her sisters Beatie, Lizzie (who was called 'Bill'), Gertie and Phyllis: each a distinct character, but getting along well enough together. Dora was closest in age and temperament to Gertie, and was especially devoted to her youngest brother, Walter. She missed him very deeply when he later went abroad to Ecuador to earn his living.

Dora describes her mother, Lizzie, as 'a commanding figure', an expression which implies she stood no nonsense. She describes her father as 'very Irish in temperament, intensely emotional at times and scrupulously just'. It was through his mother therefore that Derek and his brother and sister, Peter and Patricia, inherited just a little Irish blood to temper the staunch English patriotism that had characterized his father's side of the family.

Dora's family holidays were spent walking on the Cornish coast, or visiting France, of which both her parents were fond. Although generally strong in health, the children were not immune to the usual illnesses and set-backs that run in any family. One of Dora's brothers, Charles – named after his father – became so ill that in 1893 the whole family was obliged to move out of London to a healthier climate in the Sussex countryside. This was a turning point for Dora, then aged about thirteen. As a growing teenager with a mind of her own, she missed the life of London, her friends and her school, and she longed to return to the life she had known there. From that time on it seems she was continually resisting her parents' wishes, the accepted pattern of their lives and the expectations they had of her. Important though the cohesion of the family was to her, she could not maintain it at the cost of her own plans.

At school she became quite proficient in French and developed a taste for music. She had learnt to speak some French during the family trips to Normandy and in her teens she began corresponding with a pen-friend in Paris. Despite her parents' misgivings, she made the journey to Paris alone one summer to meet and stay with her friend; it was a journey that marked the beginning of a more independent, self-assertive phase in her life. From her mother she had clearly inherited a forceful personality, intelligence and inner strength. Gentle good looks disguised a steely determination. Derek's sister, Patricia, remembers her mother as 'very attractive . . .

with a magnetic personality'. Photographs of her as a young woman show her with shiny, light-coloured hair, a softness about the mouth but crystal-clear penetrating eyes. There is little doubt that Derek's mother, to whom he was always very close and many of whose personality traits he shared, was one of the most profound influences in his life.

In her early twenties she began to keep a diary of her life in London. She collected her memories, years later, into a book (unpublished) entitled *One of Nine*, written under the pseudonym 'Denise Lyndor' (derived from her second name Dennis and eliding 'Newlyn' with 'Dora'), which clearly shows the developing social conscience that in adulthood emerged as a more overt political stance and a career in politics. That was deemed by many to be a precarious and unpopular career for a woman in those days. Her mother and father were of the same opinion. There was no permanent rift, but there was a certain estrangement over it. Her father was ultimately less concerned about her career than about her health. Her heart was said by the doctor to be less strong than her will-power, and breakdowns in health were to frustrate her best endeavours more than once in the turbulent years that lay ahead.

Although Charles Hoblyn's success in London meant that the family were financially comfortable, resources were spread among the large, growing family. Her father was generous to her, recognizing her potential, though he was less than happy about her desire for autonomy. In a Victorian household proprieties were stronger than today. Children were more closely guarded, more strictly controlled. But Dora seems to have had her way in most things in the end and her leaning towards the bright lights and social life of London, with its opportunities for meeting people, for dancing and the theatre, all conspired to make her seek a steady job of her own in the capital. Although this created tension with her parents she still felt respect for them and remained extremely fond of all her brothers and sisters.

One day, whilst on holiday in Normandy, she witnessed the drowning of a small child in the sea. This image haunted her for a long time and she often pictured the scene in her mind's eye: the child's mother sitting there, looking out across the water, hugging herself and rocking backwards and forwards in silent grief. The seeds of compassion, awakened in Dora Worlock from that time, were given expression later in the charitable work she undertook in the East End of London. There, her local Vicar introduced her one day to people who lived below the poverty-line and in particular to one poor family to whom she began to make regular visits.

It was a very different sort of family and home from her own. The house was no more than a hovel, and one of the girls, Hannah, who lived in abject poverty, became her special concern. A victim of abuse and hardship, Hannah was only eleven when Dora first met her. She was pathetically trying to look after her baby sister, who would never know her father, and the devotion she showed to her little charge touched Dora's heart and made a lasting impression on her. All her life she never forgot Hannah's resilient and cheerful spirit which adversity could not subdue. From people like her she learnt something of the strange but noble life of the very poorest, the underclass of the East End. She had not previously known anything like those tough areas, where, she noted, 'the policemen always walked around in pairs'.

She followed, as the years went by, the sad progress of those she had visited, and from her own upper middle-class perspective found her eyes opened again and again by what she had seen and heard. Cockney phrases like 'catchin' sparrers' – by which Hannah described her latest boyfriend's means of earning a living: picking up what tips people threw to him when he was carting coal – were part of a cultural divide that shocked and saddened her. The great lesson she took from this experience was that life's resources could be shared with others but patronizing charity from do-gooders was not acceptable. Dora once asked Hannah, whom she described as 'a jewel in a dustbin', how it was that she survived such a difficult life. The reply shook her: 'Well, yer see Miss Denise, it's like this. The likes o' you was born soft but the likes o' me was born 'ard.'

Thirty years later, when Dora lay seriously ill in bed at home in Winchester, Hannah came unexpectedly to see her. The former roles were reversed, the class barriers dissolved, and the long intervening years since their first meeting in the East End melted away as they embraced each other.

As a young woman Dora visited France one summer and her indignation was sparked by the sight of a neglected wayside shrine dedicated to the Virgin Mary. She recalled how angry it had made her to think that so-called Catholics did not care enough to look after their holy places. An incipient interest in the devotion and traditions of Catholic France dated from that time and it seems that in early adulthood Derek Worlock's mother combined the Protestant work ethic with a Catholic spirituality in such a way that a practical Christian faith developed – one which would eventually find expression in adherence to the Church of Rome.

She was determined, in a society which did not favour women seeking independent careers, to find her niche in life. For a time in her late teens, she had seriously considered the nursing profession and one day reported to the Matron at St Bartholomew's Hospital in London for an interview, only to be told by her own doctor that her heart was not strong enough for such work. It was this which made her turn her thoughts and energies to social work instead. She rented a small flat of her own in London in Princes Square and from that time on began to devote herself to work which led to an active interest in the cause of Women's Rights and membership of the Women's Suffrage Society. She was offered the job of Organizer, working from an office in Victoria Street. Non-militant work for women became her principal objective and soon plunged her into the task of organizing rallies and the preparation of speeches.

Then, early in 1907, at the age of twenty-five, she met Harford Worlock at a dance in London, and soon afterwards they became engaged. Their shared interest in music, in the arts and in socio-political issues helped to draw them together, despite the fact that Harford at first thought her 'much too bright'. He, like Dora, was born in London; when they first met, his family were living at 32 Hamilton Terrace, so that it was a simple matter to meet and get to know each other. But Dora knew there was not much enthusiasm from either side of the family about their intention to marry. A man of striking, military appearance, with an air of learning, urbane and humorous, Harford Worlock had an ability for composing sketches, plays and songs, a talent inherited from the Thornhill side of the family. He was athletic as well as artistic, keen on photography and history. The theatrical and musical side of London's social milieu attracted them both, though the talent for acting was found more in one of Harford's three brothers, Freddie, who became a professional actor with a moderately successful career on the London stage and later on Broadway. Among his film appearances were minor roles in *Jane Eyre, The Black Swan* and *How Green Was My Valley,* and a part in Basil Rathbone's Sherlock Holmes series.

The *Hampshire Chronicle,* describing Freddie Worlock's film career many years later, remarked rather unfairly that his contributions were such that if you popped out for an ice-cream you would miss him completely. Frederick Worlock became better known as the husband of the much-married actress Elsie Ferguson when he retired to the USA. Derek never knew his uncle Freddie well but he knew of his career and on one occasion enjoyed regaling Radio Merseyside listeners (in an interview with Bob Azurdia) with family reminiscences about him. He had heard that one of his uncle's claims to fame was that he had featured as one of the voices behind the animated film success *101 Dalmatians* and it was that which had impressed him most as a young child.

The artistic side of the family was also seen in a cousin of Derek's, Monty Worlock, a classical and jazz pianist who used to write pieces for local orchestras, but the world of show-business was not to be the family's means of fame and fortune. Derek's father was urged on to academic success by his parents and not encouraged to seek his future in the theatre. Although he was by no means without ability in writing and adapting plays – around the time he met Dora Hoblyn he had formed his own Pierrot troupe of travelling amateurs – it was all very much a side-line. Later, when they had their own family, Harford would still encourage entertainments and write some music. Derek kept musical scores belonging to his father, including a score sheet published under the title *A Book of Play-Time Songs, by H. T. Worlock and James M. Gallatly.*

It is possible to discern in Derek Worlock something of the instinct for hosting the big occasion, of the theatrical, a sense of timing which had been part of his parents' early careers as organizers of public meetings. All this played a part in his own chosen way of life.

Whilst his brothers went into merchant banking (Ronald) and the antiques trade (Gerald), the interest Dora and Harford showed in the stage was eventually transformed into work which was to absorb them during the 1920s and 1930s – organizing public rallies and speeches for the Conservative Party in the post-war years. But when they first met it was not so much Harford's political as his religious leanings which attracted Dora. They were very similar to her own, despite their different backgrounds.

Harford had attended Loudoun House School and then Malvern College, where, as a boy of fourteen in 1897, he proved himself a capable student and a gifted athlete. He was made House Prefect at Malvern, won prizes for both academic and sporting achievements and in 1899 obtained a certificate in the Oxford and Cambridge

Examinations. In June 1900 he passed the London Matriculation, so that to proceed to Oxford seemed a natural step. It was at this point that his future prospects and religious beliefs began to take shape. His father wanted him to go to Keble College, Oxford, to train for Holy Orders following the example of his uncle. Harford duly went up to Keble, but he was there only a short time: leaving Keble but staying at Oxford, he gained a BA in History with First Class Honours, graduating in 1903.

It was three years after leaving university that he met Dora Hoblyn. She was aware of the blighted hopes of his parents, and no doubt he was aware of her own single-mindedness and independence. Dora described her father-in-law as 'a Protestant of the old school', and her view of the matter was that whilst Harford was 'destined for a clergyman in the Church of England, it was not what he was fitted for, and, much to his father's disappointment, he refused to take Holy Orders'. Dora and Harford had much in common. They were encouraged by each other's self-assured manner. In 1907 they embarked upon a long and at first clandestine courtship, which lasted seven rather unsettled years. It was something of a cat and mouse game with their parents. Without parental approval their relationship called for diplomacy and bargaining. They decided to say nothing at first, knowing the family opinion of their relationship.

At that time Harford did not have a full-time paid job. He had held a part-time teaching post in London when he first went down from Oxford but his real interest was in political journalism, and this further aggravated his father. Thomas Worlock did not consider journalism to be a suitable occupation for his son or an adequate financial basis for marriage. The compromise was to keep the engagement quiet, breaking it to their parents at a later stage when things calmed down. When they did divulge their situation, approval was grudging and they were told there was to be no engagement ring.

It was at this time that Derek Worlock's parents began their religious journey. Dora remembers Harford taking her 'to some of the most advanced churches in London' and it is likely that these included the Jesuit church at Farm Street in Mayfair, and St James's, Spanish Place. They were both devout members of their local Anglican parish but had gradually grown dissatisfied and disillusioned. Dora recorded in her journal that they came out of church one day and Dora asked 'Did it do anything for you?' Harford confessed that the service had meant little to him. Whatever divine promptings were at work in them, from that day they gradually became persuaded to look elsewhere for the fulfilment of their religious aspirations.

By 1913 the possibility of war in Europe had become a probability. Everyone was being forced to take stock and to look at their lives with a new urgency. This proved to be the final ingredient in Dora and Harford's deliberations about their future. During the long years of their engagement they had started to visit a Jesuit priest, Father Gavin, at Farm Street, and to take instruction from him. Having first approached their own curate for advice, they found that he couldn't advise them as he was thinking along the same lines himself. Although Derek often maintained that his parents received instruction from the same priest without knowing it, Dora's account shows that they acted on it together, albeit from slightly different viewpoints. It is probable that Harford's concern was with doctrinal integrity, whilst Dora was more motivated by what she felt was devotionally and liturgically correct.

Ecumenical links at this time were very tenuous. The Anglican and Catholic traditions were cool towards each other. Doctrinally the repercussions of the Tractarian Movement were still felt and socially the Catholic working-class milieu was markedly different from that of the broad sweep of Anglicanism. Harford had to convince himself, and more problematically convince his family, that it was not illogical to be a Roman Catholic and remain absolutely true to his 'Englishness'. This played an important part in Derek's attitude later, in his frequently stated 'triple principle' of social, spiritual and doctrinal ecumenism which he saw as an important part of the pathway to unity for all Christians.

During 1913, his father put himself under the instruction of the Jesuits and the influence of Catholic writings where questions relating to authority and doctrine were concerned. The personal struggle to reconcile what he considered to be contradictions in the Church of England's authority structures, and his own understanding of papal authority, were explained in two articles he wrote for *The Second Spring* (formerly *The Dublin Review*) in 1914 and 1915. He stated simply that 'Under God, I owe my conversion largely to the works of Cardinal Newman'. He soon became well-read, absorbing Purcell's *Life of Cardinal Manning* and Abbot Gasquet's *Lord Acton and his Circle*:

books which helped to instil in him what he called 'an intense long-
ing for the Catholic Church'.

The doctrinal beliefs which formed the basis of his decision to
join the Church of Rome centred on his inner conviction that the
Petrine tradition was the correct one and that it had to be structured
on the visible authority of the Pope. 'To the proofs of the Petrine
claims then I turned', he wrote. 'In addition to Newman's *Development
of Christian Doctrine*, I found the help I required in *A City Set on a Hill*
by Monsignor Benson.' He perceived that the New Testament contained twenty-nine references to authority, 'the cumulative effect of
which strongly supports the Petrine claims'. With reference to the
question of Holy Orders he wrote:

> I could not deny the force of the Roman contention that the words
> [of ordination] the consecrating bishop uses must indicate the
> particular powers conferred in the Sacraments, viz., that of offer-
> ing up the Holy Sacrifice of the Mass. The words used in the
> Catholic ritual express this definitely, whereas in the First and
> Second Prayer Books of King Edward VI there is no mention of
> anything of that kind, the word 'authority' being used only in
> connection with the preaching of the Word of God, which can
> be done by a layman.

His difficulty was how a valid apostolic succession could be maintained when the consecrating bishops had such different intentions.
In his view the matter of validity of orders was one 'upon which the
least tittle of doubt must not be allowed to rest'.

As he clarified his religious understanding, he also clarified his
personal future. He and Dora Hoblyn went out to buy that forbidden
engagement ring, and resolved that their plans to marry should now
become public at last. They felt it necessary to declare their intentions about the Church, incurring the disapproval of many of the
people they knew. The die was cast, the sacrifice was made, and in
Harford's case this sacrifice included disinheritance.

Financial reasons also played a part in delaying their marriage, and
the situation was not much better by 1914. With marriage in prospect,
they gathered all their resources together. Dora's work with the
Suffrage Society was earning her twenty-five shillings a week, organizing from the same office in Victoria Street but travelling around
the country. Many times she wondered if this was the right thing; she
did not want to cut herself off from her family at such a time. Yet her

job ensured that she did not have to accompany her parents when they moved out of London to Wrotham.

Her career meant more to her than anything else and the great names in the Suffrage Movement at that time inspired her, meeting many of them at rallies around the country. She was introduced to Maude Royden (the sister of Lord French), Helen Ward and Dame Millicent Fawcett, whom she considered 'a most remarkable woman'. Later she was to meet Emily Pankhurst. Inspired by such personalities she was resolute in pursuing her career and able to face with humour and courage the abuse and heckling of the crowds she later found herself addressing at open-air gatherings.

One heckler, evidently seeing the Suffragists merely as frustrated spinsters, shouted to her as she was speaking in Hyde Park 'the trouble with you women is, yer want to git married and yer can't – see!', to which she coolly replied, in the middle of her speech, 'As a matter of fact I'm getting married next week'. The man came back: 'Oh ar' yer? Well, all I can say is, I'm sorry for the poor bloke.'

Dora and Harford received conditional baptism, as was the custom for those entering the Catholic Church in those days, and were received in July 1913. In June the following year they were married at Our Lady's Church, St John's Wood, since by then they had managed to rent a small flat in Grove End Road. Dora's sister was to be her bridesmaid but fell ill with pleurisy just before the wedding. Another sister, Beatie, stepped into the breach. The wedding reception, held at the Great Central Hotel, was as memorable as any society wedding. Dora recalled how her father, his earlier opposition evidently softened, 'brought the car and chauffeur down to London for the occasion'. Sadly her mother was not well enough to attend. She recalled that the flat was 'full of wedding presents' and that there wasn't much space, but they had their own home and that meant everything to her. On the third-floor, the windows of the flat looked out over Lord's Cricket Ground and she was well satisfied with her 'three living rooms, two bedrooms, sitting room, bathroom and a kitchen'. She loved the flat, wanted to start a family and, with her income now £100 a year, combined with Harford's earnings from journalism, had just enough money to live on.

CHAPTER TWO

The Infant Samuel

Dora Worlock's success as an Organizer for the Women's Suffrage Movement, in which she was working full-time by 1914, had made her financial situation more secure. She insisted that she was a 'non-militant suffragist' rather than a 'suffragette'. It was not just the out-ward symbol of a different coloured sash worn by the two groups, but an important point of principle. Although a pacifist, Dora never hesitated in the least to make her voice heard and did not back away from confrontation. Derek recalled with pride how his mother was known to have 'crossed swords' with politicians outside the Houses of Parliament where, selling copies of *The Common Cause* – the National Union's newspaper – or giving out 'Friends' cards which declared 'I am a Women's Suffrage Worker', she inevitably attracted both interest and hostility. Reflecting on confrontations with certain MPs outside the House of Commons she declared them to be 'no gentlemen!'

Dora was remembered as having stood on a horse trough outside the docks in Southampton trying to persuade the dockers, as they clocked in for work, of the reasonableness of her cause. Having a natural speaking voice which carried well out of doors or in a large hall, she could make herself heard wherever she spoke in public, without the aid of a microphone. Derek remembered that she was known for speaking from notes rather than from a text. She was quite emphatic, in her own account of those days, that she 'never chained herself to railings' or 'spoiled golf-courses' as some did. By the time he was personally aware of her role as a public speaker, poor health had already curtailed some of his mother's activities and restricted the constant travelling she had once done in the 'second-hand ramshackle car' bought for the purpose.

In 1914 domestic bliss was not destined to last for long. Harford and Dora Worlock watched the unwelcome shadow of war falling upon them and the world. As Sir Edward Grey, then British Foreign Secretary, ominously described it, 'The lamps are being put out all over Europe: they will not be re-lit in our time'. And so the Great War of 1914, the 'war to end all wars', began.

Soon after the outbreak of war, Harford joined the Army as a private and mid-way through the following year he was sent to fight in France. He was then thirty-one years old. His three brothers joined up; none escaped injury whilst on active service, though they all survived. With everything directed to 'the war effort', Dora kept up her suffrage work and made time to lend her services to the refugees in London, many of them French *émigrées*. She joined the 'Queen's Work for Women', working at Battersea and concerning herself with the welfare and human rights of those who had lost both their jobs and their homes. Her knowledge of French came in useful. One young French woman was inconsolable for days and was crying continually. Those trying to find out what was wrong with her could not speak French. Dora eventually managed to elicit an explanation from the young woman: 'Mais, madame, je suis arrivée sans corsets', she sobbed.

It was during this challenging and hectic time, in the spring of 1915, with her husband away from home and her services in great demand that Dora found she was pregnant with her first child. Her son Peter (also called Walter after Dora's brother) was born on 27 December 1915, in the early hours of the morning, the day after her own thirty-fourth birthday. She continued to work until a few weeks before the baby was due, despite suffering from dreadful morning sickness. With Harford away and the house to look after she became exhausted, but doggedly refused to give up her job. Like many people, she was afraid she would not get her position back if she let it go. After Peter was born she was in a state of collapse for some time and a nanny was employed to help with the new baby.

Dora had barely recovered her strength when a crisis occurred. A report came from the Front that Harford had been fatally wounded. Unconfirmed reports of that kind arose all the time during the war and it was not always possible to get definite information. Frantically, with the help of her family and in particular the support of Harford's mother Sophie, she tried for a long time to find out the truth. After some weeks of anxiety, she was finally able to establish that her husband was alive. The relief was short-lived. Soon after this stressful event came firm news, corroborated by an officer of the

Coldstream Guards in which he had served, that Walter, her beloved youngest brother, had been killed in action. Being urged not to show her grief 'for the sake of her baby', she tried, like the distraught mother she had seen on the Normandy beach, to bear her grief as silently as she could. She was advised to 'take off her dark dress and wear something bright'. The family gave every support possible, but Dora never got over the death of her brother. As for all families during that time, it was a matter of pulling together, whatever differences and quarrels there may have been before the war.

But Dora felt the strain, and whether as the result of stress, or genuinely due to a 'sixth sense' which certain members of the family were said to possess and which Dora was certainly believed to have, she recalled vividly an experience soon after Walter had been reported killed in action. She awoke one night to see her bedroom door open silently. There was no one to be seen, but she felt instinctively it was Walter. Her reaction was not one of panic, only a feeling of calm reassurance as if she knew he had come there to check that they were all right. The next morning the maid who was helping in the house said to her, quite unprompted, that she had seen a young man in Guards' uniform leaning over the baby's cot. She too had been perfectly calm, and said 'It was Walter, wasn't it, Mrs Worlock? It was your brother, wasn't it?'

The conflict and stress dragged on, with the occasional respite when Harford and other members of the scattered family came home on leave. On 7 March 1918, shortly before the end of the war, a bomb exploded in Grove End Road. Catching up Peter in her arms and gathering together all she could carry, amidst the noise of the air-raids and the splintering of glass Dora found refuge in a nearby house until the worst of the raid was over. Peter was then aged two and a half but the trauma of the bombing affected him nonetheless, so that as a young child he would be distressed by sudden noises that recalled those traumatic days of the bombing. The effort to contain the pressure of worry about her family abroad, and the danger at home, whilst all the time endeavouring to appear calm and in control for the sake of others, took its toll. She refers to smoking a lot of cigarettes 'which I thought gave me some solace', but the close call of the bomb was the final straw for her and precipitated a move out of London to Littlehampton, where she stayed until the end of the war, with her mother-in-law and Harford's sister.

When the horror of war had subsided and the Armistice had been signed, the troops began to return home. Harford was at last reunited with his family, who moved back to the London flat. He had suffered slightly the effects of gas in the trenches of the Somme, but was otherwise unharmed. He had shown courage and a capacity for leadership which made him highly regarded, and had spent part of the war training soldiers in the use of weapons. This prepared him for a role he was to play later in charge of ground defences in Liverpool.

On returning to civilian life, he took up a post at the Ministry of Pensions at Sanctuary Buildings in Great Smith Street. Dora had been insistent that they 'had to have something more lucrative' with their increased expenses. There was not much prospect in journalism alone. Life resumed a pattern, and in the middle of 1919 Dora found herself again pregnant and, to her surprise, her doctor told her she should be prepared for the birth of twins.

It was a difficult pregnancy. Towards the end of January there seemed to be a real danger the babies might be lost, and the double birth was to be a serious test of her weakened state. After a problematic confinement, on Wednesday 4 February, with much coming and going in the house and several visits from the doctor, she gave birth to her son Derek at 8.20 in the evening, and to her daughter Patricia twenty-five minutes later. There was concern for them at first, especially for the little girl. Both babies were underweight – Derek weighed five and a half pounds and Patricia four pounds, but although they had arrived on the scene six weeks prematurely, the doctor assured Dora that with careful nursing all should be well. Exhausted, she begged someone to baptize Patricia as she seemed so frail. The doctor told Harford 'For heaven's sake, go to your wife and tell her the girl is all right – she wants her baptized or something'. Dora noted later in her diary, that 'The doctor was a dear man but not a Catholic, so he didn't understand what I was worrying about'.

Father Clement Parsons was called in to baptize the two infants at home on 12 February. He had to improvise, using a rose-bowl for a baptismal font. Subsequent accounts which suggested it was a 'pudding basin' were always indignantly denied by Derek. A rose-bowl was much more in keeping – in fact his mother states that is what it was, and that became the accepted version. However, when Derek reflected on this aspect of the day of his baptism in *Better Together*, it was clearly of much more importance to him that the baptism had been valid and that 'the water actually flowed'. His birthday was secondary to the significance of that day of baptism, which he always described as 'the most important day of my life'.

A service for the 'completion of the ceremonies', or 'churching' as it was called, when his parents received the blessing of the Church, was held at Our Lady's on 27 March, with Father Parsons once again in attendance. The godparents had been carefully chosen for the baptism: Thomas Rothmann and Dorothy Miller stood for Derek, Reginald Miller and Catherine Wilson for Patricia. Such provision was important to Dora and Harford; as relatively new Catholics they were anxious to do everything right.

It is probable that the first Christian icon that met the children's gaze was a large picture of the Madonna and Child, on a throne, surrounded by white-robed angels carrying censers. The picture, dated 1900, was on the wall of their mother's room, possibly a wedding present or a gift on becoming a Catholic. After his mother's death Derek took the picture with him and kept it in his own bedroom wherever he went to live in the years that followed. He referred to it when seventy-five years later he lay dying in a hospital bed, and although he never believed it to have any artistic merit it retained a special place in his affections, a reminder of what the saints must have known.

The post-war society into which Derek and his sister were born was one of conflicting values. The streets and buildings of London in the 1920s still bore the wounds of war. The year 1920 was one of violence as well as peace: a time of division but also of treaties and reunification. In Britain the miners were in full-blooded confrontation with the Tory Government. A deflationary budget later that year put an end to what had for a while been a booming economy. Prices and output fell sharply, whilst the number of people out of work rose steeply to over a million. The 'Black and Tans' ruthlessly enforced British law in Ireland with the resulting violence of Bloody Sunday and the imposition of martial law. In Europe the Treaty of Versailles brought into being the League of Nations and the map of Europe was gradually redrawn along the lines of the proposals of the Treaty of Trianon. A mood of cautious optimism followed the gloom and dislocation of a barbarous war.

Meanwhile the Churches were active in supporting the movement for peace which the various European treaties represented on the political level, but which not all the countries of Europe trusted.

Under the leadership of Cardinal Francis Bourne, the Catholic Church in England was making efforts to strengthen the work of healing wherever possible and the Cardinal was asked to promote the League of Nations, seeking approval for it from the Pope. The Vatican, in taking a wider view, had first to be certain that all the contributing nations would genuinely support the League. At home concerns were centred principally on education. There were two million Catholics in England in 1920 but only 40,000 places in Catholic secondary schools; the Cardinal was keen to redress the balance, for he saw education and Catholic values as key to the rebuilding of society.

The 'Great War' hastened rather than created many of the changes which were already present in embryo in British society. Most notably it was the attitude of the ordinary person towards authority figures that changed. The once hallowed personages of the squire, the priest, the factory boss, the Member of Parliament, police and parents, no longer held sway in the same measure as before. People were looking to find their guides in the new organizations, such as Trade Unions and other social movements. Organizations such as Ernest Bevin's TGWU, which emerged in 1920, found a ready-made and willing membership among post-war British workers. Derek Worlock's parents, with an increasing involvement in party politics, must have looked with some foreboding at the direction in which Britain and its political affiliations were moving and at some of the tendencies, such as Lloyd George shrewdly capitalizing on the wishes of the electorate for a policy of revenge for war-time atrocities.

In London that same year, 1920, the first official meeting of Anglo-Catholics was convened in the Albert Hall. Like many such gatherings immediately after the war, it arose from a need for solidarity in the face of common adversity and religious indifference. Demoralization, after the catastrophes that had shaken many people's faith, posed a challenge to the Church as much as to the politicians. However, the Anglo-Catholic Congress did not encourage the movement towards Christian unity. It seems, on the contrary, to have engendered antagonism in some wings of the Catholic Church. A speech by F. W. Chambers to the annual meeting of the Guild of Ransom in 1921 refers to the Congress as promoting 'the appointment of colonial bishops and safe English dignitaries to English Sees'. The presence of the Anglican Bishop of London in the Albert Hall was seen by right-wing Catholics as proof of the doctrinal liberalism being espoused, and the assembly was clearly viewed by many with great suspicion. Chambers apparently considered the Anglo-Catholics to be a dangerous group which, for example, left belief in the Virgin Birth as a matter of opinion, rather than an essential tenet of faith. A climate of closer unity among the Christian Churches was therefore still some way off; in the early 1920s, some would have gone so far as to say that ecclesiastical reunion was quite impossible.

The high profile of the Catholic Church in Europe at that time meant that many looked to it as a vehicle for resuming the path to spiritual renewal and unity; as a means of 're-lighting the lamps' – which had been put out. In fact the Lateran Treaty of 1929 would come to be seen by many as the culmination of a process of changes, a symbol of a new relationship, not only between the Pope and the people of Italy but between all the nations of Europe. It was thought of as a turning point on the road out of the embattled positions of sectarian hatred, so deeply ingrained since Reformation times. The mood of the world seemed to be swinging between alienation on the one hand and reconciliation on the other.

But if these two motifs were to epitomize Derek Worlock's future ministry in the Church, he could scarcely have been aware of it in that tumultuous year of his birth, the year in which a future Pope was also born, Karol Wojtyła, who later became Pope John Paul II.

The early concerns about Derek's health did not disappear completely in the years which followed. Throughout his life his preoccupation with health was obvious to all who knew him, and as a child he was seldom free from some anxiety in that regard, though in many ways he displayed a robust nature and a fair share of his mother's determined character which compensated for any setbacks. It is possible that his ailments, whether real or imaginary, were treated with indulgence by his mother, and that he wanted to be cosseted. His sister Patricia believed that this increased after the death of their brother during the Second World War and that their mother, in her loss, relied on, and fussed over, her second son all the more.

Dora described in her journal the two younger children during the first years of their life:

They were really fascinating babies, and I was not the only one to admire them. Patricia had absolutely golden hair, lots of it, with a donkey fringe. Derek's hair was thick, a sort of reddy brown when he was born, and curly. Patricia had bright blue eyes like Harford's, with a straight nose like his. Derek's eyes were grey like mine and Peter's and he had a rounder face and not such a straight nose. They were totally unlike in looks and dispositions, which made them all the nicer and more interesting to Harford and to me.

And so the new arrivals, and the family of five, began a new life in peace time.

Derek may have sought special attention from his mother, but in the nature of events it could not have been possible to receive it for long. Dora resumed her work and her travelling within eight months or so of the children's birth. Much of the pioneering, ground-breaking work of previous years in the promotion of women's rights was beginning to have results – another example of change and legislation speeded up by the war – and the contribution Dora had begun to make as a speaker at rallies around the country was needed.

Dora and Harford were ambitious for their children. The choice of names is possibly an indication of the great hopes which they had for their son. To judge from the official definitions 'Derek', means 'a ruler', 'an idealist who will fight unequivocally for justice'. 'John' is defined as 'a friend of God', and 'Worlock' contains the nuances of 'covenant maker, reconciler, wizard or witch'. In time, each of these meanings came to play their own particular part in his life-story. His father's name, Harford, was a long-established Anglo-Saxon word, literally the 'hare ford' from which 'Hereford' is derived. Subsequently, the full use of his name on official documents always seemed an important point of principle with Derek.

In order that Dora could resume her cherished work for the Suffrage Movement she employed the services of a nanny. Dora's commitments and Harford's work at the Pensions Office, dealing with special cases relating to the families and dependants of ex-servicemen, inevitably meant parental absence from home. When illness occurred, however, Dora refused to be away. At such times she insisted on nursing the children herself and it was a matter of honour with her that she could say 'I never had a nurse for them in any of their illnesses'. At times of crisis she was in charge.

As the children grew up they attended a local kindergarten in London, but in spite of the satisfaction she had of seeing them well started in life the stress of a growing family and the demands of her work proved too much for Dora. She took the difficult decision to leave London for a time, and to move to Bognor with the three children and their nanny. Not for the first or last time, the family were on the move and temporarily divided. Moving house was to be a regular and unsettling feature of life and it was only when he moved back to London that plans could be made for Derek, at the age of six, to settle down at a prep school for the first time. Priory House in Alexandra Road, Swiss Cottage, was the school chosen for him; he went there first on a half-day and later on a full-day basis. Meanwhile Patricia attended a local convent school, a place which appealed to Dora as it was run by an order of French nuns.

A report from Priory House School for the Easter term 1926 shows Derek (in 'Lower Transition') doing well, with 'very good' or 'excellent' in nearly all subjects, including Scripture. His spelling was considered to be 'good' and a report for the summer term showed progress, with an additional note in regard to Scripture classes: 'Dreamy at times but knows it well and the prayers too', his form teacher commented. In contrast, his French teacher had made the comment 'very attentive'. Although his mother was an accomplished student of French, languages were not Derek's strong point at school.

When the family moved again, to Blackheath, in February 1927, just after his seventh birthday, another change of school was necessary. This time it was Oakland House, where he was said to be 'much improved' in his reading and showed an enthusiasm, if not exactly a talent, for 'class singing'. His performance in Geography was said to be 'very fair', but the teaching of Scripture does not seem to have survived the move. There is little reference to religious instruction of any kind and it is probable that this was the prerogative of his parents at that stage.

The frequent moves may have had an unsettling effect on him, though in regard to his educational progress he was a bright, adaptable pupil, not easily put off his stride and maintaining a solid overall performance at school. He was serious-minded and, as the teachers had noted, a little day-dreamy; characteristics which may have resulted from a decision he seems to have made, at that tender age, about his future. Those who knew him well in later life attested to the fact that he valued stability and consistency more than most things and the need to feel secure in his own decisions and plans was an important element in his make-up. He needed to establish familiar surroundings, to have about him people who could provide a focal point, a *familia* within which he felt at ease. As he became well known in later years for his advocacy of change, this need for security was not always understood outside an inner circle of friends, and was almost certainly in part the consequence of the frequent changes of home and circumstances when he was a child.

Towards the end of the previous year, 1926, the year of the General Strike in Britain, Harford Worlock had resigned from his job at the Pensions Office and applied for a job as a Parliamentary Agent. He was successful in obtaining a post which took him first to Salisbury and later to North Cumberland for a by-election in 1928. His skills of leadership were put to use in the training sector of the Junior Imperial League and in helping to arrange public meetings for Cabinet Ministers. Both of Derek's parents were therefore fully involved in political work by the time he was eight and of an age to be aware of at least some of the issues which engaged them.

When Peter developed whooping cough and promptly gave it to the other two children, Dora was forced to give her whole attention to them. She recorded how she 'took up the carpet in the sitting room, filled sundry bowls with disinfectant, and prepared for a long spell of coughs'. In times of illness she nursed them 'all day and night', and remembered Derek suffering from 'dreadful earache' at that time, wandering around the house in a miserable state 'with his head on one side and his hand clasped over his ear'.

One of the family's regular holidays followed as part of a much needed convalescence. Cornwall remained a favourite place in which to blow away the cobwebs of sickness and city life. Peter had always been conscious of his Cornish ancestry and enjoyed his visits to his grandfather, the opportunity for travel being greatly enhanced by Dora's second-hand Morris Minor (nicknamed 'Charlie' Morris in honour of her father). Everyone loved the old car, which was still something of a novelty in those days. It opened up new horizons for them, but it was also a symbol of independence for Dora in her work, which, by the end of 1928, had come to include regular engagements as one of the first women speakers for Conservative Central Office.

At Blackheath an important development in the children's spiritual formation took place – 6 February 1927 was their First Communion day. Derek could not receive the necessary instruction for the sacraments at his non-Catholic prep school and both he and Patricia were prepared by Sister Clare at the Convent in Blackheath where he and Peter also learnt to serve Mass and assist at Benediction on Sunday afternoons. Derek informed Sister Clare, as he had been informing everyone else at that time, that he was going to be a priest and told her that he would come and say one of his first Masses at her Convent.

It was through this public avowal of his intentions that his desire for priesthood became more widely known, although it was already common knowledge in the family. He claimed that his desire to be a priest dated from the age of three. Whatever age he was, it must have been from a very early time since the 'announcement' (as his sister put it) of his intention, and the confidence and precociousness with which he asserted it, prompted his brother to call him 'The Infant Samuel', apparently to the amusement of everyone except Derek.

The occasion of his First Communion acted as a catalyst to strengthen his resolve about priesthood. The doubtful responses of those around him only served to increase his determination still more and the promise to Sister Clare was never forgotten. He intended to prove himself right in his prediction and from that day he never looked back. Confirmation, which he and his sister received at Pentecost that same year, 1927, was a further step. The sacrament was conferred by Bishop Joseph Butt, with whom the family had become good friends in the days when they had attended Mass at Spanish Place. Bishop Butt was to be instrumental in smoothing the way for Derek in the fulfilment of his boyhood wish to go to junior seminary and begin the long years of training.

For all his priestly aspirations at the age of seven, he was little different from other boys of his age. His sister recalled that he was not above childish pranks and once put chewing gum in her hair, with disastrous results; her long hair had to be chopped to get the chewing gum out, as no amount of washing would remove it. There is a clear memory too of a time when the three children set about making sweets to sell to their friends. They divided the enterprise into three parts: Peter, always the big brother, the one in charge, made the sweets, Derek wrapped them and Patricia had the task of selling them.

The enterprise seems to have been about as popular as the chewing-gum episode, but, undaunted, Peter again led the way in another exercise: a stall containing all their books which people were invited to buy. It might have been a successful venture had anyone been inclined to purchase and if Patricia had not quickly tumbled to the fact that she was being obliged to buy back her own books. Making money was not a family strength.

Reading was a passion with them. Their mother and father had a large collection of books, many of which later formed part of Derek's extensive library, and they encouraged their children to read. From the age of six or seven, when A. A. Milne's 'Pooh' stories began to be published, they needed no persuading. On the shelves was a complete set of Dickens and Thackeray, the ubiquitous Catholic Encyclopaedias and Butler's *Lives of the Saints*. Derek kept several of his parents' first editions of Chesterton, Wodehouse and Evelyn Waugh, and a collection of the novels of Graham Greene. As a child he had enjoyed reading books like *The Bab Ballads: Songs of A Savoyard* by W. S. Gilbert, which appealed to his father. *Winnie the Pooh* was the first full story Derek read, but he never enthused about *Alice in Wonderland* which he once described as 'spooky'. The Milne books provided hours of pleasure. When he went to college his affection for Pooh Bear was shared by one of his friends, Alan Wright, who nicknamed Derek 'Wol' after the wise owl in the stories. In later years Alan Wright began all his letters to Derek 'Dear Wol' but fortunately for him Derek did not return the compliment and call him Pooh!

His interest in religious books gradually extended to the lives and writings of some of the revered figures of Catholic history, such as Bishop Richard Challoner, who was closely associated with London and Winchester. The first Vicar Apostolic of the London District, Richard Challoner provided more than one generation of Catholics with devotional material, and *The Garden of the Soul* became a classic of its kind. Dora Worlock had a special interest in Challoner because he represented a time in which Catholicism had just emerged from a struggle with religious persecution and this had resonances with her own religious development. On his fifteenth birthday Derek received from his mother a copy of Challoner's *Meditations for Every Day of the Year*, a book which he treasured all his life. It marked the beginning of an interest in Challoner and awakened a more general devotion to the great spiritual authors whose lives were in some way threaded through his own.

Birthdays and Christmas were occasions of special celebration for the family. As Dora's birthday was Boxing Day and Peter's the day after, the holiday took the form of a three-day jamboree. The religious importance of Christmas Day, with the family attending Mass together at Our Lady's Church, St John's Wood, and in later years at Blackheath and at St Peter's, Winchester, was always paramount. Christmas always remained Derek's favourite time of the year and he remarked how families, no matter how poor, were generally at their best at Christmas, though he was aware that it could also be a painful time for many. His mother often reminded him about the needs she had found among the slums of London, needs that became even more acute at such times in the year. In the early years of their childhood Christmas Day itself was spent in the customary way, and on Boxing Day, if the weather allowed, a long walk was arranged to digest the Christmas dinner. But the next day, out would come a large chest full of old clothes and costumes and everyone would dress up for a concert. It was a time for music and relaxation. Patricia had a considerable talent for the piano, which her mother believed she had the potential to play professionally.

Such times, both good and not so good, were shared, in those childhood years, with Mrs McLeod, their nanny. The children loved her and in some ways she became a replacement mother during Dora's frequent absences. They called her 'Mrs Cow' – the nearest they could get to the pronunciation of her name. She became an indispensable part of the family, providing continuity, a focal point. Derek used to recall that there were times when the only sign his mother had been home overnight was that there would be a British Rail sugar cube on their plates at the breakfast table.

Peter, being nearly five years older, was perhaps better able to adapt to this situation. By 1928 he was preparing to move to another school and develop interests of his own. He even tried his hand at composing music and would ride out on his bike to see his cousin Monty to seek his approval, though the interest was short-lived and came to nothing. Derek, who looked up to Peter, had to contend with the absence of his parents and at the same time his brother's understandable wish to drift away. It was a crucial time in his formation. He developed a single-mindedness about his own future and knew he would have to be his own man. A measure of insecurity may have resulted, but there was also a spur to making up his mind about things and focusing his thoughts on the priesthood, about which his determination remained unshaken.

Dora recorded a particular moment when the twins were eight years old, when her son's thoughts about a vocation seemed to emerge with greater clarity. She recalled that Patricia 'had a most enquiring mind and from her earliest days would try to think things out'. One day she said 'I don't understand. How can Jesus be God if he is God's son?' Before her mother could answer, Derek, in a quiet, serious voice, intervened: 'If you don't understand, you'd better look at your crucifix and then you will.' Whether or not his sister was convinced by this is not known; her reply is not recorded and perhaps it's just as well. One thing is clear, she had no plans for a 'life in religion'. She was irritated by people questioning her, in view of her brother's stated intentions, 'whether she would not like to become a nun or something like that'. She would reply emphatically 'No, nothing like that'. On one occasion she told a priest, who had asked the same question, that she intended to marry early and to have a family. Like her brother, she knew her own mind.

CHAPTER THREE

A Winchester Boyhood

By the end of 1928 Derek had changed schools once more and was attending Cherry Orchard at Old Charlton. He was there for less than a year. A move out of London to Winchester the following year meant that Peter went to the King Edward VI Grammar School in Southampton, travelling daily the twelve miles from their home. It was a time of separation but the one grateful memory of Cherry Orchard School was that it was there Derek began to play rugby, a sport in which his brother had also excelled. Despite sustaining several injuries he was keen on the game and remained a fan of it all his life.

Rugby was very much encouraged in the prep school environment, and on the field Derek appears to have displayed a determined resilience, in keeping with his character but at odds with the preoccupation with his own health. Whatever health worries he may have had at other times, these did not obstruct his efforts when it came to rugby at school – an anomaly remarked on and puzzled over by his contemporaries. Rugby brought out a toughness in him which provided a foil to his otherwise shy and reserved nature. It seemed an unlikely sport for him but with a certain apprehension his mother acquiesced and his father encouraged and approved.

If rugby served to toughen him, his mother attempted to bring other, more subtle influences to bear. In her own childhood she had loved pets. She tried to encourage in her children the same interest and believed that learning to care for animals was an important part of a child's development. Peter had one day brought back to the London flat an injured bird he had found and nursed it back to health. There had been little room in the flat for anything more ambitious, but with the move to a larger house a series of larger, more conventional pets was possible. There was a cat called Christopher Robin – a name that was quickly changed to Christina

Robina when it produced several kittens. Later there was an Airedale puppy called James which, after a few years, developed hysteria. Dora had a vivid recollection of Patricia 'flying past' her in the street one day attached to the lead of the poor dog which had gone berserk. At the end of the street it collapsed and later had to be put down. To console the children another Airedale was acquired, a large affectionate dog called Corrie (Coriolanus) on which the whole family doted, especially Harford. They were devastated when it was run over one day in the road. Coriolanus was followed by another puppy, and a cat called Edgar Wallace.

Dora felt that a succession of domestic pets provided important lessons about compassion, understanding and responsibility for others in those formative and impressionable days of growing up, lessons which were important for adult life. Her efforts evidently bore fruit. When she became seriously ill with peritonitis, shortly before the move to Winchester in the summer of 1929, and had to spend some days in hospital, the family were thrown into confusion. The family doctor had serious warnings for Dora about heart failure and told her she had been seriously over-working yet again. Derek wrote to his mother in hospital: 'Mummie, never mind what the doctor says. It will be all right because everything God does is all right.' It was not the last time his mother would receive from her son the encouragement and support that helped her to recovery.

The summer of 1929 marked the end of the family's time in London. The move to Winchester that year, made necessary by the run up to the General Election in which Dora and Harford were both closely involved, was the beginning of a time of intense political activity. Derek's father was appointed Tory agent for the Winchester constituency: a position he eventually held for twenty-four years, serving no fewer than four Tory MPs. His new position meant living in the constituency, loath though the family was to leave London. The immediate question was where to live and where to find a suitable school for the children. It was decided that Derek should go to Winton House, a private prep school just outside the town, and Patricia should attend the Girls High School in Southampton. So, in spite of having his sights set firmly on the priesthood, Derek was still not yet free to receive a Catholic education in a Catholic school.

Deciding where to live was no easy matter. To buy a house outright in Winchester was beyond their means, and at first Harford arranged for them to move into hotel accommodation in the town until they were able to rent somewhere more permanent. Dora was recovering from an operation, everything was new and uncertain, a new environment had to be assimilated. However, not long after their arrival Harford was fortunate to find a house in the centre of Winchester, near the Cathedral and the imposing sombre grey walls of Winchester College, within sight of Jane Austen's house, in College Street. Dora's first impressions were of 'an old-world city full of old places and quaintly narrow winding streets with a most beautiful Cathedral', a fitting description of the ancient capital city of England.

Derek too felt very attracted to Winchester, but he had other, less pleasant memories, involving religious sectarianism. Soon after their arrival the family were walking together through the Cathedral precincts and were nearly caught in a cross-fire of stones being thrown at a group of Catholic councillors making their way in procession to the Cathedral. Roman Catholics were in a minority there and divisions were still keenly felt and expressed. It was the first occasion on which he encountered religious rivalry.

In this climate of old hatreds and prejudices, in a historic, ancient, beautiful city, the anomaly of sectarian division made a deep impression upon him. It surfaced in an even more immediate and personal way at his new school. Though he recalled no crudely hostile attitude to Catholics at Winton House, he seems to have made much of the differences between himself and the other pupils there. It seems that the choice of school was dictated by the proximity to home, and by his mother's wish that he should initially attend as a day boy, not a boarder. It was not his choice.

The living accommodation in the house in College Street was rather cramped but there were many fond memories of their first home in Winchester. In winter the scene was one of snow-filled streets, lights in the shop windows, rolling huge snowballs or tobogganing on St Catherine's Hill. In summer the memories were of picturesque Hampshire villages and long country walks. In much darker times when the pressures of a demanding life had taken over, Derek would recapture some of his childhood in the annual holidays and visits back to those pleasant scenes of his youth. The much-needed holidays would help to offset the exhaustion that often beset him in later years. Above all, he would remember his first, unexpected meeting in the garden of the presbytery in Jewry Street with one man who was to play an important part in his life: John Henry King.

In the General Election of 1929 the Labour Party came to power under Ramsay MacDonald and the decade which followed was one of political upheaval and bewildering change. The result was, of course, a disappointment to Derek's parents, even though the new Labour Government was short-lived: breaking up in 1931 and returning in 1935 under the new leadership of Clement Attlee. These developments coincided with the rise of Hitler and Nazism in Germany, the growth of Fascism and a time of general political and social unrest in Europe. Clement Attlee was the first Prime Minister of whom Derek had any personal memory and he came to consider him as a great man. In *Better Together* he describes his home in Winchester as being 'full of politics'; Clem Attlee and other politicians whose names were frequently bandied about at the dinner table were the first to stir his interest. He remembers Duff and Lady Diana Cooper coming to their house and a visit from Lord Hailsham, who was Quintin Hogg, MP for Marylebone, when his father first knew him.

There was one memorable meeting in his parents' home with Quintin Hogg, who was due to give a speech in Parliament and asked the young Derek Worlock what subject he thought he should speak about. Derek's spontaneous reply was 'fire engines'. Some time later Quintin Hogg delivered a fine speech in the House extolling the merits of the Fire Brigade, winning a standing ovation. Being told by his father about the outcome of the speech, Derek decided that public speeches were generally things to be applauded. In church, after the priest's sermon the following Sunday, he rose to his feet to clap enthusiastically. His embarrassed parents hauled him down.

Meanwhile there was a new school to go to. Winton House, founded in 1863, was originally a large country house to which a new wing had been added in the early 1900s, forming a complex of buildings that comprised a chapel, swimming baths, gymnasium and sports field. In 1929 when Derek first arrived at the school a footbridge had just been built over the busy Andover Road which divided the school from the outer playing field. The road had been a source of anxiety to staff and parents for some time, with the increase of traffic in and out of Winchester, so that the new bridge afforded greater safety and an added incentive to would-be pupils.

For forty years, from 1894, the whole tone of the school had been set by one man, the headmaster, E. F. Johns. He was a colourful, eccentric character known to generations of pupils as 'Jumbo Johns'.

Apart from his long reign as headmaster, he seems to have been famous for two things in particular. He was one of the country's leading authorities on butterflies and he had a passion for collecting things of all kinds, in particular toy elephants, which the boys used to give him as presents when leaving the school. A disciplinarian, as the boys discovered to their cost, he was well liked and respected, despite his eccentricities, and was intent on providing a rounded education based on strong religious principles. He saw his school as the training ground for future leaders of society.

Set firmly within the long tradition of Church of England prep schools, Winton House was noted for an excellent tradition of sporting achievement. Spiritual formation was not neglected either. The Chaplain at the school for most of Derek's time there was the Reverend and Honourable H. N. Waldegrave. He held a weekly service in the chapel and other local religious leaders would come to give talks. But there was little scope for someone who was the only Catholic boy. This was the setting in which Derek Worlock spent the next four years of his life, very aware that he was in some way 'different': a situation, which contributed to his reserved attitude.

It was a privileged location. The headmaster would try to attract the interest of parents by reminding them, in the school prospectus, that the school was not in Winchester itself but 'on the verge of the Hampshire Downs where, in the immortal words of the poet John Keats, the air is worth sixpence a pint'. An attractive but awesome place for a young child aged nine.

There was a great cedar tree on the front lawn and Derek remembered school photographs being taken there and eating strawberries and cream in the summer term, courtesy of a Mrs Baring, a benefactress of the school who lived at the lodge. There were picnics too in the summer at Avington Park, and at Farley Mount boys would go in search of butterflies and report their findings to the headmaster. But there is no indication that lepidoptery ever found a place among Derek Worlock's interests or priorities. On Bonfire Night a huge fireworks display was held on the field and school plays were performed at Christmas or the end of term. Other extra-curricular activities included films, walking, swimming, rugby, football and cricket, with some highly qualified sports masters, successful sportsmen in their own day, producing fine results for the school in local sporting fixtures.

The educational standard was high and emphasis was put on

learning Latin and Greek. Here Derek found at least the rudiments of the subjects and skills which would be important later in his bid to enter the seminary. The ability to write good English was one of Jumbo Johns's hobby horses. He was a stickler for correct spelling and infused his pupils with his horror of sloppy grammar and slang, often using his end-of-term orations to bemoan the passing of the English language and of the blue-blooded Englishman. He decried what he saw as the corruption of Parliament by the introduction of Americanisms that were beginning to dilute the traditional purity of the English tongue.

Winton House numbered among its pupils the sons of clergymen, politicians and the gentry. The Honourable Alan Hare, the son of the Earl of Listowel, was a pupil there in Derek's time and the roll included the names of Cleverton, Twynam, Gloster-Downing, Raynor, Le Champion, Donger and Chopney. Chopney, one of the few friends Derek made in the school, occasionally stayed with the Worlocks during holidays since his own parents were stationed in India. Another of Derek's contemporaries at the school was Peter Cave-Bigley, a fine all-round sportsman who later won a scholarship to Bradfield College. A sign that Derek never forgot his friends and schoolmates was that many years later, when he and Peter Cave-Bigley were both approaching the end of their lives, they renewed acquaintance through some mutual friends and wrote to each other about the schooldays they had shared together.

Being the only Catholic boy at the school, and his family being one of the few Catholic families in the area at that time, meant that Derek's practice of his faith called for a certain determination and sacrifice. The studies presented no real difficulty but with his sights still firmly set on the priesthood it was not a very encouraging environment for him and it is perhaps for this reason that some of his contemporaries had the impression that he was unhappy at Winton House. He felt it keenly that being at a non-Catholic school precluded him from serving Mass at his own parish of St Peter's. He would ride his bike the five miles each way to Mass at St Peter's each morning, fasting from midnight as was the custom. He remembered how occasionally, when there was an outbreak of measles or mumps in the town, 'my father would collect me in the car and take me to the chapel at Titchborne House, some eight miles away'. There they would slip in at the side door, as this gave Harford a sense of what it must have been like in the days of the Hampshire

Martyrs when the people living there had to attend Mass secretly. Even in 1930, the rivalry between denominations had not entirely disappeared.

Derek seems to have been content to join in whatever he could at the school. Although the *Winton House Magazine* does not record any spectacular sporting prowess on Derek's part, he did continue to play rugby. A good deal of illness, including epidemics of measles and chicken-pox, disrupted the sporting fixtures during his first year there. There is mention, in the magazine of 1930, of second prize being awarded to him in the sack race, and there are intriguing references to a 'bicycle tortoise race', but it is unclear whether or not he took any part in that. Second place again was gained in the long jump for the under-twelves, on Sports Day, March 1931, but that completes all the reference there is to any sporting accomplishments. He did not follow his father's success in the field of athletics. For those who had any ability in cricket Winton House gave wonderful opportunities. For example, Colonel Basil Clark, a member of staff, had played cricket for Gloucester and the Army, and had written a book on cricket for schools.

It was whilst playing rugby at Winton House that Derek broke his arm. The accident seemed to set off a chain reaction. An outbreak of chicken-pox affected all three children, and soon afterwards Derek developed appendicitis and had to be taken to hospital. His mother took him by car, and because the children's ward was full he was placed in the men's ward. She described how, with a shortage of beds, she held him in her arms until the time came for him to go down to theatre. Whilst he was recovering from the operation there was a scarlet fever alert in the hospital and she was advised to take him home at once for fear he might contract it. She recalls in her journal how Harford came to take them home, driving very slowly and cautiously 'as if Derek were a bit of fragile china!'

At Winton House he was highly commended for an essay he wrote, entitled 'Why I want to be a priest'. He was invited to read it aloud to the class, and the teacher told his mother afterwards that he had given him top marks because it was so well written. (Sadly, the essay has not survived.) As the staff at the school respected his wish about the priesthood he came to have a respect for them too. A career in the Church was not at all unknown there, but it was probably the first time there had been on the books someone aspiring to the priesthood in the Catholic Church.

There are wonderful recollections of the flamboyant character of Jumbo Johns and how he used to delight pupils by taking them out in his dilapidated, ancient car which possessed no horn. The boys would warn on-coming traffic as they turned the corner, by shouting 'Car!' at the top of their voices. Derek remembers him as a fair man but one who could offer only a restricted form of help and advice to a boy with his hopes and aspirations. When he became a boarder at Winton House he recalls a lack of tolerance and understanding of his situation from the students.

Writing in *Better Together* he noted candidly that:

> In recognition of freedom of conscience I was not required to attend the school chapel or morning prayers in the school library. I spent many a lonely hour in the corridor outside ... increasingly doubtful of the nature of my privilege. But I recall the hurt from the taunts of the other boys.

For all his eccentricities, the headmaster was, Derek recalled, 'good about what was regarded as my religious diet on Fridays. On Sundays I was allowed out to Mass in the local Catholic Church.'

One incident of punishment is recalled when youthful passion for his Catholic faith got the better of him. After a Church History class in which the Reformation had been discussed, enthusiasm – not normally associated with Church History lessons – was running high, and another boy in the class confronted Derek and began calling the Pope a rude name. Derek rose to the defence of the Pope and the two boys locked in battle. The headmaster came in and separated them, asked why they were fighting and promptly took them both out and caned them, saying he would have 'no religious discrimination in his school'. Confusing signals for a small boy who had been taught to stand up for his beliefs, and an inauspicious beginning to a priestly ministry that would one day become noted for its commitment to ecumenism.

There is a sequel to the incident which is both poignant and ironic. Returning to Winchester years later, he saw a memorial to those who had died for their country during the Second World War. Among the names listed was that of the boy with whom he had fought many years before. It gave him pause to think back to his erstwhile classroom adversary, now honoured for bravery, though he never once doubted that he had been in the right.

The only other reference in *Better Together* to correction received as a schoolboy is to being 'told off for always having an answer'. It was characteristic of Derek even in those days that he was always ready with a reply that invited no contradiction. This was, after all, something encouraged by the Church in an age when to crush your opponent with a reply to all questions was the stock in trade of the Catholic apologist. Such an approach was taken for granted until it found a moderating influence at the Second Vatican Council, where he himself was to play a part in changing former attitudes.

Throughout his life the recollections of life in Winchester would remain with him. His parents moved a short time after they had first settled in College Street. They had been looking for a larger house that was less central. There was a detached house with some land at Itchen Abbas, a small village about three miles from Winchester and Dora was very taken with it. The house was called 'Ullacombe', 'a big rambling house with a thatched roof', his mother recalled, close to the river Itchen and the chalk streams that fed the river across an expanse of placid water meadows. Derek always remembered it with great affection and nostalgia. The surrounding countryside, green and shimmering in summer, frosted over in winter, gave a sense of space and freedom.

The Itchen is a prime salmon river and he would go fly-fishing with his brother Peter during the summer holidays. It was there too that, the evening after his ordination to the priesthood, he stood and watched a salmon rise, a magical memory, an event that seemed to be timed just for that happy moment in his life, for him alone.

Unfortunately the idyllic setting of the house at Itchen Abbas was not to last for ever. It proved in winter to be a rather damp place, being so close to the river, and neither Dora nor Patricia enjoyed good health. Patricia was told by the doctor that she had a weak heart and it was eventually decided they must move. However, it was not until 1945 that they gave up the place and moved to Easton, where they lived in a house – their final family home – that bore the quaint name of 'Old Bat and Ball'. Here his parents settled but, although Derek remembered Easton well, it was Itchen Abbas – the place which had been home for him during all of his college years – which had meant the most to him.

CHAPTER FOUR

'Faith, Learning and Mission'

Many people mistakenly believe that Derek Worlock's parents opposed his wish to become a priest and some have cited the choice of non-Catholic schools in support of this. On the contrary, his parents welcomed it. Their personal journey to the Catholic Church had owed much to the help of priests. It would be more accurate to say that they were understandably protective of him, rather than disapproving of his chosen path in life. Their expectations of him were high and their hopes for his future were such that they wanted the best education they could obtain, but they knew nothing of the seminary system. He was fourteen when he finished at his prep school to go to the seminary, and his mother considered this too young to leave home. But both his parents were conscious of his expressed intent which had never altered, and were aware of the high ideals contained in such a calling. It was a question of whether he was ready to take that step. He himself claims he found in his brother and sister a ready support for what he wanted to do, and felt no pressure, at least in the beginning, to abandon his plans.

The impression among his contemporaries at college that his decision to enter the seminary was the cause of a certain alienation from his family is more likely to date from a slightly later time. In the years leading up to 1939, a rapidly developing situation brought mounting tension for the whole population, not just seminarians, with the prospect of war. In view of the spirit of patriotism his father espoused, the family's experience of the First World War and the fact that his brother Peter had, like thousands of other school-leavers, joined the Territorial Army in anticipation of active service, it would not be surprising if Derek felt a psychological pressure to abandon his plans. To do so before they could be put to the test would have been a bitter disappointment.

But at the beginning of 1934, with this challenge still in the future, he actively set out to find where and how he might begin his studies. Dora and Harford made no attempt to thwart him and made the necessary enquiries about a college for him when the time came to leave Winton House. But which college? There were few Catholics to advise them; they decided to turn to their friend Bishop Joseph Butt, the Auxiliary Bishop in Westminster, who had given the family such support in the past. It was he who arranged for Derek to apply, with his backing and recommendation, to St Edmund's College at Old Hall Green, Ware, in Hertfordshire.

There was one other obstacle: the opposition of his own bishop, Timothy Cotter. Bishop Cotter had already made it clear that he would withhold approval on the grounds that the family was not of Irish extraction. He had perhaps overlooked the fact that Dora's father had Irish ancestors, or perhaps someone had whispered the name of Oliver Cromwell in his ear. Whatever the personal reasons, he was adamant in upholding his policy of not accepting English or English-trained students for the diocese – a policy shared by several bishops in English dioceses at that time. Their view was that native vocations were not yet sufficiently developed and an Irish Catholic background, preferably with a training in an Irish seminary, was safer. It is certain that finance played the biggest part in this. It was obviously less expensive for the diocese to recruit the services of priests already trained in Ireland than it was to put boys through the long years of training in local seminaries. Students had to be adopted by a diocese before going forward and an active recruitment of candidates abroad took place in those days, with the United States and other countries sending to Ireland for candidates, which were then plentiful.

Through Bishop Butt, Derek was accepted for the archdiocese of Westminster instead of Portsmouth and so was able to gain admission to the archdiocesan seminary of St Edmund's. St Edmund's College had been established in 1793 as a direct descendant of the college at Douai, in France, which Cardinal William Allen had founded in 1569, in days when the training or harbouring of priests in England was considered treason. Exiled in France, William Allen wanted to train priests for a future English mission. When the days of persecution came to an end, an offshoot of the college at Douai – the school of St Edmund's – and the senior seminary of Allen Hall were housed in adjacent buildings, at Old Hall Green, Hertfordshire. There was provision at the school for what were called 'Church' students and 'Non-Church' students, and the opportunity to receive an excellent education. The 'Church Boys' at St Edmund's were given every encouragement to go on to do their theological training in Allen Hall.

In spite of Bishop Cotter's disapproval, Derek started there in the Lent term of 1934, just before his fourteenth birthday. At last he had his wish. For the first time he was able to attend a Catholic school: far from being the only Catholic pupil, he was in an all-Catholic institution, among young men with the same objective as himself. It was an irony not lost on Derek that Winton House had given him a good reference when there was no recommendation forthcoming from the local diocese. However, despite his keenness the move to St Edmund's was more challenging because of the lack of school friends to accompany him in this new phase in his life.

His parents travelled to Ware with him on his first day at St Edmund's, in January 1934. On the eve of his departure his mother, practical as ever, called him in to watch her pack his suitcase. 'She told me to watch carefully because this was the last time she would do it, and from now on I would have to pack my own case', he recorded in *Better Together*. It was something he did meticulously from that day on. On that January day another decisive stage in the process of growing-up had been reached.

First impressions are often very important. The fine, square building and neat, spacious grounds of St Edmund's College, set in the middle of the Hertfordshire countryside, was something far beyond his experience to date. On arriving at the door of the College, he and his parents were met by a maid whose appearance was a bit of a shock and who, he later discovered, had the nickname 'Pulchie' ('Pulcherrima' being the Latin word for a beautiful girl – schoolboy irony was evidently alive and well at St Edmund's). 'Her face was not her fortune', Derek wrote, casting his mind back to the events of that momentous first day, 'and the state of her carpet slippers left something to be desired.' So, it seems, did her manner of welcome, as on opening the door her first brusque words of greeting were 'Got an appointment?', as she pointed them to a room marked 'hospitium'.

Derek recalled being shown into a dark reception room as the maid went off down the corridor to find the headmaster. He was to discover that Dr William Purdie was something of a character and an excellent ice skater. Derek's contemporaries remember him closing the school for a day when the pond froze over, so that he could show off his skating skills. On that first day he simply said 'So, you've come then' – a remark occasioned either by the fact that Derek had arrived half-way through the academic year, or by the doubts sown by Bishop Cotter and the lack of a reference from him. As he offered to show them around the college, Derek's father informed the headmaster that it would be quite sufficient if they had a look at the dining room and the dormitory. Where his son was to eat and sleep were the important things as far as he was concerned. The rest of the school could be judged from that.

When Derek's new headmaster had taken leave of them, one of the pupils assigned to accompany them round the building informed Derek he would be in Douglass House. That was the House for 'Church students', and that meant he would be sleeping in the 'top dorm' – an euphemism for the row of tiny cubicles in the attic where, he would quickly discover, the ice would have to be chipped off the inside of the windows on winter mornings. The sight of many illustrious names emblazoned on the walls around the corridors was awe-inspiring and mystifying; gradually it would become clear that the college was divided into Houses named after great Catholic forebears, bishops who had pioneered the foundation of St Edmund's and other colleges. He saw the names of Talbot, Poynter, Challoner and St Hugh.

The cursory tour of the place and the preliminary niceties were soon over and their young guide left them. Derek's parents prepared to leave. Meanwhile Derek tried to get ready to face a new chapter in his life in the realization that it would be many weeks before he would see home again. There was one consolation, however: if the welcome and introduction he had received were perfunctory and discouraging, at least the fate that had befallen him at Winton House in his defence of the pope's reputation would not be repeated at his new school. Cardinal Bourne, who had himself been a student at St Edmund's in the 1870s, had made it a rule that Church students would not be given corporal punishment – a privilege not accorded to everyone. Other forms of deterrent existed, but this exemption was the cause of some resentment. Derek concluded that the ruling must have meant the Church authorities considered 'Church boys' to be sacrosanct and to have 'consecrated behinds'.

When Bishop John Douglass had established the College of St Edmund at Old Hall Green it had been a turning point in a long struggle for the freedom of Catholic education and the right to train priests in England. It was a struggle that had started at Douai, where the Lancashire-born Cardinal Allen had founded his college in exile and from where, in 1793, the students had been compelled to flee by French rebel soldiers who converted the building into an army barracks. Some of the students were commandeered to help run the place, but twenty-seven refugees, many of whom later became priests, came to England to serve the recusant Catholic population.

The watchwords of Cardinal Allen's brave mission for the college were 'Faith, Learning and Mission', and so they continued to be, under new management, when it was translated to England. Bishop Richard Challoner's book *Memoirs of Missionary Priests* recounts the departure of the young students and priests from France and the sacrifices they were called on to make for the Church. Challoner had been a teacher at Douai College around 1715 and, fifteen years after the failed Jacobite Rebellion of that year, he came home to face the now less vehement religious discrimination and to give badly needed leadership to English Catholics.

Bishop Challoner played a key part in the development of Catholic schools and the spread of popular devotion. He was instrumental in the process which transformed Douai College, via its temporary home in Twyford, into its English setting in the Hertfordshire countryside. Archbishop Troy gave similar impetus to the reconstitution of Douai as an Irish college at Maynooth a short time later.

St Edmund's numbered among its alumni many who played a leading part not only in the life of the Church but also in society. Three brothers of the Scholl family (of Scholl shoes fame) went through the college, including William Scholl who became president of the company. Only a small number of students reached ordination. Derek saw many come and go at St Edmund's, taking their place in different capacities as responsible members of society. But among the Catholic writers and thinkers under whose influence his generation of students grew up was Monsignor Ronald Knox, a former member of the college community. Monsignor Knox's words to the students, when taking leave of the college in 1926, captured the ethos of those days:

In such an age, to aspire to the priesthood is not to aspire to comforts or to earthly rewards. You don't want to be a priest who

41

simply does his job and knows his rubrics and hopes to pay off a bit of the parish debt. You want to be an ambassador from God to men, ready to take every opening, to follow up every trail, where there is a human conscience to be enlightened or a lost soul to be won back. You want to love souls; if you don't love souls, you will be hard put to it, in a world of so many temptations, to save your own. And even if the priesthood has no place in your ambitions, you must still want to leave St Edmund's not merely as a Catholic, but as a fighting Catholic and a working Catholic.

The words seem to have captured the spirit of a long and turbulent history, a history strewn with the blood and bones of the martyrs, with the sacrifices of Catholic families. It was the spirit from which Derek Worlock and his college friends were now to derive the motivation for their long period of study and formation, and during that time the patronage of St Edmund meant a lot to him.

Everything was set for a journey to his chosen goal in life and there was no need now for the defensiveness that had so marked his earlier years. If he had felt himself labelled as an 'outsider' before, he was now in a friendlier atmosphere. Yet, a defence mechanism had been acquired that was not to be easily cast off. An in-built shyness, which all his school contemporaries remember, contributed to a tendency in him to put up certain barriers, especially when personal criticism or confrontation arose.

He never considered the college to be a threatening place, but the experiences of his younger days had led to an exaggerated need for self-protection which, in relation both to himself and to the Church, often took the form of counter-attack. At St Edmund's he was among like-minded people, but relatively few people could get close to him. A classmate, Tony Hewson, remembers him when he first arrived, coming across as 'a bit of a grandee from the Hampshire establishment', who was 'not involved in the rag and tag of school life' but rather 'floated naturally to the top'. Several of his contemporaries at St Edmund's attest to his qualities of leadership and his ability to take on positions of responsibility in the school.

It seems, therefore, that he always retained a sense of being 'different'. Tony Hewson considered him to be ambitious but 'ambitious for the right reasons'. His absolute single-mindedness about his vocation to the priesthood was remarked on by everyone who knew him, yet he was not thought 'pious' so much as 'dedicated to prayer and to work', devoted to the college and to his teachers and ready to take a full part in all the activities of Douglass House.

The enthusiasm for rugby which had developed at his prep school was evident too at St Edmund's. He played with gritty determination. One of his school friends, Allan Wright, who was six days younger than Derek and who went on later to a distinguished career in the Air Force, retained a mental picture of him 'on a very muddy pitch, utterly exhausted, bespattered but determinedly struggling on'. He is remembered as quite 'muscular and robust' as a player, and to quote another friend of senior seminary days, Charles McGowan, he was 'someone who would mow you down on the rugby field'. As a formidable scrum forward he apparently took no prisoners. His efforts both on and off the field were evidently recognized as he became captain of Douglass First XV and Head Prefect of his House.

Staff and students were aware of his special abilities and academically he was thought to be steady and impressive. Yet some of his contemporaries recall a young man who, if not aloof, could be reserved at times, though he was not without close friends at college and there were some who understood him better and broke through the shield. Without doubt the greatest friend of his St Edmund's days, and all through life too, was Bernard Fisher. 'The Fish' as he came to be called, was a fifteen-year-old when he arrived at St Edmund's mid-way through 1935. He was just one week older than Derek, very talented academically and good at every kind of sport, especially cricket and rugby. Derek had not met anyone like him before. Their proximity in age and the fact that they were both 'late-comers' to the school, drew them naturally to one another. Bernard had come from the Jesuit school, St Ignatius Hall, Stamford Hill. Their lifelong friendship was to be a vital, mutual inspiration. Derek often went to stay with Bernard at his home in Burma Road, Stoke Newington, during holidays when, he claimed rather mysteriously, circumstances were not favourable to his going home to Winchester. It was a friendship that was to help Derek greatly on his road to Holy Orders.

On the memorable night of 2 June 1944, the eve of their ordination to the priesthood, Derek stayed with Bernard Fisher at his home and the next day they were ordained side by side in Westminster Cathedral. Their friendship was to be incalculably strengthened by the unique bond which came from receiving Holy Orders together and sharing the brotherhood of priesthood.

Among the many things for which Derek admired Bernard Fisher was his extraordinary devotion to and knowledge of the life and writings of St Thomas More. He passed on some of this interest and enthusiasm to Derek; the rapport between them also grew out of a shared sense of humour (usually the slapstick variety), and a sense of the ridiculous. 'Things seemed to happen when The Fish was around', Derek observed. It was not uncommon for Bernard to fall out of a chair helpless with laughter at some joke or to find some remark made in class so funny he would roll about in uncontrollable fits of laughter on the floor. The antics helped them through the long years of school life and they found they had similar tastes when it came to acting in or producing plays. When it came to pastoral work, they also had much in common and would discuss new ideas for children's Masses or parish liturgy. Although their paths in life took different directions and Bernard Fisher went to Cambridge before coming back to teach at the Vaughan School in Westminster, the friendship was an important factor in their later ministry.

The fact that some students appear to have found 'The Fish' quite difficult to take proved to be part of the common ground which sealed their friendship. But by the same token this set them apart from the others. Derek was thought to have his favourites, to be cliquish at times. A number of factors contributed to this, not least the fact that there was inevitably an element of *hortus conclusus* (a walled garden) about seminary life and any sense of his own separateness was further strengthened by that. The reference he sometimes made to times when he had felt excluded from his own home are not really substantiated either by his fellow students or by his sister. If there was any truth in it then it is likely to have arisen later when the issue of call-up came to the fore in 1939.

Bernard Fisher's family kept open house for students and clergy, and 22 Burma Road was known to many of them. The fact that Derek may have sought refuge there sometimes was likely to have been because of the war and the fact that Winchester became a restricted zone. The situation seems to have become rather exaggerated in his own mind; there was certainly no conscious snub by his family.

During the earlier years at St Edmund's, it is evident he stayed in close touch with his mother. There was regular correspondence between them and she would send money or presents on his birthday such as a bunch of snowdrops, the first appearance of which often coincided with the early days of February. In a letter which he wrote to his mother in May 1937 he mentioned new responsibilities he had been given in the college, including the position of House Prefect, and how this meant the privilege of having his own room for the first time with the greater privacy it gave him. That he took his duties seriously is evident from the fact that he preserved the exercise books, and the punishment books, in which he noted the names of those who had been given lines. Everything that happened under his charge was duly noted or remembered.

In this letter he refers to an article he had written for the 1937 Spring edition of the college magazine, *The Edmundian*. The article, entitled 'Witches and Warlocks', showed an early aptitude for creative writing and revealed that he had done his homework, researching local folklore and various details about witchcraft. The pun on his own name became a regular source of amusement and an ice-breaker in conversation whenever he met people; he seemed to enjoy joking about it at his own expense, advising his mother not to take the essay too seriously. It was probably his first real attempt at writing, the beginning of a life-long interest, and his imaginative turn of mind was already in evidence. He wrote:

> In some parts of Scotland where the inhabitants of warlock-infested areas were very brave, the old and ancient game of 'Hunting the Warlock' was played. In this game, all the inhabitants, armed with sticks, went up into the mountain, where the warlock was said to be living, and having chased him out of his cave, captured him and returned in triumph with him to their town and then proceeded to burn him in the market place.

It is doubtful that we can read anything into this with regard to his own experiences at school, but the choice of subject is interesting. He goes on to recount the signs to be looked for in a true witch, quoting from an old book by William Drage, which reflected the prejudices of an earlier age:

> You may consider as bewitched those who vomit, with or without torments, knives, scissors, eggs, dogs' tails, crooked nails, pins, needles, bits of wax, live eels, stones, hooks, pieces of wood or saltpetre, or who fly or run up the walls with their feet uppermost, or leap from one place to another at a great distance, also who prophesy or speak in languages they never learnt.

The article ends with a well-known prayer, a prayer which he asserts originated in Cornwall in the nineteenth century: 'From Ghoulies and Ghosties, and long-leggety beasties, and things that go Wump in the night, good Lord deliver us.' There is no record of what his mother's reaction was to all this.

The obvious enjoyment he derived from writing was given further scope in the production of school plays. Like his father, he was known to be clever at writing comic sketches, spoofs and songs or drawing cartoons about college life. This is well attested by those who were with him in his final years of the school and in the senior seminary, though he is not remembered much for his singing voice: what he lacked there was compensated by writing things for others to sing.

His contribution to college plays in the years between 1938 and 1943 seems to have reached a peak with a production of *The Amazing Doctor Clitterhouse* – the story of an infamous doctor who murders his patients. Louis Marteau, a fellow student and later a fellow priest with Derek in Stepney, played the part of the Amazing Doctor with considerable panache. He remembers Derek contributing to another memorable performance of *1066 And All That*. The attention to detail was remarkable, and in addition to writing and producing, he was very 'hands on' about stage props and work behind the scenes. A review of *1066* in *The Edmundian* magazine acclaimed its success, adding that 'only the bitterest cynic would have whispered that the props in the scene about the "space ship" were really made out of cornflake packets'. Yet, paradoxically, Louis Marteau also recalls Derek could never take a joke and that Derek was furious with him when he printed the programmes for one college production and proclaimed on the front 'A Derek Worlock Production'.

The talent for producing plays clearly owed a lot to his father. Charles McGowan recalls that he was a natural producer and a fair actor too. He remembers how they would all often be rehearsing plays when they should have been studying. In the youthful high spirits that prevailed in those years we can discern a different side of Derek Worlock, a lighter side which not everybody would have associated with him, and one which surfaced less frequently after he left college and became embroiled in so many other things. In one production he was a judge, and contemporaries can recall him sitting in judgement with a tea towel on his head as a makeshift judge's wig! At the same time his cleverness with words and sense of humour, his skill as a wordsmith and self-conscious entertainer at concerts and conferences, composer of limericks, mimic of bishops, and master of the *bon mot*, were all gifts which had their beginnings in his college days and were put to good use in later life. Years later Grace Sheppard, wife of Bishop David Sheppard, says there was always a sense of drama about him and she remembers vividly how he made good use of every movement, word and silence when he spoke at Liverpool's Anglican cathedral to mark her husband David's Silver Jubilee celebrations. He was master of the moment.

In 1937 he wrote to his mother to express sympathy over the death of his Aunt Constance, his father's sister, who had died after a long illness. He knew how close and how helpful Connie had been to his mother and assured her that Mass would be said for the repose of her soul. His father had given him an account of the celebrations held to mark the first anniversary of the Coronation of George VI; news from home and the concerns of the family were real to him and he was interested in what was happening outside the *hortus conclusus*. Nevertheless, he could be preoccupied with himself too and there are references in most his of letters to minor health problems he had: a bad toothache, headaches and sinus trouble. In fact, sinusitis plagued him throughout his life and required several painful operations.

His appointment as a prefect in the school gave him a sense of responsibility but did not enhance his popularity. The first experience of an official position of authority seems to have been marked by an overbearing approach to the task. His strong sense of duty was evident and caused both admiration and wariness in others. Yet his attention to detail and the preservation of his school papers have enabled us to know who were his contemporaries at St Edmund's.

Besides Bernard Fisher, those closest to him were Frederick Rule, Anthony Roberts, Patrick Desmond, John Widdicombe, Denis McGuiness, Allan Wright, Frank Thompson (who later became the Bishop of Motherwell), Denis McGuiness, Edward Bilsborrow, David Norris and Peter Phillips. Of the thirty students who started with him in the junior seminary at St Edmund's, twelve were ordained priest. He counted these among his closest friends.

There were 'Non-Church students' too, among whom Gaston Marbaix, Tony Hewson and Brian Hick were close friends and remained in touch with him after he left St Edmund's. The friendships which were forged in those years were precious to him, but the traumatic years that followed took their toll on the college community and he was to see many of his classmates perish in the war.

Edward Bilsborrow, who joined the seminary at Allen Hall in

1938, remembers Derek as 'a young man who seemed to know what he wanted and somehow always got it'. He remembers him as a leader, outstanding among his fellow students but not always the most approachable. He certainly supports the general impression that as a prefect at the top of the school he had a tendency to over-play his hand. Louis Marteau was three years his junior and recalls their first encounter on the train going to St Edmund's for the start of his first term. Marteau was then fifteen and was told that as a new boy 'he would have just ten days in which to learn the College Rules. After that, if he broke any, he would be punished.' There were, he remembers, four pages of House Rules to learn, including some archaic ones that had never been removed from the statute book. One was a prohibition on taking boats out on the river – 'an impossible rule to break as there never were any boats', Marteau observes. Other archaic rules had somehow remained on the books, such as the obligation imposed on junior boys 'to wear wigs powdered by the matron', and the privilege given to older boys to be allowed a pint of beer on Sundays. Such were some of the delights of an earlier era in England's public schools.

The college timetable provided a balance of academic and spiritual formation. It was not a particularly harsh regime, more lenient than many schools and colleges at that time, but certain aspects were a challenge. An early rise at 6.00 in the morning, meditation, daily Mass, prayers at various times of the day, in addition to all the periods of study, classes and recreation that were part of any school timetable. The boys were encouraged to join the various sodalities such as the Legion of Mary and the St Vincent de Paul Society. There was little opportunity or encouragement to go outside the bounds of the school, and awareness of the Church and wider pastoral issues of the day would emerge later. The discipline of a programme of prayer, spiritual reading, Scripture and Church History were the priorities which began in the school and continued into the senior seminary.

Allen Hall had a reputation as one of the more liberal of the senior seminaries, one aspect of which was the invitation given to outside speakers and lecturers to visit the college. It was from these as much as from the curriculum itself that Derek learned of the developments which were taking place in the Church. Shortly after moving up to Allen Hall, in the autumn of 1938, he remembered well the impression made on him by a visit from Yvonne Bosche, Baroness von Drakestein, who had been the inspiration behind The

Grail Secular Institute in Belgium. She and members of English Grail came to explain to the young seminarists issues which related to the Lay Apostolate, the role of women in Church and society, the new approach to ministry which priests of the future would have to adopt in working with the laity in spiritual, liturgical and biblical formation. Her words intrigued and inspired him, marking the beginning of a lifelong interest in the apostolate of The Grail and in organizations such as the Young Christian Workers.

It was not so much the subject of lay apostolate that impressed him and his fellow students in that first meeting with Yvonne Bosche as the refreshing and exciting attitude she brought with her. Her request to the college authorities that the students be allowed to smoke was popular with the students: a good ploy that was guaranteed to attract their attention and interest. In fact smoking became quite the norm with many of the students and Charles McGowan confirms that Derek was no exception. 'He smoked quite heavily, after lunch and dinner ... I would say 7–10 cigarettes a day, in spite of having sinus trouble.'

Something of a change was detected in him after moving into the senior seminary at Allen Hall. The six years spent there coincided almost exactly with the duration of the Second World War. There was a more intense concentration on his studies that meant he socialized less, except with a chosen few. Among his hobbies and recreations were reading, walking and gardening and quite a lot of time, even in the holidays, was spent working in the college grounds. He would go for walks with Bernard Fisher or Peter Phillips, who remembers how much Derek loved walking and resented the rule which had prevailed in the junior seminary that walks had to be taken in groups of three or four. It was one of the rules he tried in vain to change. In later years, he and Peter Phillips became frequent walking companions.

Although activities outside the college were limited, especially in wartime, there was plenty of scope for useful work around the grounds. In *The Edmundian* magazine Peter Phillips recorded that when fuel was rationed

> many of the trees at the College, especially around the cricket field where their branches formed the 'heart' through which every batsman longed to hit a six, were felled, and much of the wood was sold. Some of the wood was returned sawn into planks

for the refectory tables. The rest of the wood was sawn up into logs for the fires in the priests' rooms. This work was carried out by Derek Worlock and Francis Thompson and myself. We even stayed back for some time during the summer holidays to ensure a good supply of wood for the coming winter. After the war the forestry work was carried on by a group of divines led by Ralph Brown.

His companions of those days do not recall a brilliant academic but a competent student; 'an all-rounder, with a good intellect, assiduous in his approach to work' is how Charles McGowan describes him. He admits 'we were a lazy lot and only really worked a few days before exams ... there was no continuous assessment in those days. But Derek used to put in a lot of work. ... He was the most self-disciplined person I ever met.'

Another contemporary, Benedict Nixon, remembers him for his 'rock-like firmness and integrity, as someone reserved but not in the least stand-offish' and he recalls 'the gleams of his dry wit were very engaging'. Nixon recalls how Derek used to chide him about a habit he had of inscribing his name in Latin in all his books. His middle name being William, he remembers Derek calling him 'Gulie' or 'Gulielmus' and always having fun with the play on people's names. Although not bosom pals, they got to know each other well and, whilst he did not continue on to the priesthood, Benedict Nixon was present at Derek's ordination. When Nixon left the college, in 1941, he presented Derek with four leather-bound volumes of the Roman Breviary – suitably inscribed, of course, in his own hand, in Latin. Derek kept the breviaries with him among his books. Gifts from friends were seldom, if ever, thrown away.

Langton Fox (now deceased), who became Bishop of Menevia, remembered visiting Allen Hall with the cricket team from St John's, Wonersh in the early 1940s. He recalled Derek standing with him at the edge of the field discussing things to do with the Church, taking only a partial interest in the cricket match.

Others who knew him at that time talk of him as one who 'seemed to have a lot on his mind' and who was 'occasionally under the weather'. His health was always something of an enigma. On a bicycle trip to Walsingham one day in the summer term, Tony Hewson recalls how he suddenly said he would have to lie down, and proceeded to stretch flat out in a dry ditch at the side of the road, overcome with some inexplicable exhaustion. 'I had some oranges with me and I gave him one', Tony Hewson recalls. 'He seemed to recover quickly after about fifteen minutes or so.' Hewson also recalls the time when an outbreak of scarlet fever hit the college and all the students were evacuated to the countryside. He does not recollect Derek having the fever but recalls that it was a talking point for him for a long time afterwards. As for other illnesses at that time, David Norris certainly remembers him contracting chicken-pox and having to go to the infirmary for two weeks. It seems he led a charmed life: even in wartime, 'the nurse was somehow able to get him all the medicines he needed!'

Being ill at college was not something to be recommended. Heating was minimal, medicines were in short supply and food became rationed everywhere. As the college had its own farm and cattle, the community did not feel the pinch quite so much. Fresh milk, bread, pickles, soup and especially cocoa were always in good supply, though fruit was not so plentiful. There may have been deprivations but no one starved. Derek later in life developed a passion for bananas, possibly as a result of wartime deprivation: bananas were among the fruit not obtainable for several years.

The biggest concern, however, was that the war might either curtail or interrupt studies for the priesthood. Many from the college were already beginning to leave and join up, and the Army Training Corps sent personnel to address the students. Whether at the Front or in the relative safety of St Edmund's, a contribution to the war would have to be made.

CHAPTER FIVE

Approach to the Priesthood

What can I render to the Lord for his goodness to me? The cup
of salvation I will raise, I will call on the Lord's name.

(Psalm 116)

If a more academic, more serious approach to life characterized his
transition into the senior seminary, Derek Worlock continued to
enjoy his rugby and his interest in amateur dramatics. Throughout
the Allen Hall years he took a pride in his rugby, encouraged team
spirit and was able to inspire others. Commenting on a photograph
which was taken of him in his rugger kit at home in the garden at
Winchester in 1938, he said:

> The boots are interesting, not like modern boots. They were
> called Cotton Oxfords. The trousers were called 'wings' and they
> didn't seem to tear as much from the pocket. I had my hands in my
> pockets, swanky style! I used to play outside wing forward, what is
> called a flanker today. Yes, I was very keen.

The love of rugby survived all through his life. When he could he
visited Twickenham and began to collect autographs of the top
national and international players, but, uncharacteristically, didn't
persevere beyond the first five names. Years later, in 1989, he went
to Twickenham with a Liverpool priest, Michael McKenna, and
impressed Michael by knowing every player on both sides, who the
Catholics were, which schools they had attended and who their
grandparents were.

His rugby-playing days continued after ordination, until his
appointment as secretary to the Archbishop of Westminster. On
leaving college he signed up as a member-player for Rosslyn Park
and played regularly for them on Saturdays, the club sending him
fixture lists every year. But the arrangement with Rosslyn Park,

although providing a means of keeping fit and abreast of the club's activities, had its hazards. He sustained fractures at various stages in his playing career, suffering more than once from the painful condition of 'water on the knee', and the dangers involved convinced his superiors that he should not continue as a player. When he received his first appointment as a curate at Our Lady of Victories parish in Kensington in the autumn of 1944, his parish priest raised no objection to his going to play rugby each Saturday afternoon, as long as he was back in time to hear confessions at 6.30 in the evening. Even this concession was stopped the following year as the Archbishop, whose secretary he became, felt it was too hazardous and that a broken arm or leg would incapacitate him from his important work.

With Bernard Fisher he helped to edit a college magazine called *Second Tyro – A Terminal and Cultural Review*, through which he sustained his interest in producing plays. The 1943 edition records that 'Mr Worlock came into his own last year as producer of the altogether splendid "I Killed The Count"'. It is not surprising therefore to hear college friends like Tony Hewson speak of Derek Worlock as 'someone very dedicated to both work and play'. It was generally acknowledged that he did the ordinary things extraordinarily well, and the key to this was dedication. He ran the stationery shop with meticulous efficiency, not a thing out of place or unaccounted for; he sometimes managed to obtain extra provisions, sweets and cigarettes. Efficiency did not preclude the human touch, nor the knack of being able to get something special for others from time to time. It was a combination of talents for which staff and students remember him well.

The priests and teachers at St Edmund's he held in high esteem. Their ability as lecturers and the example of their prayer life were things which Derek appreciated most. In some ways he found a father-figure in those priests who guided him on his path to the priesthood. He felt distanced from his own father when Harford began to make it clear that he would like him to be an Army chaplain after ordination. The war took both his father and brother away from home and he felt more responsible for his mother who was then left alone. The sense of his father's 'disapproval' for what he was doing seemed to mount in his own mind and it is possibly at this period in his seminary days that the feeling of separation from home was most acute. The seminary and the community it provided became his home, his security.

Admiration for those who taught him was very evident. In the school he had been awarded prizes for Latin and Greek, and these had been presented to him by Father Thomas Sherlock, who replaced Father William Purdie as headmaster. The prize was less important to him than the fact that Father Sherlock, one of his heroes, had presented it. 'To my generation', Derek wrote in *The Edmundian*, 'Tom [Sherlock] was one of the "greats".' He gave students a credible vision and model of priesthood and an example they could imitate. Derek described his contribution as broadening the base of seminaries in particular and of Catholic education in general, and believed that 'it was at that time that the bogus "Catholic Winchester" pretensions were swept aside and the solid Catholic foundations were established upon which much of the school's subsequent developments have been based'.

He also had great respect for a man who not only taught him but helped to form his ideals of priestly service – Father Reginald Butcher. 'Reggie' Butcher had been housemaster at St Edmund's before going to the Vaughan School in Westminster and later returning to become President of St Edmund's in 1952. He would therefore have been Derek's housemaster from 1934. That he had the highest regard for Father Butcher is clear from the panegyric he preached in November 1975, recalling with vivid memory someone 'tall, erect, with that widow's peak of raven black hair, rather shyly professing himself as no good with small boys, yet to many of us a hero'. There was a memory of how he would come in to the stuffy classroom and 'with a pained look and screwed up nose would, to our amused humiliation, request us as a herd to open the windows'. He recalled too his sense of irony and humour. Once when a student from the College was accused of stealing items from the local Woolworth's Reggie's reaction was simply 'Oh no, not from Woolworth's!'

The reforming spirit and the desire to base relationships and authority on mature trust rather than on absolute allegiance to college rules and regulations profoundly affected Derek's own outlook. In his first year at St Edmund's Derek had been told by Reggie Butcher that if ever he was in a position to do anything to break down the barriers in the school and to bridge the gap 'between the Church boys and the Lay boys' he should try to do so. When these divisions broke up naturally after changes in the seminary structures he welcomed it as part of the death of the clericalism he tried all his life to eradicate from the Church.

Derek enjoyed Reggie Butcher's patriotism, his very 'English' Catholicism, which resonated with his own nature and background. He found there the role model he was looking for. On meeting him many years later in O'Connell Street when visiting Dublin, he asked him 'What are you doing here?' to which Reggie replied enigmatically 'Just saying goodnight to Nelson. Why is it that every time I ask someone over here the way to one of our Cathedrals, these people always direct me to the Protestant church?' It was a great sadness to Derek when, in 1963, a severe stroke took away all Reggie's power of speech and rendered him confined to a wheelchair. As it came at the same time as the deaths of Cardinal Godfrey and Pope John XXIII, that year was a traumatic one in Derek's life. He had hero-worshipped all three.

Reflecting on a meeting with Reggie during a pilgrimage to Lourdes after the Dublin meeting, he noted the fact that the stricken priest, only able to get around by being taken everywhere in a wheelchair, was 'not a tragedy ... but a trophy, a symbol of priesthood spent now in sacrifice; his intellectual brilliance, his perfectionism now sharing our humanity; the standard set now that of the cross. In feebleness, fidelity. In frailty, fulfilment.'

Another 'Reggie', Father Reginald Fuller, was also one of the key influences on the young Derek Worlock in those seminary days. Although Derek described his presentation in lectures as extremely soporific and 'dry as dust' he somehow succeeded in giving him an appreciation of the Word of God as something real, as part of life rather than an academic subject. Scripture was a poor relation in the seminary curriculum in those days; it was still seen as something for the Protestants and not 'a Catholic thing'. The sacrifice of the Mass received the most emphasis in the Catholic theology of the sacraments, although *Divino Afflante Spiritu*, the papal document issued in 1943, paved the way for a renewed focus on Scriptural studies and the importance of the Word in the liturgy. It also heralded the demise of the Modernist crisis, creating the climate not only for the greater appreciation of Scripture but for many of the other changes that would come with the Second Vatican Council.

Derek was very much more at home with the subjects that related immediately to his goal of priesthood. He was glad to leave behind the study of science, not his strongest subject, and focus on pastoral and theological matters. He recalled ruefully how his teachers at St Edmund's had once advised him to pursue a Classical education because of repeated, ignominious failure in science classes 'to carry out the traditional experiment of separating salt from sand'.

Focus on Greek and Latin was the result and in these he was thought to be a competent rather than exceptional student. He never got to grips with a foreign language in a way that would have enabled him to speak it with confidence, though he knew the vocabulary. Later in life it surprised people that even after many visits to Rome he did not have the confidence or ability to speak Italian. He was only slightly more confident in French. It has been commented that as he was a perfectionist and prided himself on fluency and accuracy in all he did, he felt it better not even to attempt to speak a language in which he could not be word-perfect. The lack of facility in foreign languages was something of a handicap in some of the work he was later asked to do in Rome; his former chaplain and close friend Canon Nicholas France recalls how on one occasion in Rome, he had to find a student to translate Derek's Synod speeches into Latin.

In the autumn term of 1940 Derek received the Tonsure in the college chapel, a ceremony marking his formal acceptance as a candidate for the priesthood. From then on he had the distinction of wearing a cassock, of belonging to the Church and to the diocese in a more visible way. His recollection of this significant juncture in his life was twofold. Bishop Cotter was still showing a reluctance to give his approval but somehow, at the last minute, he was prevailed on by the college authorities and by his Auxiliary – Bishop King, who knew of Derek's determination – to sign the necessary documents and to agree to this important step. The day after he did so, 24 October 1940, news reached the college that Bishop Cotter had died. When Derek related the story to others later, he earned himself the doubtful privilege of being dubbed 'Bishop Cotter's Last Will and Testament'.

The only other memory of tonsure was that the ceremony took place during an air-raid. In those days it included the symbolic cutting of the candidate's hair as a sign of the dedication which was being made, body and soul, to the service of God. Derek noted that the effect of the air-raid at the crucial moment caused the bishop's hand to shake and to this he jokingly attributed his premature baldness. Photographs taken at about that time show that in fact he still had a full head of hair.

From the beginning of the war demands had been made on both staff and students alike. The students at Allen Hall had been instructed to return early from the holidays in the autumn of 1939 and had been given instructions by the local Air Raid Protection about how to act in the event of fires breaking out and incendiary devices exploding. First Aid squads were organized and all the 'paraphernalia of efficient fire-fighting appeared at a number of strategic points', the college magazine of that time records. It seems that Derek took a fairly prominent part in all the precautionary work required in that first hectic term in wartime. The saddest aspect was that half of his class failed to survive the war. 'For us, to be nineteen in 1939 was the same as being eighteen in 1914', Derek observed.

One of the tasks was the long process of blacking-out all round the college, which had over a thousand windows. When it came to the chapel, however, instead of blacking-out the windows suitable blinds were put in place and the small Galilee Chapel was used for Evening Prayers throughout the war. In this way the prayer life of the college continued. The prayers which were said daily for the safety of those who had been called up soon turned into prayers for the dead.

Life could never be quite the same after the loss of friends and family in such sad circumstances, but there were occasions for gratitude even in those dark days, as when former classmates returned with accounts of their military successes. The college magazine records that on one night in August 1941, Allan Wright 'had shown great determination and skill in destroying a Heinkel 111 under conditions of extreme difficulty'. Awarded the Distinguished Flying Cross, he eventually became a Group Captain in the Air Force. Derek watched with concern and admiration the progress of his former friends and colleagues and maintained contact with several of them through the war years and long afterwards. When the fiftieth anniversary of the end of the war was commemorated he made contact with another former Edmundian, Flying Officer Neville ('Jimmy') Stack, who had piloted a Sutherland during the war and, like several other Old Boys, had a distinguished career.

In the summer holidays of 1939, Derek joined his family on a trip to Scotland. It was to be their last proper holiday together. Part-way through, news of the declaration of war reached them and they returned home to Winchester. Derek's father, who was in the Officers' Emergency Reserve, joined the Home Guard and soon afterwards was transferred to the Air Force as a Defence Officer; he was subsequently posted to Liverpool, in charge of Ground Defences at Speke. Peter, who was in the TA, was immediately called up and posted overseas to Africa, whilst Patricia, evading the medical examination that might have excluded her from active service, joined the ATS and later received a posting to Edinburgh as an Officer. Derek's mother offered her services to the WVS (Women's Voluntary Service), though she was less able than in 1914. No doubt she carried in her heart a mother's worry for the whole family.

Only Derek was unavailable for active service. He felt he should go back to college and continue his studies, as he was free to do, but felt pulled by the pressure to join up. It was a dilemma he could not fully resolve, but on balance he felt it was more important for him to return and press ahead with his preparation for ordination.

When the staff at the college became depleted and the students were all given their share of tasks, Derek was put in charge of the Fire Watch rota and had to man a rather ancient fire appliance: originally a horse-drawn vehicle but by that time operated manually and pulled by two bars. As the night-raid warden he made himself rather unpopular by going into the dormitory and shaking the bed curtains to wake people up at the least hint of a fire. The job was not without its dangers. More than once bombs landed in the college grounds: one night a bomb fell close to a sewage works but, mercifully for the college, it failed to explode; on another occasion, a landmine exploded, shattering glass in the college porch and in a chapel window.

It was to the frequent calls on him for Fire Watch duty that Derek attributed his lifelong problem of insomnia. This is probably exaggerated: as time went by, a routine was established and Charles McGowan, remembering those days well, believes that life at the college assumed 'a remarkable air of normality' considering the extra duties, anxieties and deprivations they all experienced.

When conscription was introduced there was no one to work on the land and students were roped in to dig potatoes. With little heating available there were times when hats and coats had to be worn in the classrooms during the long mornings of lectures, whilst at break-times everyone gathered round the radiators that lined the large 'ambulacrum', to stay warm. Although energetic, rugby-playing students often complained of feeling tired when the amount of food was not really adequate, there were few other complaints. It was obvious that the war years at Allen Hall were easy compared with many other places.

If Derek felt that circumstances had conspired to cause alienation from his family, there were nevertheless occasions during these anxious and exciting days when he was able to be with his mother at home. In her journal, she recalled him being with her during one of the first air-raids and coming in to the room, saying, quietly and seriously, 'Do you hear what I think I'm hearing?' No one in the house had heard it but him – the ringing of distant church bells – one of the agreed signals that an invasion of Britain had taken place. A frightening moment but a false alarm, it was an example of how he liked to dramatize.

Derek enjoyed his study of theology but referred to the four years of Church History classes in the junior seminary with less enthusiasm. The subject matter was almost exclusively a speculative discourse on what might have happened if the Spanish Armada had been allowed to land in Britain. He did not consider this a sufficient basis for a grasp of ecclesiastical history. Despite the shortcomings of the lectures on Church History, students seem to have been very happy and fulfilled at St Edmund's. He himself wrote in *Better Together* 'at St Edmund's we were generally fortunate in our lectures and in those who helped our spiritual development throughout such a long course'. In moral theology Derek's generation was nurtured on the 'Questions and Answers' textbooks of Canon Edward Mahony, a famous former pupil of St Edmund's, and its scope was restricted by a 'weights and measures' approach to moral problems, the legacy of an over-literal interpretation of St Alphonsus.

Many years later, in an article for the 150th anniversary of the Catholic periodical *The Tablet*, Derek recalled another Professor at St Edmund's, the Maltese Dominican Father Paolo Zammit. He referred to him as 'a refugee from Mussolini and the Angelicum in Rome' who gave 'terrifying but dynamic lectures in sociology'. The lectures, he explained, were 'rendered terrifying by the fact that their machine-gun burst delivery was punctuated by the periodic descent from the rostrum to demand intelligent audience participation from amongst his students'. To Paolo Zammit's lectures he attributed the rudiments of an understanding of the Church's social teaching which was to be a very important part of his own subsequent ministry.

Another professor of sociology was Fr Bernard Good, who was closely involved with the Young Christian Workers movement and who helped to keep the organization going at the college when other groups were falling away. Although keen to get involved, it appears that Derek at first found himself excluded from membership of the

YCW because his background was not deemed suitable – he was considered to have come from an upper middle-class family which was not consonant with the spirit and purpose of the movement. In spite of this unfortunate start, he became one of the leading supporters of the YCW movement in England and gave a great deal of his time to the issues of youth employment, the work of Christian formation and the promotion of family values. What was later to become the motivation of his ministry as a bishop – the social and ecclesial renewal advocated by Vatican II – was kindled by the fiery rhetoric of Paulo Zammit and those who first taught him sociology at St Edmund's.

Despite being barred from joining the YCW, he was fired with enthusiasm for its ideals by a visit to the college of Father Vincent Rochford, who at that time was a curate in Westminster archdiocese. Rochford spoke with passion about the principles that Cardinal Josef Cardijn, the founder of the 'Jocist Movement' in Belgium, had expounded. It was new ground for the students. What caught their imagination was that Rochford revealed he was wearing a red shirt under his cassock, an effective visual aid which spoke more eloquently to them than anything else about his revolutionary views and added considerably to the excitement of his lectures.

Derek Worlock's practical involvement with the YCW really began when he met and worked with Patrick Keegan in the late 1940s. Keegan, from Hindley in Lancashire, encouraged by Father Gerry Rimmer who first brought Cardijn's ideals to the north of England, eventually became National President. 'The Movement', as it was often called, beginning with the teachings of the Gospel and personal renewal, placed emphasis on the importance of responsibility for colleagues in the work-place, the right to work, and the struggle for just and proper working conditions for everyone. The fact that this was set firmly within the Church's mission in the world influenced Derek to take it as one of the central planks in his own formation and ministry. The idea of the laity working with priests caught his imagination.

Derek later encountered Cardinal Cardijn not just as a name but as a dynamic personality and effective speaker during the Second Vatican Council. Later still, in Liverpool, he formed friendships with people like Tom and Anne Casey, Father John Fitzsimmons and Owen Doyle, Ray Turner and Peggy Norris who, among others, spearheaded 'The Movement' in the north-west of England, from which grew work for the development of family life under the banner of 'Family and Social Action'. His enthusiasm for that aspect of the Church's mission became obvious to all.

A wider vision of the Church's mission opened up when a visit from Father Van Strallen, a young Dutch priest of the Divine Word Congregation, held the students spellbound with his accounts of missionary experiences in Japan. He gave them a perspective of the Church they had not glimpsed before and in a way no amount of reading could have achieved. Derek did not lose that vision and, as a bishop, put it into effect in his promotion of various missionary projects. Fifty-five years on, by a happy coincidence, Father Van Strallen, by then well over eighty years old, was in Liverpool for Derek's Golden Jubilee celebrations; he had not met him since that memorable talk at Allen Hall.

'Mission', yes, but at no stage is there any recollection of studying ecumenism. As we have seen, though, Allen Hall was considered one of the more liberal seminaries, and students certainly had access to newspapers and periodicals. In *Better Together* Derek wrote:

> It was wartime and we were allowed to be enthusiastic about the efforts of Cardinal Hinsley at Westminster, Archbishop Temple at Lambeth and Bishop George Bell of Chichester to promote, through the Sword of the Spirit – a united Christian front in face of the evils of Naziism; but this had little connection with the various penalties we learnt were to be incurred through *communicatio in sacris* [the prohibition placed upon Catholics in regard to sharing the religious rites of other Churches].

The time was not yet right for an objective look at ecumenical issues. In fact the emphasis was on apologetics, on a style and approach to the teaching of the faith which would now make most people shudder. Great orators and apologists like Frank Sheed and Vincent McNabb could hold sway at Speakers' Corner in Hyde Park and the Catholic Missionary Society provided forceful preachers to counter false doctrine. It was a time for intimidation and refutation. There were certain priorities in the early 1940s, brought into focus by the war, which tended to push into the background the finer points of theological and ecumenical development. 'We learnt from our fellow students the value of community', Derek recalled in *Better Together*, 'and we were taught to be self-sufficient and adaptable.'

Clearly conscious of the limitations of seminary life and the consequences of the exemption rule, he remembered the sorrow and loss which the war meant for him personally: 'The six-year withdrawal (rather than separation) from the world constituted in itself a considerable test. As theological students, we were classified as having reserved occupations and not subject to call-up ... When relatives and friends were killed, the pressure at least to postpone one's training was acute.' Nevertheless, he added: 'Not many of us were given the white-feather treatment ... I was most encouraged by my only brother who was soon afterwards lost at sea.'

His brother Peter had married on 20 May 1939, shortly before his parents' Silver Wedding anniversary. He and his wife, Joan Hillier, had found a place to live in London, near Kensington Gardens. Dora Worlock had been at home on her own for much of the time. News that her son Peter was missing, presumed drowned, at sea, together with several men of his regiment, the South Staffordshires, reached her at the end of November 1942, though the date of the torpedo attack by German U-boats which sank his convoy off the coast of Africa was officially given as 30 October. The news could not be immediately confirmed, and there was still a slight chance he might have been picked up by rescue boats, Dora optimistically informed the family. The more time passed, the greater were the fears, and any last vestige of hope that Peter might still be alive gradually faded.

Derek was not aware at first of the message from his mother about his brother's death. He was in the chapel at the time her phone message asking him to ring her was received at the college. Afterwards he told his mother that as he was praying in the chapel he had a sense that she wanted to speak to him. He came out of the chapel and telephoned her, unaware of the note. He was allowed home the next day and the college staff were supportive, although by then the death of relatives in the war had become almost commonplace. He and his mother were very close, there was an understanding between them and each knew how the other was feeling. Yet he would always remember the striking words she spoke in response to his efforts to console her over Peter's loss: 'Flesh of my flesh, how can a man understand!'

The fact that Derek had not gone to war had meant that he could accompany his mother through this difficult time. Together they went to break the news to Patricia, who was at that time unwell and had been admitted to a military hospital; he wanted to save his mother as much grief as possible and to inform his sister himself.

The news devastated everyone. Derek had been close to his brother and letters had been exchanged regularly over the previous three years between Allen Hall and Peter's billet in Nigeria.

He received many letters of sympathy at St Edmund's, which he never forgot and many of which he kept in his files, and he was particularly helped by the supportive letters from his sister and members of the family, from Father Reggie Butcher and Father Pat Casey (later Bishop of Brentwood but at that time living at Spanish Place), and by words of encouragement from Dom Christopher Salmon, a friend from Winchester who had become a monk at Downside. Together, the family gradually came through their grief. The practice of supporting people by letter at times of difficulty was a characteristic of his later ministry. Those who felt the loss deeply – Dora and Peter's wife Joan – became closer through their mutual grief. Joan went back with her small daughter, Penny, to stay at Itchen Abbas where her family lived; life had to resume again. Patricia took up another posting in the Army, through which she met her future husband, Paul Hayward; they were married in October 1944, soon after Derek's ordination. Derek himself resumed his studies and, against all this sadness and the persistent worries about his own health, he was eventually to reach 'that wondrous goal' of priesthood after eleven long years of training.

His sister-in-law and Penny made their own life in America after the war, and in November 1960 Penny sent Derek a newspaper cutting which reported on her marriage to Harl Piety, a lieutenant in the US Air Force. They kept in touch from time to time, as Penny appreciated the contact with her former family and through Derek she could feel closer to the father she had never known. When she returned to England for the burial of her stepfather many years later she was able to meet Derek and re-establish the link with her Hampshire roots.

Although he must surely have felt the loss of his brother very deeply, none of his contemporaries from seminary days has any recollection of him talking about Peter's death. It is possible that he found it too painful to discuss and kept the hurt inside himself.

Meanwhile, Cardinal Hinsley had visited Allen Hall and told those studying for the priesthood that they must try to continue their studies so that he could provide sufficient chaplains for the Forces and for the needs of the bereaved at home. It was all the encouragement Derek needed at a low point in his life. Besides taking on the duties of Air-Raid Warden, he joined the Officer Training Corps and after a year qualified as a Cadet Lance Corporal. His father still hoped he might become an Army chaplain but Derek had resolutely set his sights on parish work. He had carried out his responsibilities well, as a letter from the local ARP Controller, in June 1944, makes clear: 'Regarding the A.R.P., I accept your resignation with regret and thank you for the extremely able way in which you have organized the same at St Edmund's College. I acknowledge your four years of service.' The war years had given him some experience, however limited, which would be of much value later.

The diaconate was conferred on Derek at the college in June 1943. Some time before the ordination he went to make a retreat with the Cistercian community at Mount St Bernard near Leicester. By the end of that year exertions at college and worries at home had left him looking thin and pale, and he continued to have sinus problems during the winter and the following spring. In May 1944 it was arranged for him to enter hospital at Dollis Hill, London, for an operation to drill a hole in the bone of his nose to clear the conges-tion. This placed a big question mark over his ordination, due a month later.

The advice to him from the college staff was not very encoura-ging. The President told him to get off to hospital and forget about ordination for the time being. At the same time he told him that the plans there had been for him to go to Cambridge for further studies after ordination should now be discounted. Tony Hewson recalls that he and Derek were told that if they got their Higher Schools' Certificate, 'they were going to send us to Cambridge, but it didn't work out. We did our exams, but Derek's health broke down. I think it was sinus trouble.' As the President was also the Vicar General of Westminster diocese, Derek could not really question his decision. Desperately seeking the help of his patron, St Edmund, he crept into the dark side chapel where the saint's relic was kept – and where he had often ventured during the night hours on Fire Watch duty – climbed up to kiss the relic, put it to his forehead, and prayed hard for the grace of ordination.

He was aware that more than one remarkable cure attributed to the intercession of St Edmund had been recorded in the college's history. The relic had been brought there on St Edmund's Day 1861 and enshrined in the Lady Chapel the following year. A student, Paul Hemy, had been involved in a road accident in which he had incurred brain damage that left him demented. The students began a novena of prayer for him and the relic of St Edmund was taken to him after night prayer at which the students had recited the prayers for the sick. They placed the relic on the boy's head that night and again a few nights later. No visible change occurred at first, but later when the doctor was about to remove him to hospital for more specialized treatment, he suddenly and dramatically improved. The relic was brought to him a third time and he began to regain his strength and his reason. He was able to go forward for ordination some time afterwards. No one had thought to apply the relic to Derek, however, so he took it upon himself to do so!

The operation on his sinuses was successful, though not without complications. He had to stay in hospital at Dollis Hill for some days. He always recalled with gratitude that as an aid to his swift recovery one of the Sisters at the hospital, Sister Raphael, prescribed half a glass of Lourdes water and a full glass of Guinness each day. This powerful combination, and a novena of prayers being offered at the college, ensured that he was back in time for his pre-ordination retreat. It was perhaps recognized that he had overcome enough obstacles on his road to the priesthood and should now go forward without delay. Bishop John Henry King had become Bishop of Portsmouth in 1941, succeeding Timothy Cotter. This meant he would be welcome in Portsmouth diocese, but as he put it, 'the die was cast and I had joined the Archdiocese of Westminster'.

The disappointment he had felt over the loss of his chance of going to Cambridge was something he tried to play down. His academic ability, and the fact that his father had had a university education at Oxford, should have made it possible, but uncertain health was given as the reason for the change of plan. He was told he should not tackle any prolonged concentration and his doctor had said that, as he was unlikely to be able to do a full day's work in a busy parish, he should find a quiet backwater. Seldom can a prescription have proved so wide of the mark.

For the same reasons any suggestion of going to Rome to study theology had been ruled out. This was more disappointment for him. It was not that he felt a failure, more that he felt frustrated at the over-protectiveness of his superiors, the assumption all around him that he would not have the health necessary to be able to do these things. He took the frustration and disappointment with him when he was sent as curate to his first parish, Our Lady of Victories,

Kensington; it continued to rankle with him even when he went as secretary to Archbishop's House, Westminster. It appeared to him that everything was conspiring against him, especially when the priest who came to assist him there for a short time in 1947 was none other than his friend Bernard Fisher, back from a successful three years at Cambridge with a degree in History. But the work which gradually absorbed Derek in Westminster soon eclipsed these feelings altogether and possibly made him even more determined to prove his worth, Cambridge or no Cambridge.

The effect of the pre-ordination retreat in May 1944 was an enduring one. He kept a careful note of the talks given by the Dominican priest who began his opening conference with the spine-chilling words 'I suppose at no time have those approaching ordination faced a greater likelihood of martyrdom'. His prediction about the baptism of blood which the new priests were to undergo in London in the climax of World War Two was no exaggeration, but it was offset by the bliss and idealism of the young men themselves as they stood on the threshold of their ordination day.

He went forward for ordination on 3 June 1944, in Westminster Cathedral. The joy of that day did much to melt away any remaining tensions in the family, and the happiness he felt and showed was shared by his mother, father and sister who were deeply moved by the occasion. Archbishop Griffin, newly installed at Westminster in succession to Cardinal Arthur Hinsley, was the celebrant at the ceremony. Ordained alongside him were his close friend Bernard Fisher as well as others who had been his companions over the student years now ending: Charles McGowan, Dennis Skelly, Edward Bilsborrow, Joseph Law, Denis McGuinness, Denis Crowley, Franz Hope and Peter Phillips.

What were their thoughts on that great day? It was only three days before D-Day when 'Operation Overlord' was to accomplish the successful landings on five Normandy beaches. Looking back on that moment of the fulfilment of his dreams, he wrote: 'Our love of God and the priesthood burned bright that morning with an unqualified generosity. There were no strings attached. All that we had we would give and even then it would not be enough.' His mother had anxiously watched him walk past her in the procession. He had looked very pale and drawn and she wondered if he would get through the long ceremony. Perhaps her concern increased when she saw him sit down at the moment of the prostration – a message from Archbishop Griffin, who had also noticed his pale colour, gave him permission to do so. After the Mass the new priest gave his mother and father his first blessing; they had seen their son realize his childhood ambition.

After the four-hour morning ceremony, the new ordinands were expected to wait for the Archbishop to finish his breakfast before they were allowed to start their own. Father Derek Worlock then made for his home in Winchester to celebrate Mass in St Peter's Church next day at 11.00 a.m. and the day after that visited his family in their own home at Itchen Abbas. From there he set off on a round of visits to see those who had supported him along the way – not forgetting the London convent where, at the age of seven, he had made the promise to Sister Clare. A huge breakfast party was organized by the nuns there for the family despite the problems posed by rationing, which was still in force.

Back at St Edmund's again, studies had to be completed till the end of term, but he felt no sense of anti-climax. He now knew personally the truth of the words which each year he had heard from the lips of new priests as they returned to college – 'It was worth it for that one Mass.'

CHAPTER SIX

A Curate in Kensington

By nightfall on 4 June 1944 the Allied Forces had crossed the countryside on the outskirts of Rome and were poised to enter the city and free it from the Germans. The coincidence of dates gave rise to the remark often on Derek Worlock's lips that 'Rome was relieved when I was ordained'. No doubt the relief was no less a personal and real one for him after the trials and uncertainties of his years of training. Relief all round then, but not yet a cessation of conflict for war-weary Britain.

The brief visit home to Winchester after ordination brought home to him the reality of what was being planned for the beaches of Normandy. Winchester, he remembered, was part of the 'reserved area packed with invasion forces awaiting D-Day. Vehicles, supplies and equipment were everywhere and I needed a permit to go across the city.' He recalled too that 'On 6th June, as in the early hours I lay abed, I heard the creaking noise of the gliders going over as the Battle of France began'.

He had been given a long holiday of six weeks to convalesce after the sinus operation, but various factors cut this short. On 13 June the first German V1s – the flying bombs or 'doodle bugs' – started falling on Britain. He awaited news of his first appointment. He did not know then that far from being the quiet backwater or the country parish in Hertfordshire he had been told to expect, it would be in the thick of things, at Our Lady of Victories, in London's Kensington High Street.

What would otherwise have been the unclouded happiness of those special days following ordination was sadly and unexpectedly broken by his mother's collapse during a Mass in Winchester. He was in the pulpit preaching his first sermon when he saw her being carried out of church. It was just three days after his ordination and he had gone home to be with his family and the local parishioners of

St Peter's. The collapse was the onset of a stroke and a prolonged illness for his mother. Providentially he was there to help; as Dora recalled:

> Derek was wonderful; he scarcely left me; he knew what I was going through, and his calm strength helped me as nothing else could have done. When I told him it would be better for me to die if I were paralysed, and a burden on them all, he just said, 'We want you, however you are – just remember that – and you will never be a burden, so don't worry on that score.'

Her road to recovery was a slow and difficult one. The family did all they could to support her and for Derek it meant a good deal of work and concern that prevented him enjoying the prospect of an appointment to the parish work that awaited him. He was able eventually to find a suitable nursing home in which his mother could complete her recovery, and after some weeks he was able to start looking ahead.

The large and busy parish of Our Lady of Victories in Kensington High Street was to take him into the heart of doodle-bug territory in war-stricken London. His earlier pangs of conscience about non-involvement in the war could scarcely have been more comprehensively dispelled in the months that were to follow, caring for the victims of bombing in the midst of the conflict. His direct experience of the war was minimal, but at last the time spent as Cadet Staff Sergeant, and the training and discipline of his involvement with the Officer Training Corps whilst at Allen Hall, gave him something to fall back on.

Although it was significant for his later ministry, his time in Kensington was to be very brief. A first appointment is crucial and he was anxious to know what his parish priest would be like and what was expected of him. He was to go as curate to a parish priest whose initial reticence was due to shyness rather than to a dislike of his new assistant. Canon James Walton, a Liverpool man, was the rural dean and a well-respected figure in the Archdiocese of Westminster. The Vicar General at the time, Mgr Moragh Bernard, wrote to Derek on 27 June 1944 to inform him of the appointment, instructing him to get in touch as soon as possible with Canon Walton at Our Lady's Presbytery, 16 Abington Road, Kensington.

He was told that he should be in residence there by Saturday 15 July. Derek duly acknowledged the letter and wrote to Canon Walton, who replied immediately welcoming him to the parish. In fact he invited him to lunch the following Thursday and emphasized that they were a happy family at Our Lady's, and that they worked together well. They would make him at home.

On their departure from the seminary the Spiritual Director had given some advice to the young priests embarking on their first curacy, to the effect that they should 'make the parish priest their daddy'. Derek could not have been sure, in the first days at least, whether or not this could be achieved with Canon James Walton. He would have been hesitant – and James Walton very surprised – but the reference to being a family helped.

The large and demanding parish meant that there were two other priests resident there: Father Joseph Eldridge and Father John Marriott. In those days it was not uncommon for a parish to have the help of several assistants, and they were certainly needed. The area of the parish contained the Cardinal Vaughan School, a convent of Spanish nursing sisters at Holland Park, the Society of African Missions, the Assumption Sisters whose convent acted as a Chapel-of-Ease for the parish and the Perpetual Adoration Convent, plus two other smaller religious communities. The neighbouring church in Kensington High Street, dedicated to Our Lady of Mount Carmel and St Simon Stock, was run by a community of Discalced Carmelites. It was a busy setting for a new and enthusiastic priest. He gave himself to it with customary zeal, not knowing then that it was only to be his home for 'precisely eleven months and ten days', as he would often reflect, regretfully, in later years.

Derek had fond memories of his parish priest and recorded them in *Give Me Your Hand*.

> He was shy to the point that his defence mechanism was interpreted by those who did not know him as aggressiveness. We became firm friends from the moment when, a few days after my arrival, I flung him on the floor as he hung out of a window to try to see a flying bomb which seconds later scored a near miss on the presbytery. I fell on top of him just before the glass covered both of us. The barrier of shyness was not the only thing broken that day.

The church building itself was a temporary one when Derek moved there, as the original church had been destroyed in the Blitz. Now it suffered damage yet again, from the German flying bombs. Although the two priests were unharmed, fifty civilians were killed outside the presbytery in this one incident alone.

Whether he made him his 'daddy' or not, Derek recalled that he learnt from James Walton that the basis of the relationship between priests has to be trust, understanding and appreciating that each person is different. This became a principal theme of his later approach to the clergy when he was made a bishop. He noted that just when he thought the parish priest had forgotten about him or might not care what he was doing, Walton would drop a remark indicating he knew very well 'just how much or how little you had done'. This trait was seen in Derek himself later by those who worked with and for him. Their relationship was so good that Derek never found any obstacle to his regular Saturday rugby game at Rosslyn Park. The parish priest would insist that he was given a good meal – usually including rice pudding – at lunch time to fortify him for the game. The only stipulation was that he be back by 6 o' clock in the evening to hear confessions. In *Give Me Your Hand*, Derek recorded:

> When I was threatened with a move, he [Walton] wrote to the Vicar General to protest. When some weeks later I was 'told' by the Archbishop, he was the first to help me to accept the situation. It was the harder when some years later I was sent by authority to persuade him to retire owing to ill-health. He protested that I had been sent, thanked me for having told him and added that I was quite right.

Such was the fond memory Derek had of his parish priest and he was always grateful that this had been his first appointment.

Saying goodbye, even after a relatively short stay at Our Lady of Victories, apparently proved very difficult. Perhaps he exaggerated it all in his own mind, as was so often the way with him. Looking back on that moment of departure he said, in a talk to priests:

> I can remember how fed up I was when I was called to work at Archbishop's House after less than a year in the parish. The day of departure came and somehow I delayed. I decided that it would be charity to make yet another farewell call at the local convent where I had received much kindness. I telephoned the Reverend Mother, an old French lady who was used to acting as mother confessor to everyone from De Gaulle downwards. Her words to me were direct. 'What, Father, are you still here? Now remember that the only sure way of doing the will of God is to obey your bishop promptly. Now, go!'

He added: 'I went, and subsequently I have been grateful to her.'

On the home front, on 21 October – a few months after his ordination – he had the happy task of blessing the marriage of his sister Patricia to Paul Hayward. His mother was well enough to be present at the wedding. However, she was not strong enough to play any active part in the proceedings of the General Election which took place in the July of the following year, 1945, in preparation for which Harford Worlock was closely involved. From now on Dora's cherished political work and constant travelling had to be drastically curtailed and she spent most of her time at home. Home was by then in Easton, a small village some five miles outside of Winchester; it was to be the family's final home. There were very few other Catholic families in Easton at that time. Many years later, when Derek had become Bishop of Portsmouth, he returned there for an ecumenical service at the invitation of the Vicar. By then the number of Catholics had risen to seventeen and it was a memorable occasion. On that warm summer's evening the bells rang out as he approached the church: a new climate of tolerance was emerging, so different from the days of his childhood.

Never one to be idle, his mother organized the Darby and Joan Club at Easton. Her written journal – her 'apologia' – was also brought to an end soon after this. Meanwhile, Paul and Patricia went north to live in the village of Helmsley, near Ampleforth Abbey, where Paul was a teacher.

As a new curate Derek had thrown himself into the life of the parish at Our Lady of Victories. It had been a time above all for adaptation, for having some of the smooth edges roughed a little, for learning to be flexible and open-minded. The neat and orderly lessons about administering the sacraments – learnt from the text-books – were modified by the realities of parish life in the city.

The most abiding memory of his first months as a curate was that he gave the Sacrament of Anointing over fifty times before he administered it to someone who had died of natural causes. On one memorable occasion he had made his way through an excited and tearful crowd of people to the scene of an explosion. The women were saying aloud 'Poor thing. Oh, the poor thing.' Fearful of what he was to find, he made his way through with the holy oils. On the ground was a canary in a cage which had fallen from an upstairs room when the bomb had crashed through the wall of the house. Even wartime experiences sometimes had their lighter side.

Describing this culture shock to some priests, many years later, he told them how, as students, 'we had practised baptizing rag dolls and now found a loud-mouthed and wriggling baby in front of us, with more ribbons round the neck than we thought possible. We had learned the formula for absolution, without being told how to get a drunk out of the (confessional) box.' But he explained how he was fortunate to find an understanding and patient parish priest, and a 'helpful' curate 'who laughed when you asked him what to do about the bride who comes to the altar rails wearing light string gloves which she could not get off her sticky fingers!'

The beginnings of a recognition of ecumenical partnership seem to have dated from those days in Kensington, if only in a tentative way. He does not seem to have taken the initiative himself, for he wrote in *Better Together* that 'I would often come across the Vicar of Holy Trinity, Brompton, who would turn his hand to sweeping up the glass and rubble in the street. He once told me that he envied my sacramental role, but with his broom he was humbly trying to serve the local community.' Wartime had made it a matter of necessary ecumenism by virtue of a shared crisis and a shared process of damage limitation.

It is abundantly clear that Derek was far from happy to leave Kensington, even if it can hardly have been easy there amidst the bombing and the scenes of misery which dominated his ministry. But the Archbishop of Westminster was insistent that he join his staff in the summer of 1945. He was to be second secretary, as Mgr Cuthbert Collingwood, who had been secretary to Cardinal Hinsley, still held that office and had remained at Westminster. A man who came to know Derek at Westminster, Bishop Gordon Wheeler, remembers how it became known around the diocese that before leaving Kensington, and presumably before the French nun gave him his marching orders, the young curate had made, from the pulpit, a rather solemn, over-the-top, speech of farewell, thanking all the organizations and sodalities, the Society of St Vincent de Paul and Union of Catholic Mothers, the Knights of St Columba and the Catholic Women's League, expressing his great sadness at leaving them all. It was more like someone who had been there for forty years rather than precisely eleven months and ten days.

It would be impossible to overstate the influence upon the young Father Worlock of the years which were to follow and of the man who now became his 'boss' at Westminster, Bernard William Griffin.

Although there were many things in their ecclesiastical and personal background to separate the two men, and an age difference of twenty years, they came, in time, to have a mutual regard and love not understood fully except by those closest to them. The Cardinal had ordained him and had agreed his appointment to Our Lady's, Kensington a year before he summoned him to Westminster. He knew his man.

No doubt Bernard Griffin had noted certain qualities in the young priest and had watched how he conducted himself in the first difficult year: the experience of anointing and burying victims of the London bombing in that parish; the knowledge that Derek had held certain responsible positions at St Edmund's, which had meant a role of leadership among the other students, although, contrary to the expectations of some, he had not been elected Senior Divine – that position had gone instead to Dennis Lucas. He had fought to overcome ill health and worked extremely hard and single-mindedly amidst disappointments to reach his objective of ordination. Such would have been his reputation at the end of his college days.

Archbishop Griffin may have been encouraged in his choice by the account circulating that the young Kensington curate had pulled his parish priest to the ground in the presbytery – to protect and save him from certain death from a flying bomb. This augured well for the care he might expect in the future from his new secretary. When he approached Father Worlock about the job, Derek pointed out that he was not qualified for it: he could not type, he could not drive. This only made Griffin all the more determined.

In an article in the *Independent Magazine* just over forty years later, in December 1988, Derek chose to write about Griffin when invited to contribute to a series entitled 'My Hero'. Describing the time when the Archbishop invited him to join his staff he wrote: 'I was just 25, had been ordained a priest for less than a year and had no wish to give up my work as a curate in west London. So I told him that I typed badly, my foreign languages were poor and I was an inadequate driver. I had resisted for three weeks before being summoned to his presence.' He recalls Griffin's reply: 'You have obviously got the one quality I am looking for – clearly you don't want the job.' Griffin told him, in his direct manner, 'Until now I have been inviting you, now I am telling you ... you will start next week'. Despite the show of reluctance he must certainly have been secretly flattered and pleased. The expression of confidence it betokened was a much needed boost at this juncture in his life. It was more than that; it was to be a momentous watershed in his life.

CHAPTER SEVEN

Out of the Shadows

Part One

Cardinal Bernard Griffin was enthroned as the sixth Archbishop of Westminster on 18 January 1944, having been plucked from his work as Auxiliary Bishop in Birmingham. At Westminster he had succeeded Cardinal Hinsley, his erstwhile Rector and father-figure from college days at the Venerabile – the Venerable English College, Rome. Arthur Hinsley had died on 17 March 1943, aged seventy-eight. Notwithstanding the significance of the date (which, to the annoyance of the Irish community, ensured he would be commemorated every St Patrick's Day), he was in fact a Yorkshire man, from Selby. Having taught at Ushaw College, near Durham, and at St Bede's College, Bradford, before being appointed to the English College, Rome, as Rector, Arthur Hinsley had enjoyed a varied and outstanding priestly career. He had also served as Apostolic Visitor in Africa, from which he was taking a well-earned rest when unexpectedly appointed to the leading Catholic See in England in 1935 at the age of seventy.

Among Cardinal Hinsley's notable achievements was the foundation, along with the leaders of other Christian Churches, of the Sword of the Spirit campaign which later became the basis for what is today CIIR, the Catholic Institute for International Relations. The initiative was the fruit of his broad thinking and missionary experience. Remaining in office as Archbishop of Westminster for eight years, he established a reputation and status for the Catholic community in Britain in keeping with the need for a united front and high profile for the Church in Europe during the war.

At the time of his appointment to succeed Hinsley, Bernard Griffin was living at Coleshill, near Birmingham, where Father

Hudson, the one-time parish priest at Coleshill, had founded his Children's Home in the early 1900s. The care of children and the interest he took in their needs were aspects of Bernard Griffin's work that he enjoyed most among his varied responsibilities. To help the disadvantaged or orphaned children was not just a job but an expression of his spirituality, a spirituality based on the life and ideals of St Thérèse of Lisieux. He displayed incredible energy, had a tremendous work rate and effective pastoral style that made him an outstanding figure in the archdiocese of Birmingham. Even so, at the age of forty-five he was scarcely the expected choice for Westminster.

Griffin was born on 21 February 1899 into a strongly Catholic family, and the Church was always a major part of his home life. His sister became a nun, Sister Mary Philip, and his brother Walter became Dom Walter Basil Griffin, a Benedictine monk of the Douai community. Bernard Griffin attributed his vocation, and nearly everything else in his life, to the influence of his parish priest Farther O'Hagen at English Martyrs, Sparkhill, near Birmingham – a parish which had begun on a shoestring and owed its growth to the hard work of local people, including the Griffin family.

After serving in the Royal Naval Air Service, and having suffered a heart attack at the age of only nineteen in the last year of the First World War, Bernard Griffin went on to be an outstanding student at Oscott. It was here he learnt the history and spirit of the English Church that Milner, Faber and Newman had inspired, and later, in Rome, he developed a great love for the universal Church and the *Romanità* he imbibed (probably literally) on walks around the Eternal City. He did a walking tour in the Sabine Hills with some fellow students.

He returned from Rome with a doctorate in theology and canon law in 1927 – not bad for someone who had suffered a heart attack and failed his catechism test as a boy at school. One of his first Masses was celebrated at Yardley Wood but he was given his first post as parish priest at Coleshill, a place that was to be very dear to him and for ever associated with his name. The work of the Catholic Evidence Guild and the Catholic Social Guild flourished in the archdiocese under his inspiration. Archbishop McIntyre of Birmingham, recognizing his gifts – his affable nature and infectious laugh, shrewd judgement and indefatigable work-rate – made him his secretary, but the Archbishop's ill health meant that Griffin worked mainly with the Auxiliary, Bishop Barrett, later Bishop of

Plymouth, with whom he became firm friends. Under Archbishop Thomas Williams, Griffin then became both secretary and Chancellor and from there had a meteoric rise to the position of Auxiliary Bishop, whilst taking on the appointment as Administrator of the Father Hudson Homes for Children. In May 1938 he was made Auxiliary Bishop in Birmingham, and Vicar General – to the incredulity of his former parish priest and hero, Father O'Hagen.

Joseph Masterson, one of Bernard Griffin's great friends from his years in Rome, who succeeded to the position of Archbishop of Birmingham, would have been the obvious choice for Westminster but for a serious illness, of which most people were unaware. It is considered probable that, on being asked for advice about the vacancy, he put forward the name of his bright young Auxiliary whose pastoral and administrative ability were by then well known, at least in the Birmingham archdiocese. He had by then taken on the tasks of diocesan Chancellor and Chaplain to the Catholic Stage Guild, and had won a reputation as a speaker at Hyde Park Corner with the Catholic Evidence Guild. Even more importantly Griffin had acquired a reputation for raising money and influencing the right people to give to the causes he espoused; a definite asset to any diocese.

The post which he was given in 1937, after the sudden death of Father Bunce, as Administrator at Father Hudson's Homes, Coleshill, was certainly connected with this fund-raising ability. The establishment then housed 500 boys and girls up to the age of fifteen. The Sisters of Charity of St Paul, from nearby St Paul's Convent at Selly Park, ran the Home and became firm collaborators with the bubbly, young and energetic bishop. Years later, one of the sisters who knew him well and worked with him there, Sister Agnes (Bernadette Teahan) came eventually to nurse and help Derek Worlock in Liverpool – a coincidence of which Griffin would have approved.

There were several problems to be faced at Coleshill. Griffin's priorities were the orthopaedic hospital, opened by Father Hudson during the First World War, and a home for unmarried mothers, which he himself opened later to cater for a real need he had seen in the city. In addition, he found the money needed to provide for future endowment funds. Money was not necessarily at the top of everyone's list of priorities, but he was determined. The hospital and the other institutions were, by his efforts, brought into unison. He did this mainly by undertaking to give the Sisters a series of spiritual talks which became extremely popular and in the course of which he slowly convinced them of the need to put God before their internal divisions and differences.

Although he was tough in many respects, he was completely soft when it came to the care of children and their needs. They trusted him, and as Sister Bernadette remarked, he was like one of them in his childlike simplicity. As a loving parish priest at Coleshill he was a popular figure, one whose human touch remembered people's birthdays and Sisters' Jubilees. In the years ahead he was to win the hearts of statesmen and political giants with this same personal approach.

Derek Worlock once described his great hero, Bernard Griffin, as a man who believed in doing the little things as well as possible: a policy in keeping with the spirit of the saint who had provided his inspiration through life – St Thérèse of Lisieux. His family background was in farming, which had given him a deep respect for and closeness to the things of the earth, alive to the miraculous life-cycle of every day. Griffin's sister Katherina was a fine Catholic woman who kept respect for her brother's memory and retained a friendship with Derek Worlock after his death, grateful for the two men's partnership in the Westminster years. Two of her daughters became nuns.

To take the place of the heroic and famous Arthur Hinsley was a daunting prospect for the young Bishop Griffin. His reply on receiving the news, when he was asked for an immediate response, was a simple but coded one: 'Coleshill agrees – Griffin.' Despite the cryptic nature of the reply, the local post office guessed it and the news spread like wildfire, almost before he himself could reach Archbishop's House from Coleshill. He duly went to London and began to apply his energy in a new way to the onerous responsibilities there as the unlikely and unexpected leader of the Catholics of England and Wales.

Very soon his work and energy took him, in the role of roving ambassador, to Europe, Canada and the United States. He championed the cause of Human Rights, of social and spiritual rebuilding after the war. His leadership was not that of a spectacular orator but of a hard-working, level-headed man of action. As Archbishop, he maintained his interest in the pastoral care of young people and those with social needs, applying what he had learnt about the Church's social teaching from his mentor Monsignor Parkinson in Oscott.

When Father Derek Worlock, then aged twenty-five, joined the new Archbishop's staff in July 1945, as under-secretary, it was, as he records in *Better Together*, 'shortly after VE Day and a few weeks before Hiroshima'. His sense of time pressing, and of the instability of the world, are attested to by people at that time. He had a challenging and varied job description. The responsibility for winding the clocks, of which there were a considerable number in Archbishop's House, each Sunday morning, was one of his duties – a job he tried unsuccessfully to pass on to the next under-secretary when he was 'promoted'. However, he took such duties as seriously as more significant ones.

The opportunities for the pastoral work he had been doing at Kensington were now no longer open to him, though he tried to keep in contact with people there. To his regret he had to relinquish his direct involvement with parochial organizations and sodalities, such as the Scout Group. Typically, he kept on file many letters from friends and parishioners, letters which were a mixture of congratulations and commiseration.

In November 1946, soon after starting work at Westminster, he went north, by train, to Helmsley, Yorkshire for the baptism of his nephew, John. His brother-in-law Paul Hayward was teaching at Ampleforth School. On the way back to London, the train left the rails. It was not a major accident but he suffered the effects of whiplash. It was to that incident he attributed the stooped posture of his shoulders and head and the arthritis in the neck that plagued him for the rest of his life, although he sometimes referred to it as 'secretary's neck': his sedentary job had contributed to the condition.

In the course of the decade after the war, inter-Church activity progressed slowly and cautiously. The period was marked by rather strained, distant relationships, at least where doctrinal matters were concerned. Geoffrey Fisher had been enthroned as Archbishop of Canterbury, in succession to William Temple, in April 1945, but relations between Westminster and Lambeth were no more than formal. Derek Worlock would soon find himself involved in the move to greater Church Unity for which Archbishop Fisher and Archbishop Griffin laid the foundations. The surprising thing, in a general ferment of change and new initiatives to counteract the inertia of postwar days, is that progress in ecumenism was so slow.

In other ways, however, his life as secretary at Archbishop's House was quickly taken up by the engrossing business of the many strands of social reform legislation being enacted by the Labour Government. There was the little matter of the Butler Education Bill, going through its final stages in Parliament in 1944. Rab Butler, who had been President of the Board of Education, enhanced his profile when the Board was raised to the status of a Ministry. The Bill contained proposals which were to lead, among other things, to the division into primary, secondary and further education, the introduction of the eleven-plus and the raising of the school-leaving age. Cardinal Griffin's objections were to the manner of procedure and he launched into criticism of the proposals before he was officially installed at Westminster. He doggedly opposed those elements of the Bill which affected denominational freedom but was principally opposed on the grounds that it was inappropriate and unfair during wartime for a national government to hold sway over minority groups, of which the Catholic community was one. People could have little redress, at such a time, against legal provisions which were hurried through on the pretext of urgency. The Bill, as it stood, seemed ultimately to imply the loss of Catholic schools; Griffin and the bishops would not countenance that. The motives were probably not so much anti-ecumenical as a concern for minority rights and the all-important fact that the Catholic contribution to society after the war was, in the view of the Church, itself a vital one.

Griffin had already felt the Government's wrath after his public pronouncements on various issues, such as the inadequate and unjust treatment of ex-servicemen on their return home from the Front, and the betrayal of Poland at Yalta when the three great powers of America, Russia and Britain had, he believed, allowed their own mutual distrust to come before the common good. He gave stark warnings of impending sectarian violence in Northern Ireland. For the latter pronouncement, Bernard Griffin was called to the Home Office by Herbert Morrison, who asked if he wanted to start a civil war. So much for the unknown bishop from the obscurity of a parish in the Midlands.

As for the schools, there is a clear indication in Lord Butler's autobiography, *The Art of the Possible*, that Butler had more than a sneaking admiration for his critic who did not, at that time, have the full prestigious power of a cardinal to bolster his position. Lord Butler wrote:

I had just got to the second part of my speech, in which I anticipated playing against the wind, when Mgr. Griffin, the newly-appointed Archbishop of Westminster who had been enthroned the day before, was ushered into the Distinguished Strangers'

Gallery. There, with the sun illuminating his bright red hair, he sat looking directly down on me as I outlined the provisions of the religious settlement and replied to those who had criticised its compromises. 'I would ask those who feel deeply' I said, 'to dismiss from their minds the wholly unwarrantable views that the Government desires either to tear away Church schools from unwilling managers or to force them inhumanly out of business.'

The assurance was enough to prompt Griffin to send a present to Rab the next day: a set of Butler's *Lives of the Saints*.

The landslide Labour victory of 1945 brought to an end fourteen years of Conservative rule. Helped by the conditions of a protracted war, a broad-based Labour Party had emerged, attracting an electorate from a wide range of social classes, though it was remarked at the time in *The Tablet* that whilst it was secure in its majority, the new administration was 'precariously short of men of any proven ministerial ability'. Griffin, mindful of Catholic interest, vehemently opposed certain proposals in the Health Service Act of 1946 which he saw as endangering the jobs and livelihood of the many Irish nurses in Catholic hospitals. These, like the schools, were likely to be adversely affected by the legislation, winding down the provision of exclusively Catholic establishments. In this controversy he became famous for opposing, and getting the better of, Aneurin Bevan, the Health Secretary. Similarly he was at the forefront of battles, a year later, with regard to the National Assistance Act, safeguarding the needs of disabled people, and the National Service Act (1947), in particular the clause which pertained to the right of seminary students to finish their training and to be ordained without being called up for military service.

Father Derek Worlock was soon to discover that his new 'Father in God' at Westminster was a friend to many, both high and low. He had met Field Marshal Alexander whilst on a pastoral visit to the troops in Italy. 'On one occasion', Derek recalled in an article on Griffin, 'he emerged from an audience with Pope Pius XII clutching rosaries for Alexander's children.' Later, in 1947, shortly after becoming a Cardinal, Bernard Griffin, with Derek, visited the United States, where they had an official meeting with Harry Truman. Derek recalled that Griffin shared 'a bottle of Coca-Cola' with the President. More importantly, during that same trip the Cardinal received from President Truman an Honorary Doctorate of Civil Law at New York's Fordham University.

During the hectic and extensive tour of the United States they travelled 10,000 miles, sometimes taking on as many as twelve full engagements a day, which meant at least one whole night travelling somewhere by car. When they returned, news of the successful efforts to enlist American support for European unity on the democratic lines that suited Britain caused the Foreign Office to call Griffin 'Britain's best unpaid ambassador'. His young secretary cannot have failed to notice this change of tune by the new Government.

The Irish too seemed to appreciate his approach to the Irish question and his opposition to interference in Irish affairs from outside. Griffin entertained De Valera, and vice versa, both in Ireland and at Westminster. Derek recalled a dinner when a speech went down rather well, though not the whiskey he himself was given. Having to drive home, he knew he could not indulge, even if he liked the stuff, which he did. Rather than incur the wrath of his hosts 'by refusing the great tumblers of "the creature"', he emptied it into a nearby flower pot. However, his hosts took his empty glass as a sign of enjoyment and kept on refilling it.

Although Derek was an assistant secretary, under Mgr Collingwood he soon began to make his own mark. He took on many of the methods of his boss as far as prayer and work patterns were concerned: early morning meditation, serving the Cardinal's private Mass before saying his own, clearing his desk after breakfast each morning before 11 o'clock. At quite an early stage after his arrival he became involved in arrangements to ensure that students for the priesthood (whom the typist and secretary, Maisie Peachy, called 'my Theologicals') should have sufficient books and funds to be able to stay at college in those days of rationing and shortages. Derek felt he owed much to the sacrifices of those who had kept him at seminary.

There was a lot to be done in the parishes and among the Catholic population. Bernard Griffin, especially after he was made a Cardinal at the young age of forty-seven, travelled extensively in post-war Europe, but he did not neglect to travel the length and breadth of Britain as well, in the role of 'roving ambassador' given him by the Pope. Pius XII had dubbed him 'My beloved Benjamin'. As the youngest of the Cardinals to be announced on 23 December 1945, and officially presented with the red hat at the consistory on 21 February the following year (his forty-seventh birthday), Pius XII held him in special esteem.

Whilst at the English College for the official reception of his *biglietto* of appointment as Cardinal, he took advantage of the occasion, as was his custom, to make a speech calling for peace in Europe. It appears that the honour was fully recognized back in England even by Buckingham Palace. When Griffin returned from the consistory, with the new Cardinal Archbishop Gilroy of Sydney and the Canadian Cardinal McGuigan of Toronto, Derek was asked to arrange an audience for them with the King; it was readily granted. The role of the Commonwealth Cardinals was an important one in the process of reunification after the war. In Rome Griffin had rescued them from the embarrassment of being put, by a Vatican official with a poor sense of geography, with other national groups rather than being accorded their own rightful status as Canadian and Australian. They became firm friends as a result of Griffin's intervention. Derek tried his luck and asked if he and his fellow Commonwealth secretaries might be admitted to Buckingham Palace too, only to be told that his 'proposal was most improper'.

On a later occasion, marking the betrothal of Princess Elizabeth to Prince Philip, the Catholic bishops were allowed to be represented on condition that no titles describing territorial jurisdiction held by the Church were mentioned. The Ecclesiastical Titles Act forbade it. In the event, King George VI was heard at one point loudly and clearly for all to hear addressing Richard Downey as 'The Archbishop of Liverpool' to the consternation of the Court!

One of the main purposes of all Griffin's foreign travel was to persuade the leaders of other nations, and of the Churches, to adopt what has been described as his 'uncompromising Catholic Social Doctrine'. The firm convictions learnt at the feet of his professors in Oscott and Rome were quite unashamedly invoked by the Cardinal as he made his way into many of the privileged institutions and the homes of the influential. Besides getting to know and work with the top Government Ministers in this country, such as Brendan Bracken, he came to know personally many other world figures, all in a few years of relentless globe-trotting and constant work. By the end of 1945 and early 1946 Derek Worlock was inextricably a part of the back-up team.

An early visit to Poland in 1947, the first by a leading churchman after the war, was one of many subsequent visits to Europe that Cardinal Griffin made. Affairs in Poland, threatened by Communist Russia, were of special concern to him (and subsequently to Derek) as was evident in his care for Polish Catholic welfare in this country as well as the plight of its Church leaders in Poland itself. At the time of the Polish visit, Cardinal Sapieha, the predecessor of Wyszynski, was away in Rome, but sent a message to say how Cardinal Griffin had proved himself a trusted friend of Poland. In their enthusiasm, at one point the crowd picked up the Cardinal's car and carried it through the streets. Griffin was to express his support again and again for the Polish clergy and people when the Communist regime there demanded the oath of allegiance to the state in 1953. Concern for the Hungarian Cardinal Josef Mindszenty, who held out against the incursions of the state and the nationalization of schools, increased when Mindszenty was arrested on 26 December 1948. This provoked loud protestations from the English Cardinal.

In Germany, where he advised the hierarchy about how to retain Catholic education amidst the European policy being hammered out by Britain and others, Bishop Von Galen told him: 'I have fought the Germans; unless it gives us our schools, I will fight the British Government too.' 'I shall do the same', Griffin replied. Bishop Von Galen later went so far as to tell the Pope that the English Cardinal had 'saved Germany's Catholic schools'.

A turning-point in Derek Worlock's career came when Monsignor Collingwood was appointed, in 1947, as Administrator of Westminster Cathedral, in succession to Monsignor Martin Howlett. Derek Worlock moved up to be the first secretary and principal assistant to the Cardinal. One of the tasks which fell to him was the secretarial work for the Bishops of England and Wales, not only in regard to their Low Week Meeting but in the countless matters relating to the dioceses around the country. Mgr David Norris, who knew Derek from St Edmund's, also joined the Cardinal's staff as financial secretary and general secretary to the Bishops' Conference. This side of his work evolved from scratch as there were as yet few structures in place and little secretarial help. Many initiatives which he began by scribbling on the back of an envelope on his desk flowered into important projects in the Catholic Church in England and Wales. One such project was the opening up of the piazza in Victoria Street to give a full view of the cathedral façade, in 1976.

Later on, under Cardinal Heenan, David Norris recalls that he would write up the minutes after a meeting of the Bishops' Conference and show them to Father Worlock who would then change them. 'Derek liked to attribute remarks to people' but by the time they arrived on the Cardinal's desk, Norris would have changed them back again!

In those days there were two different regimes at Archbishop's House and Clergy House and although discipline was very much the order of the day, life was not without its lighter moments. Derek's contemporaries tell of a food lift called the 'Bourne Mouth Express' – a Cardinal Bourne invention. The kitchen was in the basement and the lift passed through the clergy Common Room on its way to Archbishop's House dining room. But its cargo did not always arrive safely; dishes were said to have 'disappeared' *en route*!

Cardinal Griffin left little time for leisure. He was particularly interested in social issues and showed a keen interest in promoting the Association of Catholic Trade Unionists, the Catholic Managers and Employees Association and the Young Christian Workers. Whether by virtue of the seeds of social concern implanted in him by his mother, or whether because of his growing admiration for and devotion to Cardinal Griffin in his many endeavours, this type of concern became a part of Derek Worlock's priestly ministry too. Griffin's inaugural address on the occasion of his Installation read rather like the Queen's Speech: it discussed some of the key matters of the day then before Parliament.

After emphasizing the need for a revival of Christian family life and values, he described artificial birth-control and the means to easy divorce as 'a menace that ought to be abolished'. He endorsed the call for Family Allowance and a proper, sufficient wage. He went on to use the occasion to say that Catholics – taxpayers like everyone else – were far from satisfied with the proposals of the new Education Bill which prevented parents from fulfilling their rights to a Catholic education for their children. He ended with a plea for an end to the war and a lasting peace. Not bad for a start. His various talks and sermons, between 1944 and 1948 especially, are recorded in the anthology *Seek Ye First*.

Fuelling this deep concern with social and family values and underpinning it, there was, Derek came to appreciate, a spiritual motivation for all Cardinal Griffin did: the 'spirituality of St Thérèse of Lisieux'. Griffin was devoted to the saint and her writings. He visited Lisieux whenever he was in France and used her autobiography, *The Story Of A Soul*, as the basis of his daily prayer all his life. He visited Lisieux after he had been made a Cardinal in 1946, for a memorable meeting with St Thérèse's two sisters and Derek recalled a memorable visit there in 1948 when they again met and talked in the Infirmary where Thérèse had died and in her former cell, with Céline (Sister Geneviève, in religion), and Pauline (Sister Agnes, who became Prioress of the Lisieux Community). Cardinal Griffin endorsed the spiritual outlook of doing everything, no matter how small it may seem, with utter dedication and love and finding in so doing that God brought about his purpose. Just how many 'little' things were done in those years between 1944 and 1956, years punctuated by severe illness, is impossible to calculate. He remained a firm adherent of Thérèse's theology that God is also found among the pots and pans, and that virtue is found even in picking up a pin for the love of God. Pots and pans may not have been part of Derek's lot when he became secretary, but little works of drudgery and routine certainly were.

The legacy of those years of achievement are seen today in the benefits to the Catholic community. The work done by Bernard Griffin is perhaps only appreciated in light of subsequent history. It was rather a lonely furrow being ploughed in those experimental days after the war, when the past was horrific, and the future, however uncertain, was everything. Father Derek Worlock's role in shaping that future was strengthened when he was made a Monsignor at the age of twenty-nine, in August 1949, with the title of Privy Chamberlain. It enabled him to have a little more standing in the eyes of the officials, diplomats and Church dignitaries who came in a fairly constant procession to Archbishop's House to see the Cardinal.

It has been said that Derek Worlock became over-protective of Griffin and would not let people near him for fear of them discovering just how ill he was. Gradually Derek became Griffin's right-hand man. He wrote Griffin's letters at times; indeed, the comment among Westminster clergy every time a pastoral letter was issued was 'Who's this man Griffin signing Worlock's letters!'

The years that engrossed Derek Worlock in such demanding yet interesting work were a time of consolidation and expansion of the Catholic Church in England and Wales. There was the continuing work on Westminster Cathedral, begun by Cardinal Bourne in 1895. It was in connection with the cathedral that Derek Worlock met Father Gordon Wheeler, who later became Bishop of Leeds, and who had been appointed Chaplain to the University. He lived at Westminster Cathedral after being a curate in North London, following his departure from the Anglican Church. Wheeler had trained for ordination as a Catholic priest at the Beda College in Rome and so came from a very different background from that of Derek. His task at Westminster, among other things, was to edit the *Westminster Cathedral Chronicle*, which meant that he and Derek met often in those years, as their work and interests frequently overlapped.

Wheeler remembers that Bernard Griffin was immensely proud of 'his' Cathedral. He loved the choral tradition and excellence of its music and did all he could to promote both the fabric of the building and the standard of its liturgy. Although thought of as a man of simple piety, he could also respond to the great ceremonial occasions. As might be expected, he was particularly happy to see young people using the Cathedral. He took seriously the architectural beauty of the building. He was very anxious that every step in its embellishment should be in line with the mind of the architect. In 1955 he launched an appeal for money which later enabled the mosaic in the Blessed Sacrament Chapel, where he celebrated early morning Mass on First Fridays, to be put in hand. Unfortunately, he was too ill to attend the consecration ceremony of the great alabaster sculpture of the Madonna, known as Our Lady of Westminster.

One of his favourite parts of the Cathedral was the Chapel of St George and the English Martyrs, which then contained the shrine of St John Southworth. Derek and a small group of priests were given the task of reclothing the remains of the saint's body in new vestments and placing a silver death mask on the face. He recalled that of the seven who began the harrowing yet privileged task only he and one other saw it through to completion. Also in the Cathedral, the body of Richard Challoner lies buried, having been given a Catholic burial there at the instigation of Cardinal Griffin.

Gordon Wheeler later became Administrator of the Cathedral at the request of Cardinal Griffin, replacing Cuthbert Collingwood, who resigned that post in 1954. There had been a controversy when Collingwood, who was essentially an MC, wanted to clear the view of the sanctuary and removed a rather important pillar, to the consternation of architects and cathedral devotees. In light of this the Cardinal felt it was time for him to move on. Wheeler recalls going in to tell Derek of his appointment: 'he held his head in his hands and groaned – "Oh, God no!" Later he bethought himself and congratulated me on my appointment.' He remembers Derek Worlock as someone who 'slept little and worked endlessly', a person totally committed to his work for the Cardinal, a man of unusual talent who 'could have handled almost any job he might be given'.

Bishop Wheeler also attests to the way Derek changed. During the interregnum of 1956 in Westminster, he found Derek supervising the refurbishment of Archbishop's House. He commented on the likely cost of such a project and Derek retorted 'What you have to realize is that we are preparing here a place worthy of a Prince of the Church'. There was truth in this: Griffin and his successor Cardinal Godfrey were indeed 'Prince Bishops' and represented a very different ethos in the Church at that time. But Wheeler recalls meeting Derek some ten years later as the new Bishop of Portsmouth, wearing a wooden cross and a plain black cassock, advocating a more frugal lifestyle to his clergy. Quite a change had been effected chiefly by the Vatican Council: a change of attitude and heart which had its effect on Derek Worlock.

Part Two – Into the Light

Looking back over a series of major imaginative events which were organized during the late 1940s and early 1950s, it is clear that Cardinal Griffin, with his fellow bishops and leading laity of the time, was intent on an all-out drive to bring the Roman Catholic Church 'out of the catacombs' – as he once put it in an address to students at Fisher House, Cambridge – and to place English Catholicism on the map, in a manner reminiscent of John Henry Newman's great vision.

There was an explicit desire to use large public gatherings as platforms in promoting the Church's social doctrine, not out of defiance or even in self-defence, but because it was believed to be right for all people. These were not particularly ecumenical times but neither were they times hostile to ecumenism. The time for closer unity and common endeavour had not yet arrived; the Second Vatican Council was still some years away and Archbishop Geoffrey Fisher's historic meeting with the Pope still undreamt of. So, the work of building, promoting and negotiating in Church and state affairs went quietly and inexorably on, with Derek shouldering more of the work in proportion to the Cardinal's deteriorating health.

In 1949, when Griffin fell seriously ill with exhaustion and heart failure, for the first time since his Royal Naval Air Force days in 1918, plans were underway for a large rally of 7,000 people, on 7 February in the Albert Hall, to voice opposition to the arrest of Hungary's Cardinal Mindszenty. The Protestant Churches and the Jewish community in Hungary had felt obliged to accept the authority of the State with regard to the nationalization of schools but Mindszenty had held out against it. On 26 December he was arrested by the police and in February of the following year sentenced to life imprisonment for his opposition. Cardinal Griffin's place was taken at the rally by Richard Downey, Archbishop of Liverpool.

Griffin and the English bishops believed it was a time for strength, not only for the sake of their own Catholic education but for the principle of religious and cultural freedom everywhere.

In that same year, on 1 October 1950 – St Thérèse's feast – the Catholic Hierarchy Centenary Congress was held in Wembley Stadium and this time Griffin was present. St Thérèse had played her part, no doubt, in his recovery. He was the Pope's Legate for the occasion. There was general concern for his health, as he looked frail and was lame as he walked in procession into the stadium, leaning heavily on a walking stick. But by the end of the Congress he was walking without the stick, smiling bravely at the applauding crowd of 90,000 people. Mgr Derek, with a group of helpers, had undertaken a great deal of the organizational work of these events, having to take many decisions in the absence of the Cardinal. Assuming such a powerful position was to be both a blessing and a curse.

With more public events planned for the Holy Year called by Pope Pius XII, and a visit to Rome for the promulgation of the Dogma of the Assumption of Our Lady, there were few breaks in the punishing schedule. Derek had not made it a priority to take a day off each week and the Cardinal's policy was just to keep working all the hours God sent; 'to work the maximum amount possible for the maximum amount of time' was his adage. Overwork was the problem when illness struck. Even when the Cardinal's doctor advised Derek to take a holiday himself, and he went in to the Cardinal's room to explain this, Griffin simply replied, with his usual impish humour, 'Oh, good, where shall we go?' There were few times when the Cardinal made it possible for his secretary to go away on his own, or with his own friends. David Norris recalls that even when the Cardinal was away there always had to be cover from one of the secretaries.

One place where Griffin enjoyed a break, when it did prove possible, was Torquay, where the large convent at Stoodley Knowle, home to the Order of the Daughters of the Cross, was a favourite place for a holiday and recuperation. Here Derek, giving up his own holiday to accompany the Cardinal, made friends with the Sisters and played tennis. He remained friends all his life with past pupils of the school and their families, people like Mima (later Countess of Iddesleigh) and Jennifer Middleton, a fine tennis player who won the Devon County championships in 1950. Cardinal Griffin became a firm favourite with the whole community and his visits were long remembered with affection. Like everyone else, they enjoyed his childlike sense of fun.

It was a very welcome break to get out of London's claustrophobic atmosphere, especially when, in the winter of 1951, a yellow cloud, caused by the build-up of sulphur gases from the industrial estates and factories, descended upon the city. The only saving grace of the smog which killed 2,000 people that winter was the gradual emergence of the Clean Air Act, which Griffin actively endorsed. Small wonder he and his secretary made for Devon and Cornwall – places like Tremough, where one of the Stoodley community once described the seasons appearing 'to mingle like the inter-lacing of the warm and cold waters on the edge of the Gulf Stream' and where the climate was 'more mild and equitable than is found in any other part of the country'.

Other holidays were taken in Ireland, at Derrynane and at the Butler Arms Hotel in Waterville, with Archbishop Masterson and Archbishop Murphy of Cardiff. As a result of these memorable holidays, Derek developed a life-long love for Ireland and often recalled his holidays there, even though they had not been entirely free of care and had entailed looking after the Cardinal before he himself could rest. It was on one of these trips that he first met the friends who were to become his 'second family', Henry and Maureen Joseph and their children. They remained his close friends all his life and spent many holidays together. He became like an uncle to the family and there is no doubt that they helped to keep him balanced during the long arduous years at Westminster and in his episcopal days. They nicknamed the young monsignor 'the Mon'.

More health worries were in store. In January 1951, the Cardinal had a coronary thrombosis. As before, he came through it, though more gradually, and when he went for convalescence at Torquay he was accorded the privilege, by the Bishop of Plymouth, of having the skull of the martyr Cuthbert Mayne in his room for two weeks. Just as Derek felt at St Edmund's that the prayers of his patron had helped him, Griffin attributed his recovery to Cuthbert Mayne's intercession.

Once well again, he threw himself into the busy round, with Derek at his side now more and more in the role of supporter and aide. Deep trust and mutual friendship grew up from those days. A prime concern was the care of the clergy of the archdiocese and their spiritual needs. Days of Recollection were begun at that time. Nor were the needs of the laity overlooked, both the Cardinal and Derek, in his own right, were very busy promoting the full role of the laity in the life of the Church, in local and central government and in the community in general. This concern was something which would grow for Derek in the following years when he was to accompany another Cardinal, William Godfrey, to Rome for the Second Vatican Council.

With the title of Domestic Prelate being conferred on him in January 1953, and his work load undiminished, more and more Derek took over the running of the archdiocese and as David Norris remembers, did so 'very well', but in the process was in danger of alienating himself from his contemporaries. Too much power inevitably attracted enemies. He was viewed at the time as being careful, efficient, but unpopular. The problem was that he himself did not see it, or if he did, chose to tough it out and ignore the comments. This was his way; anything else would have been seen by him as failure. His loyalty to the Cardinal was intense and the obsession with work was borne out of a sense of duty and of the need to protect the Cardinal's good at all times. At a Rosary Rally a few of his former college friends met him, sitting waiting in the Cardinal's car, and got in to join him for a chat but he was not interested in small talk; he got them saying the rosary instead.

It was an integral part of bringing the Catholic Church out of the shadows to be present at Catholic occasions around the country, at events which would provide a platform for pressing home the message that Catholics were a strong and vital force in society. The ceremonies themselves on such occasions were in Derek's capable, not to say ruthlessly efficient, hands. Later, in Godfrey's time, his established position as the Archbishop's MC meant that clashes with other people were inevitable when it came to planning liturgy. Father Michael Gaine remembers encountering Derek in Leeds at some big diocesan celebration; it was soon after Archbishop Heenan's appointment to Liverpool in 1957, and Michael Gaine was his secretary. Derek was secretary to Godfrey, who had not yet been made

Cardinal. There was a dispute about whether the two Archbishops should each have a throne in the sanctuary; Michael Gaine arranged for two thrones. When Derek arrived on the scene the night before the ceremony, he asked for one to be removed. It demonstrated he was a stickler for protocol.

Cardinal Griffin's strength and his range of work were diminished but he surprised people again and again by his resolve. The Family Rosary Rally led by Father Peyton, the Marian Year and 1950 Holy Year celebrations, as well as the great Vocations Exhibition at Olympia, in July 1953, at which the Cardinal ordained 30 priests, all helped to bring Catholics out of the 'catacombs', out of the siege-like position in which they had been for so long. At Olympia he prayed that more vocations to the priesthood might be granted: at that time the Westminster Province alone contained one million Catholics and there was an acute shortage of priests to serve them.

Derek made the care of the clergy his special concern. He often remarked that, at the age of twenty-nine, he was 'the youngest Monsignor in the world'. Accompanying the Cardinal to the International Eucharistic Congress in May 1952, he was at the centre of a historic occasion. Some two years later he was present at the ceremony, in Wembley Stadium, of the crowning of the statue of Our Lady of Willesden, a shrine that had been ruined at the Reformation and was proudly restored to its former glory. Such events helped to restore the morale of clergy and laity.

Changes were also being tentatively introduced into the liturgy, with the Dialogue Mass, and the advent of evening Masses (which increased the round of parish visits), whilst the Friday abstinence laws were also revised. Relations with the Anglican Church were also beginning to move forward slowly. For the occasion of the Coronation of Queen Elizabeth II in 1953, the Papal Legate was asked to take his place in a specially constructed box opposite the entrance to the Abbey, rather than being allowed inside. A slight thawing of the ice that had surrounded ecumenical attitudes at this time, however, came in the form of a recognition, on the part of Catholics, that the new Queen, Elizabeth II, could be the subject of prayers and that Masses could be offered for her in every Catholic Church in the land. On the part of the Anglican community, permission was given to the Catholic bishops to go into the Abbey, during their annual gathering at Westminster, on 13 October 1953, to pray at the shrine of St Edward on his feast day.

The Catholic Church had not yet quite come out of the shadows. The visit took place after dark, as the Abbey was officially closed during this period for refurbishment. The Dean, Dr Don, left a side door open at Derek Worlock's request, and the bishops crept in. He described it as 'a moving moment when all of us trooped silently into the Abbey and went to the shrine to pray for reunion'. One bishop walked slowly round the sanctuary singing 'Kyrie Eleison' in the belief that it might have been 'the first time those blessed words were heard inside the Abbey walls since the Reformation'. Unknown to Derek, at that moment his mother lay dying at home in Easton.

In the morning a row broke out in the Press over a publication entitled *Infallible Fallacies* which purported to be a rejoinder to recent Catholic statements of belief or 'propaganda'. Coping with the news of his mother's death, he handed the press enquiries to Father Christie, a well-known Jesuit apologist who replied with a pamphlet entitled *Anglicans Anonymous*. This 'point-scoring' went on for some time and set relations back.

In the middle of this busy and controversial time the sudden bereavement took him unawares. He had been so close to his mother and this was a hard time for him and his family. The funeral, at which he was the celebrant, three days later in St Peter's Winchester, was attended by Cardinal Griffin and the Bishop of Portsmouth, Archbishop John Henry King. There were Members of Parliament, members of the organizations and local groups with which she had worked, together with a large number of priests from Portsmouth and Winchester. Although she had been in poor health since the war, Dora Worlock's death obviously came as a shock and a source of very real grief to many who knew her. She was laid to rest in St James's Cemetery, Romsey Road, just outside the city of Winchester, where some famous people are buried, including the mother of Bishop Challoner, and Bishop King of Portsmouth.

It was here that Derek came to bury his father, in 1957, and many years later his closest friend, Father Bernard Fisher. For Derek is was important to mark the passing of his loved ones with special care for their burial place. He took great pains over having a worthy memorial stone for his mother – a stone cross depicting the figures of St John and the Virgin Mary, which he designed himself down to the last detail of the type of stone and lettering to be used. Later, after Bernard Fisher's death, he ensured that the family were able to erect a proper headstone for the grave and was helped in this by his

Chaplain, Canon Nicholas France, who was also a great friend of Bernard Fisher. The hope of resurrection was strong in him on such occasions and he saw that external signs were an important reminder of this to the passing world.

After his mother's death, Derek's father, who had retired in 1952, lived alone at Easton until his death four years later. He too was by then highly esteemed in both political and Church circles. Not only had he been the Tory agent for four successive MPs, but he had also been a leading member of his local parish, a strong and active Catholic to the end.

Derek heard of his father's death in an abrupt way. He had been visiting his father in hospital for a number of weeks. He had just been making one such visit and returned to Archbishop's House, Westminster, when the phone rang. The voice on the phone simply said: 'Is that Monsignor Worlock? This is the hospital. Your father was a patient at this hospital.' It took a few moments for him to realize the significance of the past tense. It seems that when he lost his brother, mother and father, he did not allow himself time for mourning and preferred to keep his feelings to himself, immersing himself in work as an antidote to grief and suppressing his feelings.

Along with the sadness caused by the loss of his parents there was the worry he increasingly felt on account of the many voices which said that Cardinal Griffin was too ill to continue and that he should retire. This might well have happened had it not been for the protective and supportive role of Derek himself, who had increasingly become the Cardinal's eyes and ears. Much of the work and speech-writing, correspondence and representative work was now being done by Derek, whom Griffin trusted absolutely. This, for good or ill, made it possible for Griffin to remain in office. It did not make for the best of relationships with the clergy of the archdiocese, many of whom felt that Derek was taking too much power on himself and preventing, in the process, what some undoubtedly considered to be a much-needed change of leadership. Instead, one of the Auxiliary Bishops, Bishop Myers, was made titular Archbishop with the right of succession. This move secured the Cardinal's position further, and meant that Derek retained his post as secretary at Archbishop's House.

Before Cardinal Griffin's final illness, when Derek was always closely in attendance, Archbishop Masterson died in Birmingham. His funeral was at St Chad's Cathedral, and Griffin preached an emotive panegyric for his old friend. The loss of his great companion must have added considerably to the strain that he was under at that time. In this panegyric he looked nostalgically back and remembered Archbishop Masterson 'one evening standing on the shores of Derrynane looking wistfully at the country he loved so well and gazing longingly at the sea'.

Griffin presided at the Low Week meeting after Easter 1956, and led the National Pilgrimage to Lourdes in May; he even attended a ceremony in Rouen in honour of St Joan of Arc. One of his last visits to Westminster Cathedral was on 28 June. The occasion was a Service to mark the bravery of Catholic holders of the Victoria Cross and give thanks for their work. Incredibly, he preached that day whilst experiencing a heart attack, remaining in control throughout and collapsing later in the house. He rallied again from this illness but arranged soon afterwards, on the doctor's advice, to go for a complete rest. He decided to use a holiday house called Winwalloe that had been rented for him at Polzeath, near St Minver Highlands, on the sands directly overlooking the sea to Pentire Point. He made the journey by train on 7 August – Derek, together with Bernard Fisher, having gone ahead to prepare things. He relaxed and seemed better. But there was little warning, as he retired for the night on 19 August, of the heart attack that was finally to kill him in the early hours of the next day: the feast day of his patron, St Bernard. Derek remained with him and held a crucifix to his lips as the final prayers were said. He anointed the Cardinal from the oil-stock he had carried with him for this eventuality since 1949.

At his funeral on 24 August in Westminster Cathedral, Archbishop Grimshaw of Birmingham said of Griffin that he was an intensely loyal Englishman but believed in the brotherhood of man, which, he used to say, was only possible with belief in the Fatherhood of God. He described him as 'a genuine product of the true democracy of the Catholic Church'. The Cardinal's death left a real gap in the lives of Catholics and the life of the nation, and his passing was described by Monsignor Ronald Knox as being 'like a determined dash through the net of watchfulness that surrounded him'.

CHAPTER EIGHT

The Vatican II Experience

You know my heart, Lord, that what you have
given to your servant, I desire to spend
wholly on your people and to consume it all
in their service.

(St Aelred)

Part One

No one felt the loss of Cardinal Griffin more than Derek Worlock. The Cardinal had been a loyal friend to him, a mentor. He now had to prepare for the next phase of his life, and awaited news of the successor at Westminster. There was not too long to wait. In December, the appointment of Cardinal William Godfrey was announced. A Liverpool man, from the Kirkdale area of the city, and a distinguished former pupil of the English College, Rome, William Godfrey – 'Uncle Bill' as he was known by many – brought with him fourteen years' experience as Apostolic Delegate with all the diplomatic skills and the necessary *figura* that gave him.

Derek Worlock, staying on as secretary, greeted a robust, serene and imposing man as his new Archbishop; a man in vigorous health who claimed he had never had so much as a headache in his life, let alone a day in hospital. Godfrey was described as a prudent, cautious man 'of sober judgement', much slower in decision-making than his predecessor, an altogether different personality. Derek once made the comment that Bernard Griffin had been five years ahead of everyone in his policies and Godfrey took five years to decide on any pastoral development, so it did not make much difference in the end. 'By then everyone had reached the same conclusion', he commented.

Writing about Cardinal Godfrey, years later, for the Venerabile magazine, Derek Worlock said of him:

Certainly no one could live long with Cardinal Godfrey without realising that his priesthood was the very centre of his life. His daily meditation and his punctilious preparation and thanksgiving for Mass were a byword. His frequent use in public addresses of quotations from the Mass exemplified its position of supreme importance in all that he did each day.

He went on to describe how, at a parochial visitation,

he would scrutinise registers, confessional grills, the inside of ciboria and the number of members of the Blessed Sacrament Guild. But when the ceremonies were complete, he would remind the priests that a parish visitation was a joyful mystery and he would relax happily in their company, leaving them delighted and encouraged by showing them that he was their brother priest as well as the local ordinary ... he was renowned for his equanimity of spirit.

He described Godfrey as a man with 'an infectious spirit of serenity' and someone who never missed a chance for quiet prayer. He became known as approachable and personable, often sitting at the back of an almost empty cathedral in a plain cassock, ready, if asked, to hear a confession or direct the way to a chapel. Among his great pastoral attributes was an outstanding record of sick visiting, of both priests and parishioners.

These reflections, written by Derek after the Cardinal's death, show the main characteristics of the man who came to succeed Bernard Griffin as Archbishop. Derek himself had to adapt quickly from being the confidant and nurse of a sick man and the arbiter and executive of nearly all Bernard Griffin's affairs, to being once again alert to the commands of a new challenge, a different agenda and, in some respects, a new era in the Church. The first instruction he received from Godfrey was to cancel all the evening Masses which his predecessor had introduced. Knowing the outcry this might cause, he succeeded in stalling until evening Masses were accepted anyway.

William Godfrey had great regard for the one whose place he was taking at Westminster and maintained many of the same key policies, building on the excellent work already done. The knowledge and experience which Derek, though still not thirty-seven years old, had gained stood him in good stead for his new role. Recent years had brought expansion for the Catholic Church in Britain and considerable development in the spheres of science and technology, population explosion and social change. In the archdiocese of Westminster thirty-seven new churches had been built; 11,000 more children attended recently built Catholic schools. The new Archbishop picked up the work involved in visiting all the schools, parishes and convents of the archdiocese. He was especially keen in promoting the Days of Recollection for Clergy, started by his predecessor, and determined about introducing, in the summer of 1957, a new four-year Syllabus of catechetical instruction for the schools, building upon the Syllabus Cardinal Griffin had authorized for Westminster four years earlier.

The new Syllabus was intended for all sectors of the school community and was accompanied by guidance for teachers. The emphasis at that time was on a formal list of subjects and on the use of stories from Scripture, on the need for memorization, but not on bland repetition of Catechism questions. It was far from being autocratic and laid the stress on the teacher's freedom, within the formal guidelines, to build up the images and language suited to different age-groups. The beginnings of a new approach were already in evidence. Many years later, Derek would face controversy over another RE programme with similar aims, *Weaving the Web*.

Pastoral letters, sometimes ponderous, seldom world-shattering, were, nevertheless, full of doctrine and solid spiritual advice. There was a notable, almost infamous exception: one letter, which Derek referred to as the 'Poodle Pastoral', caused quite an uproar. It was designed to encourage a collection for Family Fast Day in the dioceses (Family Fast being a forerunner of CAFOD, the Catholic Fund for Overseas Development), and did in fact help to raise a total of £25,000, but the controversy came from pet lovers everywhere. The Cardinal had dared to suggest that less might be spent on pampering our pets and more on the needy people of the world – 'plump and pampered poodles prancing in the park might run all the more gaily after a reduced diet or simpler fare'. This method of encouraging people to look at priorities and at the practice of self-denial backfired rather badly, as the recommendation happened to coincide with Crufts Dog Show that year. The furore which ensued was predictable. He was more circumspect and watchful of coming events in his future pastorals. It was possibly as a consequence of this that when he came to a position of authority himself, Derek Worlock would always look ahead carefully to see if any local and national events might result in an awkward clash of interests.

The duties which had absorbed him before now continued without loss of pace or intensity. There were the Hierarchy Meetings to prepare, visits to other dioceses around the country – visits which had a pattern to them and involved carefully arranged meetings with civic leaders, parishioners, clergy, and diocesan representatives. He was virtually the Press Officer for the Catholic Church, since media interest tended to focus on London, but had to combine this work with his many other duties. One of his contemporaries recalls Derek dealing 'with some episode with the press which would certainly have rebounded very badly on the Church, concerning a priest'. He remembers Derek interviewing the journalist from a national newspaper with himself in the background as a learner. 'I must say, he dealt with it very effectively with a little mixture of sugar and threat. The man backed off. He had no reason to, he was from a national newspaper and not a Catholic-controlled paper.'

On one occasion he had to pacify angry reporters who asked Cardinal Godfrey for some words on a particular issue. Godfrey instructed Derek to take a text from among those he had placed in his files from earlier occasions. When the reporters queried whether this was one he had used before, he asked 'Is it a good text?' 'Of course, Your Eminence,' to which he replied 'Worth repeating, then'. Some measure of diplomacy was called for as a result.

Constant travelling was an aspect of his life, as Visitations of dioceses throughout the country were undertaken. There were many long journeys, by car or by train, both in Britain and abroad, and air journeys to many parts of the world. One of the most memorable of these must surely have been the visit to Rome for the Consistory of 17 December 1958, at which Cardinal Godfrey received the 'red hat' from the new Pope, John XXIII. Godfrey received the news whilst at Hare Street House, his country retreat in Hertfordshire. He had been at St Edmund's College the day before the announcement, celebrating the college's patronal feast. Derek had accompanied him to his Alma Mater for the feast day which was always very special to him.

They set out for Rome on 9 December, the two Auxiliary Bishops of Westminster, Bishops Craven and Cashman, seeing him off at the airport. At Rome airport he was met by the British Ambassador to the Holy See, Sir Markus Cheke, and all the staff of both the English

College and the Beda. Also in attendance was Mr Anthony Bartlett, the Cardinal's Gentiluomo for the occasion, as on many subsequent ones, and Wing-Commander Robert Grant-Ferris MP, representing the British Government. Those were days of greater ceremony and solemnity than today. The new Cardinal-elect, in a speech at the college, said: 'In receiving this favour, I am well aware that it is at the same time an honour to England, my native land, to the Archdiocese of Westminster and to the Venerable English College wherein I have been privileged to spend sixteen years of my life.' In the years that followed, during the historic meetings of the Second Vatican Council, it was possible to say of William Godfrey that 'few Cardinals outside the Curia have been held in such affection in the Eternal City'. As a former Apostolic Delegate, and later the leader of a large and prestigious archdiocese he found favour on all sides.

Derek loved the experience of a Roman ceremony with all its splendour and pageantry, something he secretly revelled in (though he claimed not to) and believed to be an important expression of the Church's authority and collegiality: two themes which were the principal aspects of this period of the Church's history. It was at this time that he became acquainted with many of the members of the papal entourage and Masters of Ceremonies, people like Bishop Van Lierde, the Papal Sacristan, and Monsignor Nasalli Rocca, Master of the Papal Household. Later in life, when he was a bishop himself, he was always happy to be part of the great Papal Masses and occasions in Rome, with an unashamed sense of the sheer triumphalism of it all and a sense of the Universal Church which Griffin had given him. However, in later years he recognized that this triumphalist liturgy was not necessarily well received by the other Churches.

The consistory of 1958 proved to be a prelude to the many liturgies which Derek was to attend in St Peter's during the Second Vatican Council. There he was to take on the role of secretary to the Eng-lish bishops and during the final session become a bishop himself. The historic announcement of an Ecumenical Council came unexpectedly from the caretaker Pope, John XXIII, on 25 January 1959, the feast of the Conversion of St Paul.

Twice in the autumn of 1958, Derek had been in Rome with Cardinal Godfrey: for the funeral of Pope Pius XII and for the Coronation of Pope John. At the time of the historic announcement from Rome, Derek was at The Grail in Pinner giving a talk to a group on the Lay Apostolate. As he returned to Archbishop's

House Bishop David Cashman greeted him by saying he had better pack his bags as he would be off to Rome again. 'Pope John has really done it this time: he has called an Ecumenical Council.'

Above all, it was the atmosphere and the experience of the Council which left the deepest impression on Derek Worlock and changed him. These were things which no amount of words or documents could adequately convey. Being part of an historic event which was in many ways epoch-making was profoundly significant for him. The sheer length of the event was awe-inspiring. The story is told of Cardinal Cushing leaving the Council in frustration after the first few debates in St Peter's and returning to his diocese of Boston, claiming he would do better by being at home and raising money for various good causes. When reporters in Boston asked him how the Council was getting on he replied 'I give it two hundred years'. In *Better Together* Derek recalled that

> the first announcement of Vatican II caused some confusion. My instructions were to emphasise in any press statements and in response to enquiries that this meant a General Council of the Church, whereas the media insisted that it was about Church Unity. While many bishops throughout the world had their own hobby horses to ride, it was soon evident that the main focus would be on the nature of the Church.

However when the Holy See established the Secretariat for the Promotion of Christian Unity and the Archbishops of Canterbury and York appointed representatives to the Vatican, it was hard to convince the public and the media that the agenda was not wholly that of relationships between the Christian Churches.

Archbishop Heenan of Liverpool was appointed to the Secretariat and Derek always felt that he did much to reinforce this false notion. Pope John XXIII made it abundantly clear from the start that the first meaning of the word 'ecumenical', in the context of the Council, was 'general'. He had first mooted a local Synod of Rome and then, thinking bigger, his vision growing wider, he felt all the world's bishops should be invited to contribute. He appointed the somewhat bemused, though highly efficient, Cardinal Tardini, his Secretary of State, to head the first organizing body, the Pre-Preparatory Commission, as it became known.

In June 1959 all the world's bishops (about 3,000 of them) received an invitation to state the points they would like discussed at such a

Council of the Church. Pope John's encyclical letter 'From the Chair of Peter' spelled out the likely topics: the renewal and spread of the Catholic faith and morality and the updating of Church structures and disciplines in a way suited to the modern day. The bishops' replies were asked for by the end of August. It was hardly the most welcome bit of holiday work. Derek accompanied Godfrey to Hare Street, his summer residence, to prepare his submission. Word then came that the bishops of England and Wales should draw up their response at their autumn meeting. Although a general response document was prepared, it seemed that the Secretariat in Rome wanted every individual bishop's response as well, and would not be happy until they got it. In all of this, secrecy had to be observed; information coming to the Cardinal from Rome was all in Latin, marked *sub secreto*. It remained one of the paradoxes of the whole Council, leading to some frustration and cynicism, both inside and outside the Council itself, that the vision of open windows and greater trust associated with Pope John's wish was paralleled with this secrecy.

Derek Worlock had an abiding memory of his first sight of Pope John XXIII. Recalling it, during an interview in 1994, he told Bob Azurdia of Radio Merseyside that he had thought of Pope John as 'Dumbo'. From behind it was seen he had very large ears. Ironically, without intending any reference to this, he had written about the background to the Council saying: 'Already the press were full of stories about this new and unorthodox Pope. But this time he had them by the ears.'

The machinery of the Vatican Curia that sprang into action in 1959 began, in typical Vatican fashion, with the 'Pre-Preparatory Commission', already mentioned. This was designed to prepare and send out the general invitation to the bishops of the world to say what subjects they wished to have covered at a future Council, and a prelude to the Preparatory Commission proper which would comprise Curia and diocesan bishops and experts. The bureaucratic machine took on its own relentless momentum from there. In the years prior to the opening of the Council there were many trips back and forth to Rome for meetings. Cardinal Godfrey was a member of the Central Preparatory Commission. Cardinal Alfrink in the Netherlands was quoted as saying that this Central Commission might turn out to be even more important than the Council itself. It was meant to act as an objective 'sieve' for filtering ideas and views from the world's bishops into the Council agenda. It became very evident in these early exchanges, however, that the hobby-horses, not to say entrenched positions and interests, of both Vatican and diocesan bishops were heading for a collision. The unity issue was to the forefront in the discussions alongside questions of authority and infallibility – where the First Vatican Council had left off.

Ten separate Commissions were set in place, co-ordinated by the Central Commission: a Theological Commission, one for the Role of Bishops, for the Discipline of the Clergy, for Religious, for the Sacraments, for Liturgy, for Seminary Studies, for Foreign Missions, for the Eastern Church and for the Lay Apostolate. Each one had a Cardinal or very senior ecclesiastic in charge of it and the task of each was to prepare the discussion documents – schemata as they were called – which would in the fullness of time become official pronouncements of the Council. It is noticeable that Christian Unity was not the subject of a Commission but had something of a lower status as a Secretariat. Certain English bishops and consultants were chosen as members, including Bishop Dwyer, Archbishop Heenan, Bishop Holland and Mgr McCreavy from Ushaw. Archbishop Beck, whose father had been a journalist, and who was at that time Bishop of Brentwood, was chosen to represent the English Church on a Secretariat which was convened to deal with press, TV and radio.

It seems it was not as deadly serious and turgid as it looked on paper. At a meeting of the Liturgical Commission the Pope himself was present. To illustrate the need for renewal and the shedding of inessential frills he told the story of the shipwreck in which all the passengers were recommended to throw one thing overboard. The captain got rid of his wife, the chaplain threw away his breviary. Pope John often lightened proceedings in this way.

Derek, who formed part of the team of people to act as a Secretariat for the English and Welsh hierarchy and whose other principal role was as support to Cardinal Godfrey, enjoyed describing the scene at the opening ceremony of the Second Vatican Council, in Rome, in 1962 – an unforgettable and historic day for him, and for the whole Church. As with everything else that happened during the Council, he kept a detailed personal account:

It was a Thursday, it was the eleventh of October. It was the Feast of the Motherhood of Our Lady, and the historians were quick to link this with the teachings of the Council of Ephesus. My diary for the day adds quite simply that it was raining in Rome when we got up that morning at 5.15 am.

It seems that Pope John XXIII had acquired a reputation not only for sanctity and for springing surprises but also for attracting bad weather. The bishops called to take part in the Council were accorded the privilege of saying Mass in the evening. Their assistants or secretaries were not, hence at the crack of dawn there were individual Masses, at altars around the tribune or gallery of the English College chapel.

Having been assigned the task of arranging transport by car or bus from the college to the Vatican for the English contingent of the Council Fathers, Derek described the 'purple blood transfusion' of bishops injected into St Peter's Basilica. It was to be a daily feature, and the spectacle of nearly 3,000 bishops getting back into their buses soon after the midday exodus became one of the tourist attractions of Rome. He recalled leaving the Cardinal's car in the Cortile San Damaso 'with the same feeling of hopelessness with which one abandons a car in an irretrievable position in the car park at Twickenham'. It appears to have been a chaotic situation, made worse by the rain. With the papal MC desperate to keep to time for the Pope's arrival the procession of bishops was stopped temporarily:

> The College of Cardinals began their ordeal down the Scala Regia, each step about a pace and a half. It was difficult enough to negotiate at the best of times. For Cardinal Godfrey, an unhealed wound in his side from a recent cancer operation, it must have been agony ... television viewers in England were falsely reassured by his smile as he leaned heavily on me down the length of that formidable staircase.

Then he recounted the great gesture of Pope John XXIII when 'he dismissed the Sedia at the entrance to St Peter's and, as Bishop of Rome, walked up the nave amidst his brother bishops to the more simple chair which had been prepared for him before the high altar. In that moment was set the tone of much which was to follow.' The first sight of the 'incomparable debating chamber' which St Peter's Basilica had become was breathtaking. It was a picture the world would become familiar with. Despite all the talk of a new order, a renewed Church and greater equality, the attendant secretaries were 'banished to the side aisles by guards and "gentlemen" in evening dress', he noted, testily; 'it was like being shut out of Wembley Stadium as the winning goal was about to be scored.'

However, it was not all frustration. Soon afterwards he managed to gain admission to a bench containing diplomats and special envoys. He was warmly greeted by the Irish Prime Minister, Sean Lemass, and by Cardinal Willebrands 'who hastened to greet me and then turned to a functionary and said 'They can't stay here'.' Room was needed for the ecumenical representatives, and the secretaries had to defer.

The long ceremony included the singing of the 'Veni Creator', and the Pope's inaugural and famous address about the Church as the Rock of Peter, the need to dispel the prophecies of gloom always forecasting disaster as though the end of the world were at hand, and the belief that 'in the present order of things, Divine Providence is leading us to a new order of human relations ... which are directed to the fulfilment of God's superior and inscrutable designs'. Also included was a profession of faith, in the name of all the Council Fathers, by Cardinal Pericle Felice. During all this the secretaries had to stand for a long time on the sidelines, with no reception of Holy Communion except by the celebrant, Cardinal Tisserant (a practice retained throughout the Council).

After the Mass came the frustration of retrieving the car Derek had borrowed for the occasion. The damp weather had affected the engine and it wouldn't start. 'On that day of all days', he recounted, 'I had the humiliation of having to seek help for a push-start beneath the papal windows. So we juddered and shuddered into the world and into the promised new order. It was 1.45 p.m.' After that experience, it seems he took papal ceremonies in his stride.

The memory of Pope John's opening speech remained with Derek for the rest of his life and found expression in all he was to do later. The Council, he always said, was the most significant event in his life, after his baptism, and the longest in-service training course in history. It was also an event that opened up more friendly relationships with other Churches, which Derek greatly welcomed.

Perhaps in that momentous opening ceremony he thought about his own ecumenical experience, an encounter with Archbishop Fisher at Lambeth Palace, an experience that had bitten deep into his soul. He had gone on behalf of the Cardinal to discuss the joint recitation of the 'Our Father' at a united gathering in the Albert Hall and had been rebuffed by Archbishop Fisher who, having resolved that the Lord's Prayer should be said by all in the full Anglican version, interpreted Derek's suggestion that the prayer be prayed in silence as 'Roman aggression'. He told him: 'Haven't you Romans been in this country long enough to know that we are the established Church and you must toe the line?' Relations had thawed out considerably by the start of the Council, helped enormously by Geoffrey Fisher's visit of friendship to Rome at the end of 1958.

It seems that understanding between Catholics themselves prior to the Vatican Council was not always easy. The story is told of Godfrey praying one day in the cathedral when a gentlemen of the road, the worse for drink, came up to ask what time the Mass on Good Friday would start. The Cardinal explained kindly that there was no Mass on Good Friday but a Service at 3.00 p.m. The man insisted about the Mass and Godfrey again patiently explained why there was no Mass. 'In Ireland there's Mass', cried the man indignantly, 'and the priests take off their boots.' Godfrey replied, 'Well, you come along here at 3.00 p.m. on Good Friday and you'll see the ministers remove their shoes at the Service.' 'Ah', said the man, 'I'm not talking about the ministers, I'm talking about the Roman Catholic priests.' The Cardinal gave up. This became one of Derek's favourite stories in ecumenical gatherings to indicate Godfrey's efforts with the 'man in the street'.

Whilst having the common touch, ready to talk to all comers, Godfrey was at home with the very highest officials in the Church, and with the Pope himself. When he entered the Pope's study for an audience one day the Holy Father stood up and shouted 'Bravo' as he entered the room; Godfrey's reputation in Rome was very strong. Before the audience, Godfrey had asked Derek if there were any points to be raised and Derek had mentioned the case of a blind seminarian seeking permission for ordination. The Papal audience lasted more than 40 minutes. Wondering about the application for ordination Derek asked hopefully how it had gone, Godfrey replied 'We talked all about the Precious Blood'. Nothing more happened and some time afterwards Derek asked if there was any chance for the student's request. 'Oh, that's all going through', Godfrey said, casually.

Part Two

Although Cardinal William Godfrey was in many respects his own secretary, going to great pains to master every detail of the preparatory papers for the Council personally, very competent in several languages, not least in Latin, much of the ongoing work around the diocese had to be taken over by his staff.

The Council preparation, with bulky documents in Latin sent from Rome, was hardly an all-important matter in the everyday life of Catholics. Despite the surprise announcement and added workload, Godfrey went ahead with plans, in 1960, to set up the Parochial Development Commission and the Schools Commission, both of which demanded a lot of behind-the-scenes work. There was a great deal to do also in carrying on the good work of Bernard Griffin in relation to work on the Cathedral: the marbling of the pillars and the completion of the mosaic in the Blessed Sacrament Chapel.

There was, as ever, money needed for these projects. A priest of the diocese who later became a colleague of Derek in Stepney, Father Louis Marteau, recalls being summoned to the Cathedral for the sole purpose of fund-raising, but no one was to know the reason why he was there until the appeal for £225,000 was officially launched. It resulted in eight months of isolation and secrecy for Marteau: saying a private Mass and not joining the others at Clergy House for the recitation of the Office. Eventually the appeal was launched, with Derek Worlock overseeing the whole process.

In the midst of these major projects, pastoral commitments and the preparatory work for the historic Council, came the unwelcome shadow of illness. Derek Worlock must have thought history was repeating itself when he saw the Cardinal falter in the late summer of 1961. He accompanied Godfrey to Hare Street House in August and travelled to Ampleforth for Mass on 8 September, for the official opening of the Abbey, by which time the doctors had already arranged a date for him to go into the St John and St Elizabeth Hospital in London. Cardinal Godfrey's only concern was that he should be fit enough to attend the Vatican Council and to see it through to the end. He made it to a crucial meeting of the Central Preparatory Commission in November 1961, and went to Rome again in the early part of 1962 on Council business, also attending the Sixth Centenary celebrations of the English College there at Trinity, 1962.

There were to be several more spells in hospital and operations for cancer in the groin, and just as many sheer acts of determination to get back on his feet, before the great day dawned when he and Monsignor Worlock set out for Rome and the First Session of the

Council in October 1962. Not only they but virtually the whole hierarchy of England and Wales went too.

The work of co-ordinating the needs of the bishops, their accommodation at the English College, the paper-work and the medical care of a sick Cardinal were all now part of Derek Worlock's remit, but now he had to work in Rome, at the centre of a whirlwind of activity both in and out of the Council Session itself. His own diaries were meticulously written by him each day, and typed by members of The Grail, a community of committed lay people who gave their services completely to the Church, and whose members had formed a Secretariat for the English bishops in Rome. That Derek felt a great debt of gratitude to The Grail is clear. He noted that

> they have provided invaluable help in the typing and duplication of speeches and background papers, not to mention help for the bishops in dealing with the inevitable correspondence from the home country. The arrival each morning at the college of large envelopes and parcels was proof of their industry (late into the night).

Derek Worlock's personal diaries have been preserved and give a detailed account of the first three Sessions of the Council. They show clearly how very busy he was personally during the Council, how he was pulled in many directions, and how demanding life was for the 'Council Fathers', as they became known. The special position he held as secretary to the English bishops in Rome introduced him to some hidden aspects of the Council. He loved to relate the scene when a group of American bishops objected to the delaying tactics of some of the Curial Cardinals who occupied the chair at the main debates. They had taken the document on Religious Freedom up to the rostrum, under the very eyes of the Cardinal in charge, and on to the lift that led to the papal apartments, demonstrating that they intended to have it approved personally by the Holy Father himself.

As secretary he was also able, with his Commonwealth and American counterparts, to lobby and gather block votes from the English-speaking bishops on certain issues and carry through some important reforms in the structures and rules of the Council. Within the restrictions that existed he had a powerful position and greatly enjoyed the intrigue and the manoeuvrings in the corridors outside the Council debating chamber.

Above all, Derek Worlock's contribution in the First Session of the Council was that he helped Cardinal Godfrey to survive it. There were almost daily, secret visits to the Salvator Mundi Hospital; the Cardinal's doctor was in attendance for part of the time. In fact, with this support and reassurance, Cardinal Godfrey was able to make a great impact on the early proceedings of the Council, even to the extent that he was hailed by some of the Fathers as 'a second Manning', so eloquently and powerfully did he speak on many different subjects in the general debate.

The first subjects under discussion centred on *De Ecclesia*, the nature of the Church, on the place of Scripture in the Church and in the liturgy, and about the best way forward from Vatican I, at which the role of the Pope's teaching office was established but the concomitant role of the bishops, priests and laity left unresolved. Continuity was a vital ingredient in the whole of the Council preparatory work and the debates and radical call for change were always tempered by the calm approach of caution and diplomacy. This was borne of long experience but in some measure also due to over-bureaucratic structures at the centre. A decentralization of the Church was perceived by many, particularly in the West, as an essential part of progress and a right understanding of authority. By many Vatican and Curia Cardinals, however, it was seen as a potential disaster. Hence the dynamic and struggle that ensued throughout the autumn of 1962.

For Derek Worlock himself there was a great deal of activity behind the scenes: organizing a meeting of the Commonwealth bishops, the English-speaking contingent of the Council, lay people at the Council and the meetings at the English College of the English and Welsh hierarchy. The College Rector, Monsignor Tickle, and the Rector at the Beda, Monsignor Duchemin, did everything to make their long-stay guests feel at home. It was really like the hierarchy in exile.

It was thought at first that the only way of accommodating the influx of bishops in Rome was to dismiss the students for the Michaelmas term. Many people were of the opinion the Council would not last that long any way: wishful thinking, perhaps. In fact, the students stayed and helped to furnish the apartments which were to house the dignitaries – their bishops – for the next four years.

Writing in the Venerabile Magazine Derek describes how 'The Rector cast covetous looks across the cortile and the magic name of

Paolozzi [a local architect] was heard, if not actually seen, upon his lips. Inside walls were tapped, outside walls were guarded. Marco appeared on the scene – and after a decent interval a certain number of articles appeared such as scaffolds, hollow bricks, chandeliers, hat racks and wardrobes.' So the transformation of part of the college began, in a way that never would have happened but for the historic nature of the bishops' gathering. In return for the college hospitality a new lift was installed (to the advantage of everyone) and the refectory was refurbished with wooden panelling, a gift from the bishops at the end of the Council.

Cardinal Godfrey and Monsignor Worlock came home from the First Session on Monday, 10 December 1962, and by the following Saturday Godfrey was in hospital for his fourth operation for cancer. He struggled through the Christmas ceremonies but on 19 January suffered a mild coronary. Bishop David Cashman, his auxiliary bishop and close friend, came to anoint him. Derek, in much the same way as he had done for his mother many years earlier, gave him words of consolation; he told him he had given everything to the Church. 'He looked at me and said, "I hope so, Oh, I hope so." '

It was his last illness. The doctors could do no more for him. Death finally came on 22 January 1963, at 5.00 in the evening, at the very moment when Archbishop Michael Ramsey arrived at the door of Archbishop's House to visit him. Derek had received a call telling him of the intended visit and replied that it had better be soon. Michael Ramsey was too late to see the Cardinal before he died.

It is worth recording here part of the tribute in the *Daily Express* at that time: 'Cardinal Godfrey was one of those leaders of his Faith who have helped to make the Roman Catholic Church once more an accepted element in the nation's life. Combining immense kindliness with an inflexible adhesion to the Church, the Cardinal was the right man for an era of warmer understanding between Christians.' With the Vatican Council still to run its course, the change in climate in inter-Church relations boded well for the future and was to be much closer to the top of the agenda from that time on.

The death of Cardinal Godfrey did not signal the end of Derek Worlock's years at Westminster and Archbishop's House. There was still a role for him on the staff of the new Archbishop of Westminster, John Carmel Heenan, who arrived there in September 1963. With Archbishop Heenan, the Liverpool connection continued. He had been Archbishop in the north for six years before being appointed to succeed Cardinal Godfrey. Once again Derek had to adapt, learn the new man's style of leadership and relate to a different personality, a new and vigorous leadership after the years of Godfrey's decline, in ways similar to 1956. This time, however, it was clear that his role was to oversee the transition. His own position there had become problematic, as positions of power often do when they continue too long. Besides, Heenan had his own style and Derek found he was having to give way. One contemporary describes the relationship as 'cat and dog' and adds that Heenan was certainly not one to take directions from a secretary!

But Monsignor Worlock had by now established himself as a considerable personality and an effective administrator in his own right, generally admired with gratitude for the wonderful care and secretarial service he had given to two Cardinals, but also well connected to all that was going on in the archdiocese and beyond. This was both his strength and his weakness. He had forged links with many different movements in the Church, especially the Lay Apostolate. Furthermore, he already knew John Carmel Heenan well, from their work in Rome at the Council, where Heenan had been the Cardinal's right-hand man, second-in-command as it were among the English bishops during the Council's deliberations.

Cardinal Heenan was aware that Derek had also made a big impact as the behind-the-scenes man at the Council, an impact that had been noted and appreciated in other circles in Rome. Pope John XXIII himself had embraced Derek warmly one day on account of his friend Cardinal Godfrey and joking with him. He referred to him as 'Monsignor Strega' (Italian for 'witch') since Cardinal Godfrey had once introduced him and explained the name Worlock to him. Despite the different spelling, the explanation that 'warlock' meant a witch was enough to associate the two words for ever afterwards in the mind of Pope John.

In 1963 the old Pope, dying of the same disease which Godfrey had suffered, called Derek to recount all about the death of his friend and how it had been for him at the end. At the end of the audience, overcome with emotion by the interview, he embraced a rather bewildered Derek Worlock with great and genuine affection, even sending his secretary after him down the corridor to 'tell that young man that when I embrace someone I mean it'.

Derek's growing expertise and capacity for organization were recognized at many different levels in the Church, and with Griffin and Godfrey he had acquired a good knowledge of other cultures and other lands in his many travels. Heenan therefore did not see it as expedient to lose him too quickly, despite his desire to make a fresh start. In any case, the work for the Vatican Council, which was only one session old, required Derek's unique experience if only for the sake of continuity. Yet Heenan saw Derek's competence, both at home and abroad, as useful rather than necessary, and Derek knew it.

Cardinal John Carmel Heenan was the third in an outstanding trio of Cardinals at Westminster. In their different ways they each profoundly influenced the direction and priorities of the Catholic Church in England. They also shaped Derek's own approach to priestly ministry. Although very different in character and temperament from his predecessors, and not always at one with the accepted view of things in the archdiocese, Heenan's great qualities were quickly recognized. Long involvement with the Council's affairs and a good knowledge of its procedures and pronouncements made him the right man for the times. He was another incredibly hard-working man, in the tradition of those who had gone before: restless, full of purpose, zeal and new ideas, very prayerful, practical and shrewd. He had a reputation for possessing a brilliant memory and also for being quick-acting – even impetuous some would say, yet not one to move without that deep theological and pastoral know-how that had also characterized his predecessors.

Another era was dawning in the Church. There were exciting times ahead, but Derek recognized his own situation. As he would remark later, 'He had "buried" two Cardinals already'. The third one must surely have been watching his back!

Although their time together at Westminster was relatively short – a matter of six months – Derek discovered a sense of the informal, ordinary friendliness and readiness to share for which Cardinal Heenan was recognized among the clergy. Despite the pressures of high office and leadership, which often led to some alienation, this is something Cardinal Heenan is remembered for – the camaraderie and ability to relax and to talk as friends. It was a key ingredient in the improving climate of ecumenical relationships, and the Archbishop of Canterbury and the Bishop of London were frequent guests as well as firm partners in inter-Church events. Heenan's experience in the Secretariat for Promoting Christian Unity played a part in this.

In the Second Session of the Council, in the autumn of 1963, the struggle for the soul of the Church, a struggle for priorities and for power, still formed the backdrop. The terms 'progressive' and 'conservative' were being bandied about too easily. Derek noted that 'a number of us, perhaps understanding the far-reaching effects of what was happening, settled for being described as "radical"'. There was an effort to channel what might be seen as in-fighting into something of a more positive nature such as the true needs of the Church, and in particular of the grass-roots clergy and laity at home.

The Preparatory Commissions had been juridical in approach, whereas people were getting impatient for change. The word *'Reservata'* on the working documents and drafts of decrees hardly acted as a spur to the hopes that many people had for radical action and open debate.

Derek was to find this bureaucracy one of the great challenges. To cool the ardour of some of the more 'progressive' bishops the Secretariat of the Preparatory Commission had called meetings in Rome at impossibly short notice or at awkward times of the year. Cardinal Godfrey, however, had never missed a meeting. A key factor, besides the Council Fathers' readiness to meet the canonical requirements and demands, was the failing health of Pope John, who was now desirous of progress and who was still determined to abide by the spirit of his original vision and to open the windows. He wanted to let the Spirit breathe freely through the Church.

In all the bureaucracy, signs of the Holy Spirit at work were to be found. Before Derek left Archbishop's House, after nineteen years, he found himself as a guest at Lambeth Palace. He was invited by Archbishop Michael Ramsey to mark his farewell and departure from Westminster after his long years of service. This helped to redress the hurt of the earlier episode at that same house in Geoffrey Fisher's time. He had enjoyed a good rapport with the Archbishop of Canterbury, as with other Church leaders, as the climate of unity and understanding grew during the late 1950s and early 1960s. The Council had acted as a catalyst in this but the change was also being precipitated and encouraged by the other Churches. It would be wrong to forget that there are always at least two sides to a relationship: change comes about through experience of hurt.

The next time Derek was to visit Lambeth Palace was a less hospitable occasion. After his appointment to Portsmouth, his secretary, Cormac Murphy-O'Connor, recalls how he drove Bishop Derek to meet the Archbishop on a delicate matter concerning the mixed marriage of the daughter of the Bishop of Portsmouth to a Catholic naval officer. Archbishop Ramsey wanted the girl's father to officiate, but Derek could not agree and wrote about the matter to the Nuncio. Ramsey rang and said he wanted to see Derek. The end result was that the Archbishop did not win – they agreed to differ; three years later the rules concerning mixed marriages were changed. Another step towards unity had been taken.

In Derek's final year as secretary at Westminster, he was anxious to hand over to the right people the various aspects of the work which had flourished there. Such concern for continuity was characteristic of him. Often it became something obsessive and he seemed to be concerned more with secrecy than with trust. The new regime at Westminster that helped to shape policies and priorities made much better use of television and radio for conveying the Christian message. Heenan was acclaimed as a master in every way of talking to camera. Catholic readiness to use this medium was to be a significant factor in the years ahead. In other spheres, ecumenical approaches to social issues in London, such as housing and unemployment, served to unite the Church leadership even if, with some exceptions, it did not get noticed at the grass-roots level.

The quiet work of reconciliation and pastoral concern for individuals in delicate situations was something in which Heenan excelled. Nevertheless, despite the real regard for 'priestly' concerns, one of Derek's recollections of John Carmel's approach to priests wanting to leave the priesthood in order to marry was to dismiss their motives as simply lust. The climate was against seeing it as anything else. Concern for priests in difficulty was to be a hallmark of Derek's ministry from this time: he had seen many misunderstood, hurt or unfairly treated. Face-to-face dialogue was part and parcel of his whole approach, both as parish priest and later as bishop. Despite his conservative approach to the laws of the Church, he had a pastoral concern.

By 1963 he was eagerly anticipating parish work. At this point in his life, however, the overriding pressure on him was to see the Council work through. He had been appointed a *peritus*, an expert adviser, at the Council's Second Session in autumn 1963, chosen especially for his practical interest and expertise in matters relating to the Lay Apostolate. His interest in this had not been merely academic. He had, for several years been working closely with a group of committed laymen, who were known as 'The Team', and included men like Patrick Keegan, Maurice Foley, Michael Foley,

Frank Lane, Eric Tykke, Romeo Maione and Kevin Muir. These laymen had pledged themselves to daily Mass, an annual retreat, and regular confession, in addition to specific apostolic work in the parishes and in foreign countries. Keegan committed himself also to a celibate life. They met frequently at Archbishop's House, Westminster, and this involvement enabled Derek to help Cardinal Heenan play his full part in the Council's debate on the laity and in the contribution to the Decrees on Priesthood, Religious Freedom and the document concerning relationships between Christians and Jews.

Cardinal Heenan served on the Secretariat for Christian Unity from the earliest days, but now he also put the role of the laity in 'secular' affairs firmly to the forefront. Such priorities were an integral part of Derek Worlock's life also. The association with 'The Team', or 'My Team', as some recall him saying, even before the days of the Second Vatican Council, helped to earth him in the practical working out of what lay commitment to the Church could mean during the rather rarified debates in the Council chamber.

By the early 1960s, however, he had begun to see the potential of all this for his own work as parish priest in Stepney, to which his thoughts now turned. There, in the East End of London, among the dockers and high-rise flats, he was soon to begin what he always claimed were 'the happiest days of all for me'.

CHAPTER NINE

Stepney:
Peritus *and Parish Priest*

Don't try to be one of us, just be with us.
(The dockers in Stepney)

The combination of the pastoral role he was to play in the East End of London, and the dramatic setting and atmosphere of the Council debates far away in St Peter's, Rome, created an interesting and challenging contrast for the prospective parish priest. During the long weeks in Rome he must often have focused on the dockland parish with its varied problems of poverty and unemployment, and the day-to-day anxieties of parishioners. Whilst he was out in Rome for the Third Session of the Council, in October 1964, he received a letter from Paul Mullins, a colleague and friend in Stepney, demanding that he 'get a move on with this Council. Remember that for us it means flesh and blood.'

The difficulty of trying to satisfy this kind of frustration felt by people at home who were not personally involved in the Council, and the whole question of relevance – what difference will it make to us? – were things Derek Worlock was acutely aware of. When he did have time to give himself to the parish he tried extremely hard to bridge the gap of misunderstanding and the querulous cynicism about the Council's deliberations. The key connection for him was the very purpose of the Council itself – the *aggiornamento* (that elusive Italian concept), the whole thrust of pastoral and spiritual renewal, a new awakening for all people in the Church in their own locality. Pope John's vision and enthusiasm had infected him profoundly, but how to communicate it was the problem. The shortcomings of the Council lay in the fact that its implementation and infectiousness depended very largely on the ability of individual bishops to convey its message.

What was to be brought back home to Stepney therefore was not the written word so much as the living reality of this *aggiornamento*. The fruits of deliberation had taken the form, in the First Session of the Council, of a long hard look at the liturgy and at the profound matter of Divine Revelation, with the added ingredient of Bishop de Smedt's intervention calling for an end to triumphalism and clericalism in the Church. In the Second Session, in the autumn of 1963, it had continued into new areas of debate, cognizant of the changing times, on questions about the role of the mass media. It was a session described as laborious but enjoying freedom of expression. As well as a Decree on the Mass Media, the vital Decree on the Sacred Liturgy had emerged from the protracted debates.

A certain impatience began to dictate a faster pace and a streamlining of the debating, drafting and voting procedures by which the Council schemata, the discussion documents, eventually became agreed documents for publication. The Third Session, opening in the autumn of 1964, expressed the principle of renewal in the many and varied areas of the life of the Church and its relation to the world. To date the subjects covered had comprised: Ecumenism, The Eastern Churches, The Lay Apostolate, Marriage and the Family, Religious Liberty, The Jewish People, Christian Education, The Missions, Religious Life, The Bishops, The Priesthood, Training for Priesthood and the next stages of the Schema *De Ecclesia* which included the place of the Blessed Virgin Mary.

As if this were not enough to tax the minds of the bishops, lay auditors and observers from all over the world, there was to be the famous 'Schema XIII' at the end, dealing with the impossibly wide-ranging subject: 'The Role of the Church in the World Today'. This would introduce the tricky but more exciting questions of war and peace, poverty and social justice. This was to be the objective of the Fourth Session of the Council, together with the rounding off of several items of unfinished business. A very long in-service course indeed.

Monsignor Worlock was now fully engaged with it all as a member of the *periti* (a role which, to Derek's irritation, was treated rather dismissively by Cardinal Heenan). The speeches which undoubtedly inspired him most were those of Heenan on Religious Liberty and Patrick Keegan on the Lay Apostolate. On the former, Cardinal Heenan gave an address, much acclaimed, about the need for Christendom to rid itself once and for all of the attitude of mind which accused the Jewish people of deicide. He pointed out that we would not presume to condemn all Europeans as guilty of killing Jews in Germany and Poland just because one extreme faction in Europe had done so. As for the Keegan speech, Derek had forged a strong mutual friendship with Pat Keegan and it was a very proud and moving moment when Pat took the platform for the first ever speech by a layman from England at the Vatican Council.

Pat himself used to describe how he had bought some new shoes for the historic occasion and was acutely conscious of them squeaking and sliding as he made his way across the floor to the dais. He spoke well about how the Lay Apostolate 'cannot be an isolated entity in the Church', and how it 'reaches its fullness in close collaboration with all the other members of the Church'. He appealed for the active help of priests in the lay organizations as vital to the work of formation, and the need for continual exchange between lay people and their bishops as a necessary way of bringing the real-life needs of today's world to bear on the decisions taken by the hierarchy. The phrase 'family dialogue' summarized the purport of his speech. These were matters close to Monsignor Worlock's heart. The symbolism of the layman's intervention was just as important as the content. Whilst Derek himself was not yet free to make a speech, not being a bishop, his friend and collaborator was allowed to do so at length. A shift of emphasis had taken place which was, in Derek's view, crucial for the future Church.

The pageantry and the machinery of the Council were still intact, but even there things were becoming a little simpler, less bureaucratic, more streamlined. Among the Council Fathers themselves there was a move towards greater collegiality in the way authority was structured and exercised – now no longer just from the top down, but by individual Conferences of Bishops in their own country, and bishops in their own dioceses. The local parish was seen as the Church, every bit as much as the Pope in union with the bishops.

There was both innovation and consolidation of the past certainties in the Council: married men were to become permanent deacons, though priestly celibacy remained; debate continued on the use of English and other vernacular languages in the 'Mass'; and a far friendlier approach was being adopted in relation to what had been called 'our separated brethren'. There was a growing, perhaps in some cases a reluctant, recognition that other Christian bodies were exactly that – Christian communities, or, as Pope Paul called the

Anglicans, 'a sister Church'. The new emphasis was on what the Catholic Church could learn from other Churches and other faiths. The refreshing breeze Pope John had asked for brought with it a recognition of sin and blame and shame on the part of the Catholic Church, of responsibility shared with other Christians for some of the hurt and tragedies of the world. Forgiveness, given and received, was the strange new language being spoken in the Council chamber. No infallible statements were being made, a less rigid legalism was evident in all that was said, religious opinions and conscience were to be treated with utmost respect, lay people were invited to speak and make decisions, and the priest and deacon were defined in terms of service to others rather than as rulers of the people. It must have been a bewildering and fatiguing experience. In his Council memoirs, Derek Worlock recalled the phrase of one American bishop who declared that 'The happiest *dixi* is the Friday noon-day' by which he referred to the blissful sound of the last speech at the end of the long and exhausting week's debate.

What had not really been thought through adequately was to whom the Council's findings and pronouncements were addressed. Pope Paul VI was alert to this. The Council addressed itself to all people of good will everywhere; how could this be given focus and bite? The answer lay in saying that these pronouncements were what the Roman Catholic Church believed, how it wanted to relate to the world, how it saw itself in the world today. The result was a masterly exposition of the nature of the Church but without the anathemas and condemnations which had attended previous Councils. This delicate balance was for some a momentous triumph, for others a recipe for disaster. Derek Worlock took the former view.

Because he was personally involved in the drafting of part of the Decree that became known as *Gaudium et Spes*, the 'Church in the Modern World', this remained for him the most exciting of the Council Documents. If all the Council's pronouncements flowed from and were fed by the document on the Church, *Lumen Gentium*, then *Gaudium et Spes* provided the practical conclusion and rallying call of the Church to implement the whole spirit of the Council. It spoke about 'the treasury of the Church's doctrine' and its purpose of helping all people to 'understand better their vocation as a whole'. Its aim was to make the world 'more worthy of the surpassing dignity of man, to aspire to a wider and deeper brotherhood and under the impulse of love to try generously together to respond to the urgent demands of our age'. Derek and his Polish colleague Karol Wojtyła worked together on the document and it was in the process of this close work of drafting, in small groups late at night, that the two became firm friends.

In March 1964, on St Patrick's Day, some seven months before the fourth and final Session of Vatican II, Derek moved from Archbishop's House to the parish of St Mary and St Michael, Commercial Road, Stepney, a significant and enriching move for him. He had, for the first time, the freedom to be his own man with his own table. Even more important to him was the fact that he had his own team of assistant priests with which to start the mammoth task of ministering to the huge parish and putting his ideas to the test. His qualities of leadership and organization were already proven, even if he was subject to the inevitable criticism that he had no parish experience.

Fr Louis Marteau was again called in secretly to prepare the parish for Derek Worlock to take over from the much-loved Canon Fitzgerald who had just retired. There was also some 'dirty work' to be done in handling the problem of an allegation of child abuse against a member of the laity in the parish. A caretaker also had to be evicted from his house, but even trickier was the case of a boy who had been mauled by a lion at a zoo while on a visit with the parish Scouts. The boy's parents, Fr Marteau recalls, were having to sell their house to pay for the legal costs in taking action against the zoo and the Scouts. Derek Worlock heard about the case and got in touch with a contact he had on the zoo's Board of Directors. The result was that the case was settled and the family did not have to sell their house. The right contacts proved invaluable then as they did many times subsequently.

Stepney could scarcely have provided a bigger contrast to Westminster. This was the place where the famous John Colet had served as a Vicar at the great 'Sailors' Church' of St Dunstan's – 'the Church of the High Seas' as it was sometimes called. It was a place of poverty that had replaced the smart dwellings of the gentry of an earlier age. It was the land of the East End dockers. Within a quarter of a mile of the Catholic church there were, in the 1960s, dosshouses and a brothel, derelict buildings, the remains of bombed houses where meths drinkers gathered, streets full of litter and debris. With an irony not lost on the incoming parish priest, the Tory Party poster for the General Election of 1964 had been put up across the road from all this mess. It read: 'Don't let Labour ruin it.'

Derek Worlock came there as parish priest and rural dean, to rub shoulders with Trade Union leaders like Jack Dash, a Communist and champion of the cause of the East End dockers and their families. He saw his move as a sign of contradiction. As George Scott observes in his book *The RCs*: 'No one came to Stepney, not even the Irish immigrants, it seems. The common opinion was that anyone with any go in them got out of the Stepney area.' The population was mixed Catholic and Protestant, and 'mixed marriages' were two in every three. The figure of 80 per cent lapsation from the faith is given for the period of the 1950s and 1960s. Any clergy arriving there faced a situation of deep scepticism and indifference in matters of the faith, and any other matters as well. George Scott's description of the young Monsignor Worlock on his arrival in Stepney is revealing:

A spare willowy man who impresses as a man of inner toughness, of candour and passionate sincerity. There is no trace of condescension in his manner – just as well in an area like Stepney where (in words attributed to Derek himself) 'people don't want to be bloody patronized'.

In Stepney he was conscious of the need to get the balance right, the correct approach to people attuned to their mentality. This effort could of course have seemed patronizing in itself. He was clearly more one of the gentry from Westminster than the working class of the parish. However, when the nuns in the local convent, who helped the priests in the pastoral work of the parish as part of a team, proposed calling the new Youth Centre the 'Holy Child Centre', his reaction was 'Call yourself that and see how many come!' As he was to find in Liverpool years later, there was an intense dislike of being patronized or of having things done to them 'for their good' by well-meaning outsiders.

The 'Commercial Road experiment' embarked on by Mgr Worlock and his team of priests and sisters was a risky enterprise. As leader of the team his underlying motivation was to translate the up-dating process of the Church (Pope John's *aggiornamento* of the Vatican Council) into parochial terms and to do so as a family of priests and people in a once family-centred area. There was much ground to be recovered. He was concerned to bring a proper plan for the future. Now the old battle lines of the previous sectarian divide were to be revised in an alliance of all Churches against secularism and materialism.

Derek felt strongly that the Church had lost its mass popular appeal when it lost its role in social welfare, now taken over by the Welfare State. The Church had been most attractive when it combined the religious and the social agency roles. The clergy team at Stepney included Fr Jack O'Connell, a late vocation, who proved to be a good anchor man, and Fr Brian Nash who was described as being 'incredibly good with the kids in the East End'. He was also a great believer in the team praying together. Derek recalled Brian Nash, at the end of a long day's pastoral planning and discussion, hitting the table fiercely and shouting 'How can we really work together if we don't bloody pray together?'

Also in the team was Paul Mullins, who later suffered temporary blindness and had to be treated in hospital. During this time of crisis Derek often visited Paul and a strong bond developed between them. It was Paul Mullins, he would say in later years, who really taught him to pray. The new parish priest passionately wanted the team idea to work and put a great deal of effort into it, but there were misgivings about what was seen as his rather inflexible approach. Louis Marteau, another member of the team, recalls having to be in the Common Room every night at 10 p.m. for night prayers. At that time he was also chaplain to the Royal London Hospital and liked to do a night round to see patients who were due to have operations the following morning. Nevertheless, he says he still had to be back at Commercial Road's Common Room for the 10 p.m. deadline; the same was also true for Brian Nash, who would have to leave the kids in the Youth Club.

It was probably no exaggeration to say that the parish diary was so formal and full that if a tramp or an unexpected caller came to the presbytery, Derek's diary would be affected for a fortnight! Team meetings were held regularly and were whole-day affairs. If someone arrived late they were frowned on. Louis Marteau remembers arriving late after having driven to Ealing to see someone who had taken an overdose, and on returning to Commercial Road being told he had missed lunch, and that was that. It was too late for him to have even a sandwich. 'Derek's problem', he says, 'was that he couldn't adapt to parish life, but the parish realized that and allowances were made. The East Enders showed a great loyalty to him.' They responded to his earnestness. 'He was a remarkable person – extraordinary – but could not be one of them', claims Louis. 'In their eyes Derek came from the posh class.'

The class divide that his mother had been so sharply reminded of with her friend Hannah was a lesson he too had to face. Stepney had an extensive area of slum tenements and poor people, but equally it contained generous hearts. People responded to any care shown them and co-operation came through mutual trust. There had to be give and take in the parish and in the team-work between the priests.

The others in the presbytery attest to his insomnia. Lying awake at night, he knew when a call came from the hospital because he would hear every footstep of the priest on duty going out to answer the call. He would be able to tell him exactly what time he had gone out and what time he had come back. Yet he was up before anyone else and raring to go at breakfast time.

Despite the fierce loyalty, his time at Commercial Road was not without conflict, especially when it was decided that the open-air processions should cease. There were practical problems with these, not least the increase in traffic, and they had become occasions for the Irish to make a show of strength rather than prayerful exercises. Compromise was reached with a Rosary Rally being held behind the church. Parish council meetings were started and Derek would con-sult members of the laity as well as his team about suggestions and plans. 'After people had come up with ideas, he would say "I have a little scheme" and then we would find he had everything mapped out in detail', recalls Louis Marteau.

Fr Marteau has one little anecdote which he believes sums up the Commercial Road period in Derek's life. Mindful of the growing role of the media, Derek had arranged for an outside radio broadcast to be made from the church. There were children playing flutes, a psalmist and an accomplished organist all assembled. Beautiful music resounded throughout the church while Derek, supervising every detail, strolled up and down the sanctuary. Forty Hours devo-tions that week were also being held in the church, and at the back a book was kept for people to sign their names. Amidst all this, Louis Marteau vividly recalls two little kids dashing in with rubbers in their hands. 'Sister' had sent them to erase an offensive word they had written in the Forty Hours book! 'Everything about the East End was to be found there', he adds. The sublime and the ridiculous went hand in hand.

In many parishes the Church seemed only to spell out mortal sin, and to have adopted an almost punitive role which was gradually losing relevance for people who had enough to contend with in their daily lives. The new team of priests' message was: it is different now at SS Mary and Michael. They had to prove it. A systematic visitation of the parish; strenuous efforts with the school-leavers that first summer of 1964; changes of Mass times to suit the early working hours of the dockers and their families; and plans for a new nursery and junior school behind the church, as well as the normal practice of visiting the sick in hospital (there were three hospitals in the Stepney parish) – all this was part of the work-load.

The transition may have been difficult and Derek was naturally sensitive to any challenges to his own ideas or to the outspoken complaints of people who were used to speaking their mind. And speak their minds they did over the re-ordering of their church, especially when it came to the pulpit being dismantled! No one can have the perfect answer for every situation. What mattered was his absolute commitment to the people who now formed his first parish and who recognized that they had a gifted and able pastor. Amidst the dereliction of the war-torn East End he and his team set about rebuilding the spiritual lives of people, cognizant of their own need for priestly renewal and unity.

If St Dunstan's was the 'Sailors' Church', the imposing building of St Mary and St Michael's Catholic Church might have been thought to have its own maritime flavour. It was often abbreviated in writing to 'SS Mary and Michael', and represented at that time much more than just a religious focus for a dispirited community in a battered part of London. It was an important centre of unity for the area with many traditions, even if it was now standing in the shadow of devastated housing estates and poverty. Derek and the other clergy set about the task of reclaiming the lapsed. As they visited the area the children would run up to them and the priest would say 'Take me to where you live to meet the family'. The children running on ahead might come back as they approached and say 'Mum's got the kettle on', or alternatively 'Mum says she's busy, she's in the bath', depending on how welcome or unwelcome they were.

Here Derek got to know families who remained his greatest friends and supporters for the rest of his life. Years later when he came to celebrate his Golden Jubilee of priesthood, at least two families, the Mahoneys and the Wilcoxes, travelled up to Liverpool to share in the celebrations, and they were also present to mourn his passing at the funeral, in 1996. They never forgot his kindness, his interest in their problems and sorrows. The Mahoneys' son, injured in a road accident, was of special concern to him and he was frequently at their house to encourage their dedication in caring for the boy. The time he gave to parishioners' instruction and formation was of central significance. The formation which is rooted in faith and deep love never dies and bears fruit for years afterwards, and Derek recognized that the social reconstruction of the area went hand in hand with spiritual rebuilding. The 'Don't let Labour ruin it' tag served only as a spur to him in his alliance with Labour councillors to improve the conditions of the area. There was a great deal to do in the regeneration of the material and spiritual life of the place.

Family groups became a feature of the formation work. There would usually be groups of young couples helping each other to reflect on shared problems, though this was not intended as marriage guidance. Strength came through being together. People were sent out from Mass to 'bring back a lapsed Catholic – a neighbour or relative'. When someone came and reported 'I've got one, what do I do now?', the answer from the clergy was 'Go and get another one'. A certain trust was built up between the clergy and the Stepney parishioners, so much so that the annual showing of parish accounts was greeted with the remark 'We're not interested in what you do with the money, Farver, just let us know how much you need'.

The dockers gave him two gifts when he left the parish. One was an oil painting of the Curé of Ars, St John Vianney, patron of the diocesan clergy. In presenting it to him they said 'Stay like him Father, and you'll be all right'. The other gift was a small metal disc with a 'no left turn' symbol on it. He appreciated the sentiments of both gifts. He would often recall the wisdom of those warm and caring people who once told him: 'Don't try to be one of us, Farver, just be with us.' He made this a matter of principle later as he came to realize that he could not be the same as the poor, the unemployed, the homeless, the black community, but he could love them in all their situations and celebrate Christ's presence with them.

There was a lot of revising and re-learning to do in the dockland world where ethical and social principles were dictated more by expediency and the need to survive than by reference to moral text-books. It left a lasting impression on him when he discovered the tactics of the dockers who, whenever some accident occurred to a fellow worker in the shipyard, would immediately and loudly proclaim 'I done that', as there was no compensation for self-inflicted injury. He remembered too the expression 'knockin' off Watneys' to describe the practice of pinching bottles of beer from the brewery. A long way from the ideals of Vatican II. Yet the simple approach to pastoral care and moral integrity learnt at the feet of Cardinal Griffin were a practical reminder to him.

In the parish, at the start of Advent 1964, a special Year of prayer and reflection was arranged to coincide with the last year of the Vatican Council and draw together some of its teachings and ideals. It was organized around the theme: 1964 – A Year of Conflict and of Change; A Year of Hope – 1965. The title was carefully worked out by Derek and his team of priests and people. It was a kind of parish mission and each week a programme was set up for talks, meetings, prayer in the homes, and parish visiting street by street. This approach to pastoral renewal, the pattern and structures of a time of special prayer, were to be hallmarks of his later ministry and can be seen reflected in the Pastoral Congress and the Year 'In Communion With Christ' much later, in Liverpool.

During this testing yet happy time, the social concern and commitment which his mother had demonstrated when she worked for the Suffrage Movement in London forty years earlier stood him in good stead for his new ministry. He loved all the usual aspects of parish life, First Communion classes, catechetics, the school visits – and new school building projects, the processions and parish meetings. Twenty-five years later, when he celebrated his Silver Jubilee as a bishop he made a point of going back to the scenes of those wonderful times and, despite the changes, looked fondly around at what had been his beloved parish. Team work was the order of the day for him in those days and he always valued the spirit of co-operation between clergy and laity wherever this was possible. He soon came to appreciate the special talents and contributions of his fellow priests who taught him much.

Paul Mullins, one of his assistant priests, was very socially aware and involved in the lives of the needy people of the parish. Derek described how Paul came back one night from a visit to a young mother whose husband had walked out. He was strumming loudly on his guitar in a state of frustration; so Derek went in to see what was the matter. Paul told how the house was in an awful state, but how he went round all the local pubs, found the husband and persuaded him to come back. The same thing happened again some time later. Paul went to the house, cleaned the place from top to bottom, made a meal, dressed the children. As he was leaving the house, with this practical example for her to follow, he remarked 'And if I were your husband, I would have left you'. He regretted saying it afterwards, going back to the presbytery in a bad mood. To such incidents Derek owed a lot of his own pastoral style – trying to help people to help themselves in this way.

However, the new parish priest was clearly the one to whom all turned for guidance. Even as a busy parish priest and dean of Stepney he had to go back frequently to Archbishop's House, Westminster, to carry out some of his residual duties there, and of course he accompanied Cardinal Heenan to Rome for the Council. Together he and Cardinal Heenan witnessed the rather controversial end of the Third Session, when three American bishops walked out in protest at the slow progress being made on the document on Religious Liberty. The Council's work was far from over.

Louis Marteau was nearly always on hand to meet the twosome on their return from Rome and went out with them for the Fourth Session of the Council. In those days it was possible to fly a car and passenger to Geneva for less than a hundred pounds. They landed in Geneva for their planned car journey down to Rome and stayed at the Hilton, one of the few hotels which could guarantee safety for the cars and their valuable documents. They could not fail to notice the party of African gentlemen attending a cocktail party in their colourful robes, only to discover the purpose of their gathering was to discuss Third World poverty!

The following morning the cars set off in convoy with Louis driving. The weather was appalling: blinding torrential rain, so heavy that part of the road they travelled was later washed away. But Louis recalls that even if Derek was feeling somewhat nervous, he made no comment; neither did he complain of the pain he was suffering in his back. His emotions were always under control, and even if he seldom saw him laugh, Louis can remember him getting visibly excited when he was in the *peritus* box listening to some theologian speak.

It was while Derek was at the Final Session of the Council that the news came of his appointment to Portsmouth. Louis, always one for a prank, had prepared his own farewell at Stepney by placing skulls, a small lifeboat (because he was going to Portsmouth), buckle shoes and a label on the dressing table drawer proclaiming 'Papal Briefs'. But much to Louis' disappointment, this elicited no response, except that all the items were returned to his own room without comment.

There were many memories to be taken from Stepney, and the day he left the nuns got all the children from the nearby school to line the road and wave farewell. It was one of the few moments when Louis Marteau saw him really touched. 'I told him to "remember this experience every time you move a priest".'

Marteau believes Derek's greatest achievement in the East End was to put into effect the changes of Vatican II and to do it in one of the most difficult places, where people were resistant to change. He won the people's respect and loyalty. But Louis also saw in him a great disciplinarian, who had such a control over himself that he didn't know when to let go and enjoy himself. He never knew him to upset anyone and he expected complete loyalty from his 'team'.

There was some regret though that he had not been very successful on the ecumenical front. 'Ecumenical relations in Stepney were varied', he wrote in *Better Together*:

At monthly meetings of local clergy there were always a number of apologies for absence, often because two clerics of the same denomination would not meet. The Methodist was in particular demand by all of us because he alone was practised in the new art of public spontaneous prayer. The Presbyterian taught us that the care of the sick and needy did not have to be restricted to 'your own'. We also had a very High Church Anglican neighbour who flew the papal flag and rang his bell to coincide with the consecration of the Mass in our church.

In *Better Together* Derek also described the occasion when the Rector of Stepney, Edwyn Young, walked home with him from a civic function one evening and was conscious that they were being observed from nearby windows by their respective parishioners. He ventured to suggest they go their separate ways, but Derek replied they should walk together down the middle of the street. Edwyn Young moved to Liverpool soon afterwards, where he became Rector of Liverpool Parish Church. As a parting gift Derek presented him with a papal medal, as 'a form of protection as much as a token of friendship'.

The experiences of those Commercial Road days stayed with Derek all his life. Among the most significant events of this fruitful time was meeting David Sheppard for the first time. David was then a young Anglican priest in Canning Town. In the light of later developments, the significance of this meeting cannot be overstated, though it was brief and seemed at the time to have little immediate consequence. Derek describes the ecumenical scene in Stepney at that time in *Better Together* and it was clearly of central importance to him, though it was not a particularly fertile ground for inter-Church activity. There were certain breakthroughs, but the greater opportunities came later when he exercised his role as bishop and bridge-builder in Portsmouth and Liverpool. David Sheppard recalls that it was through being invited to do the *Epilogue* for TV that he first came into contact with Derek Worlock. Derek's memory was that Archbishop Ramsey had said he wanted them to meet. 'Anyway, I went to an evening meal with him at the presbytery', David recalls. 'My memory is a clear one of talking into the night and realizing we had a lot in common in our thoughts about inner city ministry.'

There was not, however, universal acclaim for Derek's efforts in the 'Commercial Road experiment'. There were those who saw it as superficial. He certainly spent most mornings away from Stepney, commuting across London in his car – a black Triumph Herald – to put in a morning's work at the office at Archbishop's House, Westminster. He was still secretary to the Bishops' Conference and because of his long years of experience had retained an office there and a door key. He also had the unfinished business of the Fourth Session of the Vatican Council to deal with.

The Final Session of the Second Vatican Council opened on 10 October 1965. A group of people saw Derek off but the parting was more heart-rending for him than they were aware, for he carried with him the secret that he would not be returning to his beloved Stepney. A month earlier he had been called to see the Cardinal at Hare Street to be given this saddening piece of news.

He had assumed that Cardinal Heenan intended him to become his Auxiliary Bishop in Westminster, residing still at Commercial Road and remaining parish priest, whilst secretary to the hierarchy. Despite the heavy work-load this would entail he was happy at the prospect of remaining in Stepney. On the day of his meeting at Hare Street he had been meeting with his priests and parishioners to discuss the plan for the coming year and had already talked with them about a five-year pastoral plan for the area. This had been an ecumenical enterprise too and in his capacity as Dean he had made a point of involving the whole deanery. In what was to become a characteristic manner he had been urging the people to stay and fight for their rights and for their corner against proposed demolition in the area. The priests should stay and fight with them, he had declared. Now he was told he would be leaving. It was heart-breaking for him, and he felt it would be a big let-down for the people. But, as he later reflected, he was only thinking of his own plans and not reckoning on God's.

Not knowing what was really in store for him, he went out to Rome with a heavy heart. It was essential to concentrate, nonetheless, on the task in hand, the resumption of his work for the Council, for the English bishops in Rome, with his added responsibilities as a *peritus* involving him closely with the preparation of the document on The Church in the World Today (*Gaudium et Spes*).

In any spare time, which was rare and precious, he did broadcasts on Vatican Radio. These were later published as *English Bishops at the Council*. He also performed an amazing array of chores on behalf of the bishops who were living, as many of them had been throughout the Council, at the English College. He was very excited about the various schemata which expressed the findings of the Council Fathers on a variety of subjects, but the most significant ones for him remained the Decree on the Laity and *Gaudium et Spes*. The latter was to become the charter for his future work as a bishop to the end of his days. Actually helping to draft a document which would be promulgated to the world and have a profound influence on the Church's ministry was an exhilarating task, and an exhausting one, with many late nights spent at meetings. More than once he succumbed to heavy colds and a bad throat and had to retire to bed for a few days.

Among the myriad tasks he had was the preparation of documents on Secular Institutes and their relationship to religious and lay organizations. He thrived on all this, though he was often in poor health, but he had the capability to keep many issues going at once, seeing them all through to completion in their every last detail. There was even time to give the occasional talk to students at the English College.

Pope Paul VI brought the Council to an end in December 1965. In his closing address on 7 December, the day before the Feast of the Immaculate Conception which saw the final day of the whole Council, he had these words for everyone: 'For the Catholic Church, no one is a stranger, no one is excluded, no one is far away.' The Council, in contrast to the Council of Trent, had issued no anathemas, no condemnations. Its tone had been conciliatory and all-inclusive, it had taken its lead from Vatican I in affirming the infallibility of the pope but had put this in its proper context of collegiality between the pope and bishops and the unity in faith of all the Church's members. It had opened new vistas for ecumenical dialogue and understanding and had affirmed the indispensable role of lay people in collaborating with the clergy, emphasizing their distinct place in society as well as in the life of the Church.

The Pope concluded:

This Council can be summed up as nothing other than a pressing and friendly invitation to mankind of today to rediscover in fraternal love, the God, to turn away from whom is to fall, to turn to whom is to rise again, to remain in whom is to be secure, to return to whom is to be born again, in whom to dwell is to live.

There was truth in his words that the Council:

has spoken with the accommodating friendly voice of pastoral charity, to be heard and understood by everyone: it has not merely concentrated on intellectual understanding but has sought to express itself in simple, up-to-date style, derived from actual experience.

Although the opening ceremony was in many ways a liturgical disaster, and 'ceased to be amusing after the first four hours standing in the passage', the recollection of it, and of the equally historic but lengthy final ceremony too, always gave him the satisfaction of knowing that he had been part of the process. His enthusiasm and sense of Church greatly enhanced, the Council nevertheless took its toll on him in at least one physical way. He recounts the final scene:

The Feast of the Immaculate Conception, December 8th 1965, was one of those bright but cool days in Rome which justify holding a religious ceremony in the open air and enable participants to risk sun-stroke and pneumonia simultaneously. With less hair on my head than that with which I had processed into St Peter's for the opening of the Council three years earlier, I was fortified by the instruction that for the first time in my life I must wear a skull-cap: but not yet an episcopal ring.

The four years of the Council would bring about great changes in him, not least the loss of hair. Relationships were also changing. The triumph of the Council lay in the balance which had been struck between the progressive and the conservative elements with which it had been bedevilled three years before. It had produced instead of these opposing tensions a radical Council, in the sense of one that went back to the roots of the faith and doctrine of the Church, the sources of the Church's inspiration and purpose in Christ. The overall concern was to look out upon the world, not in on itself; at its mission, not just at its structure; at relationships and worship not simply at its regulations and its rules. The Church, in Pope Paul VI's view, was a servant of humanity, a teacher and pastor, enlightening people about God by means of an enlightened view of mankind. Derek Worlock was now to take this 'enlightened view' with him to the Diocese of Portsmouth.

CHAPTER TEN

Bishop of Portsmouth

According to the grace of God given to me, like a skilled
master builder I laid a foundation, and someone else will
build upon it.

(1 Corinthians 3:10)

Part One

In view of the stirring words of Pope Paul VI at the close of the
Second Vatican Council, and his own experiences there, it is possible
to see why Derek Worlock, as the newly elected Bishop of
Portsmouth in the autumn of 1965, chose for his episcopal motto
words from the Council's Decree on the Pastoral Office of Bishops:
'Caritas Christi Eluceat' (Let the charity of Christ shine out).

It was a time for mottoes and catch phrases, of which 'The Age of
the Laity' was to be a prime example. Derek chose this particular
motto because he wanted to enshrine in it his personal mission
statement and what he considered the role of a bishop to be. He
saw that role as helping the members of the Church to look outwards
at the world rather than inwards at themselves.

His reaction to the news of his appointment, on 18 October 1965, the
feast of St Luke, was that he felt 'knocked endways by it'. He had no
indication up to that date as to where he would be bishop. There had
been talk of Menevia, and one of the bishops in Rome, when he was at
the last session of the Council, mystified him by asking what he thought
about being sent so far away. It was in a state of some bewilderment
therefore that he returned to London at the end of October before
those final words of Pope Paul were heard closing the Council. Louis
Marteau met him with a car at the airport, and drove immediately to
Stepney. The parish was the only thing in his mind and he had no
thought of seeing anyone else, though he had been away many weeks.

At Commercial Road people had gathered in the church to await his return. There were some who congratulated him warmly, with emotion – he remembered their phrase about being 'right choked'. There were those who felt aggrieved at the news and at the prospect of losing their parish priest so soon. His friend and fellow priest, Paul Mullins, said he could not believe this was God's will – they all had such hopes for the future of the parish, with their five-year plan, and now those hopes seemed to be dashed. Derek himself had no choice but to take a different approach. He tried to see it, welcome or unwelcome, as the will of God, which did not and could not depend on individuals and their private wishes.

When he left the parish in Stepney many of the parishioners were in tears, as he was. But there was no turning back. The love affair with Stepney was over, even though he would retain many happy memories of it and keep surprisingly good contact with some of the dockers and their families. A week after the announcement in Rome, he had told a reporter for a Catholic newspaper: 'Whatever the future, nothing can eradicate the inspiration of my time in Stepney.'

Whilst he had his admirers, his 'love affair' with Stepney was regarded with scepticism by many, especially those who had borne the heat of the day in those difficult areas of London. Looking at it from the outside, eighteen months was too brief a time to have put down roots or established a rapport in a complex parish like St Mary and St Michael. He had been constantly in a form of 'shuttle' activity between Stepney and Rome. The contrast between the poverty of the London tenement buildings and the grandeur of St Peter's Basilica, between the everyday concerns of the dockers and the rarefied speeches of the Council chamber, all within the space of eighteen months, did not seem conducive to a proper grasp of the reality of the parish.

He no doubt saw things very differently. He had found there a genuine rapport, even if not total empathy. His chaplain in Portsmouth, Nicholas France, remembers the summer of 1968. He was newly ordained and serving his first appointment at St Edward's, Windsor, when an 'away day' was held for the dockers and their families. About thirty families came from Stepney and enjoyed a lovely day in the church grounds. Derek had tried to heed the advice of the dockers not to try to be one of them but just to be with them, and had had some measure of success. The very issues which had occupied his mother a generation earlier in the East End, issues of housing and unemployment and poverty, were also his major concerns when trying to relate people's material needs to their faith.

The unsettling and unwelcome shadow of change had moved over him again. He had given to people the mandate he had given to himself: to carry on with the vision and practical living out of the Gospel according to the ideals the Church had offered at the Vatican Council. It had not proved possible to do all he had wanted to do in Stepney; there was much unfinished business. Yet, as he set his sights on Portsmouth, and the beginning of a new chapter in his life, he could look back on some achievements with satisfaction.

One measureable result of the brief East End sojourn was an increase in Mass attendance in the parish. There were 2,200 people at Mass on Sunday by the time he left the parish, which represented an increase of 500 people in less than two years. What was less measurable was the renewal of life and faith which, he hoped, God had set in train through the ministry of his committed team of clergy and parish helpers.

In the middle of November he flew back to Rome for the final stage of the Council. With the closing ceremony on 8 December, 'the longest in-service training in history' as he called it, came to an end; the more difficult work of implementing it was only just beginning. In December, he drove back to England laden with many papers, and with gifts from well-wishers and grateful colleagues. By now he knew the route across Italy and France very well; however, this would be the last time he would make the journey for the purposes of the Council.

The residual duties of what had been an unprecedentedly long tenure of office as private secretary at Westminster, and the demands of follow-up work for the Council, made inroads on the time he would have liked in order to gather his thoughts after Rome. There were invitations to send out and arrangements to be made. He had no doubt at all that the families of Stepney must be represented at the consecration ceremony, set for 21 December in Portsmouth Cathedral. They would lose two days' wages for absenting themselves from work, something they could scarcely afford to do a few days before Christmas. But there were those who wanted to be there and it was worth the sacrifice. He got some hint of what had happened over the wages and promised to return to say Mass in one of their homes as soon as he could after settling in Portsmouth. Stepney was not going to be shaken off so easily; the parting of friends was not going to mean the end of a valuable relationship.

In Portsmouth there was a mixture of jubilation and sadness. The new bishop – at the age of forty-five one of the youngest in England and Wales – was a welcome and exciting choice, but his coming meant that the 25-year reign of the revered Archbishop John Henry King, an octogenarian with a long white beard and a father figure for so many for so long, was over. Of the man whom he had first met in the presbytery garden in Winchester thirty-five years before, Derek said 'I can never replace him but I hope to continue his good work'.

Archbishop King had lived at St Peter's in Jewry Street, Winchester during those years and had known Derek's father well. He had lived there mainly because the earlier bishops' residence in Portsmouth had been extensively damaged by a bomb. It had been partially restored and occupied in part by the clergy. The incoming Bishop, despite his earlier family connections and his love for Winchester, opted to live at the Portsmouth house in Edinburgh Road. It was rather cold, had no central heating, and was unfurnished. There was a lot to do to make it habitable but he accepted that challenge. The Vicar General, Monsignor Mullarky, and the Chapter of the diocese welcomed him to his new responsibilities and celebrated Mass together with him in the cathedral. A new era was opening up for the Church in Portsmouth.

On Tuesday 21 December 1965, in St John's Cathedral, Derek Worlock was consecrated and installed as sixth Bishop of Portsmouth. The date in the liturgical calendar was the feast of St Thomas the Apostle. This was the first major feast day and the most suitable date he could think of for the consecration ceremony. Cardinal Heenan presided at the Mass, Archbishop Cyril Cowderoy of Southwark preached, his principal co-consecrators were Bishop Ellis of Nottingham and Bishop William Power of Antigonish in Nova Scotia – a good friend from the Council days. Also in attendance were his great friend and helper Patrick Casey, many of the English and Welsh bishops, and his former curates from Stepney. The priests from Stepney, and Bernard Fisher, acted as his chaplains. With 2,000 people present, 280 priests, sixteen archbishops and bishops from all corners of the world, he was well and truly seen in. It seems he had succeeded in reproducing a microcosm of the Vatican Council! He had also made every effort to add the all-important ecumenical dimension, on which the Vatican Council had been so emphatic, by inviting the Anglican Bishops of Portsmouth and Winchester and the local representatives of the Free Churches and the Jewish community. This was to be a feature of all the big occasions in the future. To complete his happiness, alongside his friends the faithful dockers and their families, there was Maurice Foley (a former member of 'The Team' he had chaplained in Westminster days), by then the Joint Parliamentary Under-Secretary at the Department for Economic Affairs. Maurice Foley was later to go on to represent Parliament in Europe. There, in all their finery, were the Lord Mayor of Portsmouth and the Mayors of Winchester and of Tower Hamlets. The whole ceremony was in the capable hands of Father Raymond Lawrence, who became one of the Bishop's financial advisers and close helpers in the diocese.

After the Mass it was revealed that Cardinal Heenan had brought with him an envelope which was to have contained a cheque for the new Bishop from his fellow bishops. In fact, the envelope was empty; Bishop Cashman had failed to get all the contributions in on time. Heenan, to Derek's amusement, had hastily put in a note which read 'I.O.U. whatever I can get out of the bishops'. Derek liked to regale people with the story and comment: 'It's the thought that counts.'

The new Bishop had come to a diocese which had been founded in 1882, formed from a portion of the Diocese of Southwark and consisting of the counties of Hampshire, Berkshire, the Channel Islands and the Isle of Wight – equivalent to the ancient Catholic See of Winchester. He came as successor to a respected scholar of recusant history: a difficult act to follow but helped by the fact that Derek's father had worked with him and had been a personal friend.

In the tradition of Cardinal Allen, John Henry King had helped people to understand how the diocese was founded on the sacrifices of the Martyrs – men like Swithun Wells – and the faith of Catholic families dating back to the 1580s. Parts of Portsmouth diocese had been home and refuge to many Catholics in hiding. St Edmund Arrowsmith had been arrested at Lyford Grange. The giant figures of Challoner and Milner, pioneers of Catholic revival, were hallowed names closely connected with the area. In his long reign as Bishop, John Henry King had guided the diocese through a time of rapid growth and change, not least an increase in the Catholic population with the consequent needs for schools and priests. The years of expansion, during which many new churches were built, was also marked by the urbanization of the region: notably at Southampton, where the demand for teacher training led to the establishment of La Sainte Union College, and at places like Waterlooville and later at Basingstoke. Another lasting legacy of Archbishop King (whose title of 'Archbishop' was a personal one, given by Pope Pius XII in 1954) was the founding, in 1953, of the Diocesan Child Welfare Society.

Bishop Worlock therefore was fortunate to inherit a sound situation on which he was to build and move forward on the lines of the Vatican Council. However, in latter years Archbishop King had been rather relaxed with the clergy: Derek's secretary, Cormac Murphy-O'Connor, and chaplain, Nick France, both remember that the clergy were independent. There were rumours that some even arranged their own exchange of parishes. Cormac says: 'During King's time they didn't get *ad clerum*s and were moaning that nothing ever happened. When Derek came they got *ad clerum*s every fortnight and said they couldn't cope!'

On the evening of his installation there was a reception for Bishop Derek Worlock in Portsmouth's Guildhall, attended by the Lord Mayor of the city and the Mayor of Winchester, along with many of the bishops, priests, leaders of other Churches, relatives and friends who had been at the ceremony that morning. Derek's address of thanks was a typical example of his anxiety not to leave anyone unmentioned and to make sure that all had been acknowledged. He launched into a litany of thanks – first to God for the gift of the fullness of the priesthood, to the Pope for putting his trust in him, to the memory of his predecessor, John Henry King, to the Cardinal who consecrated him a bishop, to Archbishop Cowderoy for preaching, to the two bishops who were his co-consecrators, to visitors from abroad, his fellow bishops, Mgr Carlomagni representing the Apostolic Delegate, to Mgr Etchegaray his colleague from the Council and secretary of the French bishops. He then went on to thank the Westminster clergy and the Portsmouth clergy, his official and personal guests, his sister and her family, many friends from Stepney and Kensington, members of Cardinal Griffin's family, the team of laymen he had worked with from the days of Westminster and all those who had arranged the day for him, the priest, choir, singers, organist and servers. This litany ended in a rather grand fashion: 'My brethren, ancient and modern, conservative and progressive, old established and new found, to all of you my thanks and the humble pledge that I will do my best to live up to the wonderful start you have given me'. It was worthy of a closing Council speech in the aula of St Peter's, Rome.

As their newly-appointed Bishop, Derek Worlock was asked by the priests and people who gathered to meet him at different venues in the diocese what he would be hoping to do. His reply was 'We shall try to do the lot'. He did not believe in a pick-and-choose approach; after all, the Vatican Council had been extremely wide-ranging and thorough. His intention was to follow the clear lines laid down in each of the conciliar Decrees as they affected the life of the diocese. The touch-stone of orthodoxy and confidence for all of them was 'follow Peter', follow the lead of the Pope and Council Fathers. The principle of collegiality, so positively learnt at the Council, should apply now in the local Church which was the diocese, and everyone had a part to play. 'We must', he told reporters, 'try to provide our priests with the opportunity to study the Council documents, and together with the laity, we must work out a means of implementing them.' But Cormac Murphy-O'Connor also remembers just how exhausted he was after the Council. 'He could hardly bring himself to preach for about two months – he had done so much work at the Council helping bishops, morning, noon and night and it took its toll.'

The Decrees of the Vatican Council were to form his charter for the years ahead, and it was soon understood by everyone in the diocese that this would be the agenda for the foreseeable future. How the Decrees and Constitutions would be translated into action in the local parish setting remained to be seen in 1965. What was not in doubt was his determination to make the Council work and to shed the light of it on the part of the world of which he now found himself to be bishop. Very quickly, thanks to Derek Worlock, Portsmouth diocese was to be described as 'the shop window of the Second Vatican Council'. It was both Derek's strength and his weak-ness. Derek's Achilles' heel was his inability to cope with criticism of his plans, and when some wag dubbed him 'the aggiornamentoed bishop', the defences came up. The self-understanding and nature of the Church expressed at Vatican II were not negotiable – that was his problem. Soon after his appointment, Cormac Murphy-O'Connor remembers attending meetings held at The Grail, in Pinner, with fifteen priests from the diocese to work on a plan for pastoral coun-cils, clergy training, involvement of lay people, and delineating where the diocese was going. Team ministries were later introduced, but Canon Nick France remembers them being disliked – with the exception of those in Southampton, where there were university, college and seafarers' ministries. More were introduced in Basingstoke and Guernsey.

People reacted in different ways to the new scene that was emerging. It was not something that could be mapped out in a blueprint, nor could it ever be imposed from outside. The renewal process, the Council's great purpose of 'going back to the roots' of everything, had to be translated into the reality of people's lives. The lessons of Stepney applied in Portsmouth and everywhere else too. What the new bishop had to say about his hopes for ecumenism bore this out, even if the reality was still to be painfully faced.

The Council's Decree on Christian Unity he described, during a Mass for Christian Unity at Holy Rood Church, Folly Bridge, as 'a clear charter for immediate action'. The Week of Prayer for Christian Unity in January 1966 gave him an early opportunity to stretch his ecumenical wings in the new freedom of his episcopal ministry. He said, in a sermon on 26 January,

> Let us be clear that by joint action we mean such matters as housing, care of old people, care of the poor and of inadequate families, world hunger and international peace... We must work together for the community at large not just our own Catholic community... Guided by charity and the search for truth we need have no fear as we move steadily forward on the path to unity.

His approach was a practical one, comprehensive and eclectic. The mission of all Christians, at home and abroad, was the emphasis and vision he wanted to convey, but unfortunately it was not understood or appreciated by everyone.

In the challenge that faced the Church in Britain, Derek was keenly aware that his hero and friend, Patrick Keegan, had given him the lead he needed in saying that the whole issue of the Vatican Council was 'whether it is able to show to the world the face of Christ'. The same point had been impressed on the Council Fathers when, as they prepared to leave St Peter's for the last time and the Council ended, Pope Paul VI had taken all the bishops to an exhibition in which the face of Christ was depicted by artists from different countries throughout the world. There were many portraits, varied according to each country's culture and artistic traditions; but it was the same face, the same person: Christ, for every place and time.

During the first four years Father Cormac Murphy-O'Connor was his secretary and companion. Bishop Derek greatly appreciated his pleasant and competent style of priesthood. In Father Cormac, the link with the English College, the Vatican and Rome, where Cormac had been a student, was maintained, as were the diocesan and personal connections with Ireland.

Ireland was a country full of associations for Bishop Worlock, a place where he had enjoyed holidays, met and talked to clergy, a country that would always remind him of Cardinal Griffin and of his friends, the Irish President and many of the bishops, and also of his great friends the Josephs. It was a country which had been a source of priestly vocations for the Portsmouth diocese, especially since the days of Bishop Cotter. Many trips to Ireland were to follow in the next years. Cormac also recalls a 'secret meeting' held during the summer of 1966 in the New Forest. It was in fact just one of many meetings Derek arranged with lay people impatient with what they saw as lack of progress in the Church. Pat Keegan was among the group of about eight people present at this meeting.

As well as diocesan meetings there were a number of annual 'fixtures' for the new Bishop. The fixtures included two meetings of the Bishops' Conference in London, at Low Week and in the autumn. When he became Vice-President of the Conference in later years, with Cardinal Hume as President, the work entailed in these meetings increased. They formed, along with the meetings of the Standing Committee of the Conference, two focal points in his yearly round which were indispensable. He was anxious to ensure that the principle of collegiality which had been established by Vatican II would work and be seen to work in the local church too.

Also fixed into the annual schedule were trips to Rome to attend meetings of the Council for the Laity and the Committee for the Family. These meetings usually took place in the autumn, during a ten-day spell in October when the departments in Rome began to open again after the summer break, but it was not unusual for him to be in Rome on three or four different occasions during the year. The habit which had come about because of the Vatican Council was now totally part of his annual agenda. Only in later years did pressure of work and problems with health necessitate cutting down these visits.

The meetings of the Laity Council enabled him to resume his friendship and collaboration with Karol Wojtyła, who became the Archbishop of Cracow in January 1964. There were happy and memorable occasions in Rome in his company. At one meeting Karol Wojtyła came in to the meeting and put his leather gloves on the radiator to dry. It was a very wet and cold day in October. As the discussion progressed a pungent smell began to permeate the room. The group looked at each other in puzzled embarrassment, shifting uneasily in their seats and looking around for the source of the stench. Eventually the gloves were discovered on the radiator, bubbling with the heat. The incident was often recalled at future meetings. Once, several years later, when Wojtyła was a Cardinal and Derek was Archbishop of Liverpool, the incident was recalled amidst howls of laughter, over a glass of Polish vodka. Such events did more to seal the friendship and coherence of the group than all the theological insights they might produce. Anyone who believed that Derek Worlock could not relax and that he lacked humour should have been a fly on the wall that day.

At home it was equally important to keep to regular appointments. These included the annual gathering of seminarists at Park Place, the annual pilgrimage to Lourdes in September or July, the annual clergy retreat at Douai Abbey, the Octave of Prayer for Christian Unity, from 18 to 25 January, the National Conference of Priests in September. In addition there were the meetings of the Portsmouth Diocesan Pastoral Council, and the newsletters and pastoral letters produced for Vocations Sunday and other fixed occasions in the year. Each Sunday and Monday was set aside for a parish visitation and confirmation, something which he looked forward to and enjoyed most of all. 'He was the only person I knew who could keep twenty balls in the air and never let one fall', recalls Bishop Cormac. 'It was admirable the way he dealt with something: whether it was a letter from Rome or a letter from Mrs Bloggs, he would pay as much attention to one as to the other.'

As part of the visitation programme he loved to visit the Channel Islands, which formed part of the diocese, and was anxious that the outposts of the diocese, Jersey, Guernsey, Alderney, Sark and the Isle of Wight, would not be deprived of the episcopal and fatherly care that other parts of the diocese on the mainland enjoyed.

He needed the security of these fixed events, but they did not prevent him taking on countless other things week in, week out. The appointments diary for 1972 shows him attending meetings of the Hampshire Development Planning Committee, the Diocesan Education Council, Portsmouth Family Welfare Association, several consecration ceremonies for new or reordered churches in the diocese, meetings of the National Catholic Fund, Deanery Conferences, Ordinations at Douai Abbey and at the Beda College in Rome, masses for teachers and other groups, meetings with his Episcopal Vicars, the Diocesan Council of Priests, meetings of Diocesan Commissions of Justice and Peace and Liturgy, with Lay Trustees of the diocese, with local MPs like Frank Judd, meetings with ecumenical colleagues such as the Bishop of Portsmouth and the Bishop of Oxford, schools meetings, gatherings at La Sainte Union Training College, endless private interviews, and social and liturgical functions all over the diocese. The travel involved was considerable: a 100-mile journey was not unusual. He was also committed to fostering ecumenical relations and not long after his arrival in Portsmouth accepted the kind invitation of the Provost to what was to be a memorable Christmas Day lunch. Unfortunately this occasion was not memorable for the right reasons: he got lost on his way there, and a woman guest got drunk.

Derek continued to enjoy regular visits to Ireland and in April 1972 he set off to maintain the link with priests from Cloyne diocese in that country who traditionally came to Portsmouth. The visit began with a trip to All Hallows College, Dublin, Maynooth, Thurles, Killarney and Middleton in Cork. Cormac Murphy-O'Connor went with him and they travelled down to Cork where they met some of Cormac's relations including two uncles who were parish priests. Cormac recalls one was a fat, old-fashioned priest who smoked throughout the meeting and kept dropping ash into his hat. They listened while Derek talked about the Council. When he had finished, the uncle – who was parish priest of Ballinspittle, and not noted for his diplomacy – told Derek that the Council was 'a lot of rot' and that he could have the first vocation that came out of Ballinspittle.

Back home, there were innovations to be made, decisions to be taken. These were to do with pastoral policy and the structure of parish and deanery which would allow his hard-won priorities of the Council to find expression. It meant changes of clergy and appointment of new deans, trustees and other officials in the diocese. This was bound to encounter opposition. He was more than prepared to face this, though his sensitive nature was easily hurt when confronted or crossed.

The enthusiasm of a new bishop, fresh from the rarefied atmosphere of the Vatican Council, was not necessarily going to be shared by everyone. He sensed this to a degree but somehow did not always appreciate the strength of people's feelings. His own natural shyness providentially served to endear him to others rather than repel, as they recognized, after a time, his complete integrity in the midst of his human weaknesses. That first summer there were a lot of moves, but some doubted the wisdom of moving some of his most able priests to the outskirts of towns. Later he reversed this trend, realizing that strong leadership was needed centrally.

It needed time and love to bring everyone through in a spirit of long-term co-operation. His very first pastoral letter as Bishop in Portsmouth – written in Lent, two months after his arrival – was essentially a call for co-operation and collaboration in the work of implementing the teachings of Vatican II. It would be almost impossible to find a statement, pastoral letter or any other communication and talk from Derek Worlock which did not contain at least one reference to the Council. Everything he said and did was imbued with it. In that first letter he explained his chosen episcopal motto as an expression of his hopes that all in the diocese would work together to serve others in need and let the light of Christ's teachings shine forth in the world, but always with charity.

He also made a plea that Holy Week that year should be an opportunity for all in the diocese to make a retreat in the form of reflection on the Council. Talks were arranged in the deaneries to facilitate this. The Pope's call for a period of reflection and thanksgiving for the Council could be answered in this way. Thus the tone of his ministry as bishop was set: renewed personal spiritual fervour was necessary for all other aspects of renewal.

If the late 1940s were a time for reform in social legislation, the late 1960s were marked by very profound changes in the legislation affecting moral behaviour. It was a time which heralded the emergence of what was called the 'questioning Church'.

The Abortion Reform Bill and the legalization of homosexual activity rocked society very deeply. Some people saw things sliding into degeneracy on every side. When the MP Leo Abse, who was Jewish, proposed changes in the divorce law in 1963 all the Christian Churches united in opposition to him, fearful of the consequences for marriage and family life. The controversy aroused by his Bill continued throughout the 1960s. When asked about the unprecedented united stand the Churches had taken in their powerful bid to prevent some of his proposals for easier divorce, Mr Abse replied

'It took a Jew to found the Christian Churches and it has taken a Jew to finally unite them'. This climate of moral concerns created the ethos for all that took place, in the Church and in society, in the way of renewal, culminating in the furore over contraception as part of the Catholic Church's official response to the new moral liberalism.

Some of the priests and parishioners who did find the going hard in those first years came in due time to see the wisdom and value of the changes that Bishop Worlock proposed. Yet many remained unconvinced, some even resentful. Any new 'regime' would feel threatening and unsettling. It was, in any case, a difficult time for the whole Church, coming to terms with some radical changes wrought by the Council, alterations to a long tradition of liturgical practice, and to traditional ways of relating to non-Catholics and other religious faiths. The use of Latin in the Mass had been part of the cherished ways of life in the Church, part of a Catholic culture and a pattern of doing things, indicative of a certain fixed relationship between priests and people, for many centuries. Derek related well to the younger clergy, many of whom were more easily persuaded of the value of the Vatican II reforms. The ordination of such men was one of his greatest joys. In turn they knew and appreciated that he took a personal interest in them and was genuinely concerned for their welfare.

Although the Council had certainly not called for an abandonment of Latin, those who saw the vernacular Mass as the thin end of the wedge could easily criticize the Council for this. From the heart of the disturbed feelings grew the 'questioning Church' mentality, which wanted to challenge the Church's authority structures, and in doing so was questioning the nature of the Church itself. The loss of cherished traditional ways of doing things was seen by many as the result of pressure in society, rather than Church teaching.

Bishop Worlock was not unsympathetic to the difficulties people were experiencing, especially where his clergy were concerned. Priests of his own age and background would naturally find the changes a real challenge. His overriding desire to forge ahead may have obscured his empathy with them; it cost him a great deal to assimilate the changes, but then he had had the benefit of being part of the change, the ground-breaking process of the Council itself. In a pastoral letter for Pentecost 1966 he wrote: 'At the present time there are many tensions and difficulties which beset the priest. The world

Harford Worlock, Derek's father. Derek described
his home as being 'full of politics'

Dora Worlock, Derek's mother, played a courageous
part in the emancipation of women

Aged 18, 1938. The rugby player: 'open-side wing forward', in the garden of his home in Winchester

Derek Worlock in France with Cardinal Griffin, 1949

Better together? Archbishop Worlock with Bishop David Sheppard after they both had received honorary degrees at Liverpool John Moores University

The Queen's Silver Jubilee, Liverpool Metropolitan Cathedral, 19

In South Africa, 1989

With Mgr John Furnival, *en route* to Lourdes in a private plane, 1993

With Archbishop Carey in Warrington after the IRA bomb, 1993

ogether in thought. Bishop Sheppard and Archbishop Worlock at
iverpool City Council, *c*. 1981

ie Liverpool Three. Bishop Sheppard, Archbishop Worlock and Rev.
r John Newton, Liverpool Metropolitan Cathedral, 1994

With his life-long friend Fr Bernard Fisher, Alresford, *c.* 1988

is full of bewildering and rapid changes and the Church itself is undergoing a period of self-examination and renewal.' He stressed that the leadership and authority of the priest were 'matters of service rather than of personal power' and called for sharing of responsibility with lay people. He knew that for the Church at that time the priority was 'a better understanding of the role of the priest' and the letter made reference to the perennial need of more vocations.

Part Two

This new climate of questioning was to find its most controversial expression in the 'contraception' question a year or so later with the publication of the encyclical *Humanae Vitae*. Bishop Worlock was reluctantly propelled into this controversy. August 1968 was one of the most testing times, not just for him but for the whole Church. The issue really hit the Press. Most of the bishops were away on holiday and Derek had to draw on all the experience and cool-headed wisdom he was known for to handle the Press enquiries and the furore that continued to affect priests and people over the next few years. It was a delicate time, full of emotion, anger and resentment, but also shot through with some high-handed approaches from those who wanted to make compliance a test of orthodoxy.

This was a time of the three 'Rs' in the Church as well as in society: Renewal, Reform and Revolution. A rather heady mixture of all three had somehow to be taken on, sustained and lived through. Derek Worlock's long experience in Westminster had equipped him with stamina for this challenge. It had enabled him to understand how the Church, guided by the Spirit and led, temporally and spiritually, by the Pope, was like a great and deep river. Pope John's fine opening speech of the Council had drawn the distinction between the deposit of faith itself and the manner of expressing that faith in a variety of cultures and languages. At the Council's conclusion Pope Paul VI said that the Council had issued 'not anathemas but invitations' and had prayed 'May this ray of divine light cause us all to recognize the blessed door of truth'. It was from these perspectives that Derek chose his way forward.

He had been intrigued by a telegram he had received at the time of his consecration as a bishop from Archbishop Thomas Roberts of Bombay, which read 'May the spirit of St Thomas uphold you'. The date of episcopal ordination had been 21 December, the feast of St Thomas the Apostle. That may have been the sole significance of it. Perhaps the Jesuit Archbishop was warning him that doubts might arise but could be overcome: difficulties lay ahead but the sense that times were changing rapidly, contrasting sharply with the more certain era he had lived through in Westminster, urged Derek Worlock to find a new model for the Church in the modern world. He would rely on the spirit of St Thomas then, but it was St Edmund whom he took as his inspiration and patron in those challenging times. He felt that he owed his vocation to the prayers of St Edmund, fondly remembering his old college, and recalling the saint's origin from the town of Abingdon near Oxford, part of the Portsmouth diocese. He always invoked St Edmund in prayers before a pastoral enterprise or important meeting.

January 1967 saw him preparing to go out to Rome again, not for a meeting this time but to renew acquaintances and carry out business arising in the diocese. Rome was always like an extension of the diocese for him. He was keen to revisit the English College, scene of his labours for the Council, and he wanted to visit the students at the Beda College. The timetable he and Father Cormac set for themselves for that week was almost frightening in its intensity, and was to be the pattern for many future visits.

They took the Alitalia flight to Rome at midday on Monday 9 January. He had become a familiar figure on this service over the years, though some of his trips for the Council had been made by car, carrying bundles of the Cardinal's papers. He was welcomed to the English College by Mgr Leo Alston, who had been appointed there in 1964 from his post as headmaster at St Joseph's College, Upholland. A visit to Gammarelli was called for to buy some episcopal socks and *zucchetti*. That evening, in the college there was Mass with the students. Next day he attended a press conference and met some of the Roman Monsignori he had known at the Council. In the evening he had a meeting with members of The Grail.

The next morning he met Bishop Marcinkus, head of the Vatican Bank, and Monsignor Laboa, an old friend who later became Nuncio in Manila. Back for lunch with the students at the college, taking time afterwards to see his Portsmouth students individually, then more meetings with Laboa and others that evening. On Thursday 12 January, he had meetings with Mgri Tucci, Palazzini and Ransing, lunch with the British Ambassador, Frank Doria Pamphili, and gave a talk to the students at the college in the evening. There were more meetings the next day with Bugnini and Castelli at the Holy Office Vicariate: in the evening he met with some of the religious with whom he was acquainted and whose orders had members in his diocese. Saturday morning saw him at the Congregation for the Sacraments, the Council Secretariat, more meetings with Castelli and Bugnini, lunch with Father Charles Burns, archivist at the Vatican and spiritual confessor at the English College. That evening he went to Beda to give a talk to the students there. On Sunday he was main celebrant at the Concelebrated Mass in the English College. Next day, Monday 16 January, he sped off, exhausted no doubt, for his plane home at 1.00 p.m. The diary thankfully records a blank day on Tuesday.

Looking back, Bishop Cormac reflects on how he saw Derek grow in the episcopate and become a great planner. 'He was able to get into a rhythm and that helped when he went to Liverpool.'

The timetable at home was really no less frantic than it had been in Rome. He had quickly established a pattern to the week, though every week held something different. He would give most Sundays and Monday mornings to the visitation of the parishes. At each Sunday Mass he would preach and usually administer Confirmation at one of the Masses. He would build in to the programme visits to sick parishioners in their homes, visits to convents, and a meeting with the parish council in the evening. He found some interesting and amusing reactions on his rounds. He often recalled how some parish priests would drive all round the area by the most tortuous routes, to give the impression that the parish was much bigger than it was.

He once visited a house with the parish priest, who prided himself on knowing his parishioners well, and who had told him beforehand that the old lady they were to visit was crippled and house-bound, quite unable to get out to Mass. They waited on the doorstep; nobody came to the door. They were about to leave and call for assistance when the 'frail old lady' arrived, walking very sprightly up the garden path and laden with shopping! On another occasion Derek arrived at a house and the priest with him explained that he often went there to visit the man. The man came to the door and engaged the bishop in conversation on the step. Quite openly he asked: 'By the way, whatever happened to old Father So-and-So who used to be in this parish?' Derek rejoined 'Let me introduce you.'

One of his most memorable house visits was to a man who really was house-bound and suffered from emphysema. The parish priest explained that the man's greatest pleasure in life was the racing on television. As expected, a little white dot was disappearing on the television screen as they went into the sitting room. 'Were you watching the racing?' Derek asked him. 'Did you back the winner?' The man was silent, still catching his breath, then he said 'I saw in the paper there was a horse running in the 3.30 at Ascot called "Benign Bishop"', the man told them. 'As you were coming today I put a lot of money on it – I thought it was a sign.' 'What happened?' Derek enquired, expectantly. 'The b ... horse fell at the first b ... fence', the man shouted in disgust.

Monday mornings were dedicated to the children in the parish primary school, and a meeting with the mothers and toddlers. The rest of the week's programme varied, with a large number of speaking engagements, meetings of all kinds, interviews and desk work. The volume of correspondence was always high, his letter writing was so thorough and painstaking that it became a full-time industry of its own – a constant factor in his life to the end.

In the development of his work in the area Derek came to value the friendship and co-operation of the Labour MP for Portsmouth, Frank Judd. Together they often visited homes and places of work in a kind of joint ministry of religion and politics. The blend was an interesting one; Derek claimed to learn a great deal from Frank Judd's kind yet penetrating style of questioning and operating, whilst he was able to introduce Frank, who was not a Catholic, into some of the mysterious inner workings of Catholic sodalities, prayer groups and confraternities. The Catholic social teaching he was applying fitted quite comfortably with the objectives of Frank's brand of socialist policy. It was a friendship that continued right to the end of Derek's active ministry, though Frank Judd's work for Overseas Development, Oxfam and then in the House of Lords, prevented them from meeting much in subsequent years.

Cormac Murphy-O'Connor does not recall Derek relaxing very often. When he was not working at his desk, he would turn up at school speech nights and often make up a limerick on the spot. He was excellent at off-the-cuff speeches and on one occasion excelled himself when he was invited to speak at a dinner for 500 bankers held in Bournemouth. 'There were eight speeches and he was the last and everyone was getting fed up', recalls Cormac. 'He got up and said

"I'll tell you a little story – and after four minutes you can go". He was brilliant. He could be excellent at things like that.'

Two months after the busy January visit to Rome he was there again; this time for the first meeting of the newly-established Council of the Laity, one of the Pontifical Advisory Councils which the Pope had constituted after Vatican II. Like the other new Councils and Committees, there was usually a Cardinal or a senior bishop in charge, and membership comprised clergy and lay people appropriate to the particular brief and expertise involved. The first meeting took place at Santa Marta on 13 April 1967, with a plenary session with the Pope in the morning and a meeting of the Council itself that evening. Afternoons in Rome were usually not occupied by formal sessions of any kind, though Derek rarely took a siesta and worked on papers for the evening meeting instead.

Occasionally they would be more relaxed affairs. He would sometimes go up to one of the hill towns outside Rome, like Nemi and Rocca di Papa. At Nemi you could buy strawberries in the famous restaurant called Specchio di Diana, where, if the visitors' books were to be believed, people like Mussolini and Hitler had dined. Italy, especially Rome, was full of such places. Patrick Keegan was with him for the Laity Council meeting, and he also spent time with Peter Coughlan, an old friend whose family Derek had known for many years. As on most trips to Rome he gave time to the students of the English College and the Beda; he confirmed some young people at San Silvestro church, the centre for English and Irish residents in Rome.

Bishop Worlock wrote regular newsletters to the priests of the diocese as a way of improving communication with his clergy. In the letter for April he described his Rome visit and the way that Pope Paul had spoken to the members of the Council for the Laity about the 'joy of serving Christ in the Church'. This, he said, should offset the 'prophets of gloom' against whom Pope John had warned at the beginning of the Vatican Council.

He reminded the priests that Pope Paul had called for a special 'Year of Faith' and study, from the feast of St Peter and Paul onwards, to deepen the understanding of the Council Decrees and to renew faith for all God's people. It was decided that the bishops of England and Wales would concelebrate Mass at Westminster Cathedral on 20 June to launch this special year.

Practically, he recommended in his letter a study of the

Constitution on Divine Revelation, the study of God's Word in the Bible. It was a part of the Vatican Council's determination that the Scriptures should be given back the prominent position they once had in the Mass and in the whole life of the Church. Even when Derek had been a student at the seminary, the Bible had been very much secondary to other subjects. Its re-emergence in the celebration of the sacraments and in the general activity of Catholics would also help in bridging the gap with the Protestant and Evangelical Churches.

As another way of getting the year under way in Portsmouth diocese he invited the Apostolic Delegate, Archbishop Cardinale, to visit the diocese for two days in July. Among the engagements prepared for him was the dedication of a window at St Peter's, Winchester, in memory of the late Archbishop King, a Mass and lunch with all the priests of the diocese, and a talk about the Pope's special 'Year of Faith'.

He attended the Synod of Bishops in Rome in October 1967, which, in addition to a focus on Scripture, was to look at the subjects of mixed marriages, the Code of Canon Law, the liturgy and seminary training. This was to be the first meeting of the World Synod of Bishops following the Council. It was clear that the Pope did not see the Vatican Council as over but continuing in its application and its influence. Because of his close involvement in the Council, Bishop Worlock was a natural choice to represent the bishops of England and Wales at the Synod. The subjects on the published agenda were to be underpinned by reference to the principle of collegiality between the Pope and the bishops.

This principle formed a more central theme at the next Synod, in October 1969, at which Derek was also one of the Bishops' Conference delegates. The authority structures in the Church – the new relationships and issues which had formed since the Council – were by then under considerable strain in the aftermath of *Humanae Vitae*.

Reporting back to his diocese afterwards he remarked:

> Happily the wounds of just over a year ago were healed. Hope and confidence were restored. With the principle of subsidiarity upheld – that the higher power does not intervene unnecessarily in a work which a lesser authority is carrying out adequately and in an authentic manner – we are able to see better the relationship between the See of Peter and the local Churches.

This was the principle on which the Bishop placed his own determined efforts to establish a diocesan council, deanery councils, and where practical, parish councils throughout the diocese, which were representative of membership and relevant in their subject matter for the real needs of the people they were meant to serve. However, the hurt caused by *Humanae Vitae* ran very deep.

One central plank in this rebuilding in Portsmouth diocese was the establishment of a Pastoral Centre at Park Place, near Havant, in which he placed great hope for the future. The advantages this gave, as a focal point and source of unity for the diocese, as well as a place for formation and training, were incalculable. The setting up of a properly constituted Diocesan Pastoral Council, fed from below by parish and deanery councils, was the way forward as he saw it, for he recognized the need for structures to implement the ideas, and to give visible expression to the principle of 'one Church for all'.

Close to his heart was the role of the laity and all that he had learnt from 'The Team' in earlier days, not forgetting to take forward in an imaginative way the ideals of Christian Unity at a local and national level. It should be remembered that it was not just the Catholic Church or the Council which was pressing forward with these changes. The whole of society and the whole world order were changing. Vatican II both reflected and articulated this, whilst attempting to preserve the fundamental beliefs which had underpinned the Church down the centuries. Bishop Worlock summed it up nicely in a book published twelve years later: 'It means an end to "churchiness" and "outside-churchiness", an end to clericalism and anti-clericalism, an end to Sunday-suit religion and weekday secularism.'

As in former days he had seen Cardinal Griffin use particular occasions as platforms for conveying ideas, events and gatherings were part of the daily fabric of Derek Worlock's episcopal work, just as surely as the 'structures' he set in place. In March 1967 he preached at the Mass to mark the 800th anniversary of the first church in Portsmouth. In a substantial address, he set out what might be called his stall for the Portsmouth years. Whilst he appeared in a hurry for change and opposed standing still in any form, he also valued personal stability and a sense of security which would enable him to carry through his plans properly. On the occasion of the 800th anniversary he spoke of the importance of looking back over many centuries in order to appreciate the history of the Church Christ had founded and in so doing understand the present time better. One of Derek's greatest strengths was his love and acceptance of the Church.

The foundations, built on Christ, gave the clue to the way forward now for the future direction and life of the Church. Part of almost every sermon was a reference to ecumenism, stressing the need to do far more than attend the services arranged at each other's churches during January, at the time of the Week of Prayer for Christian Unity. Of great importance too was the knowledge of Scripture and sharing study with others as a prelude to action, according to the proven method of the Young Christian Workers movement, based on 'See, Judge and Act'.

But the principles of collegiality and authority were tested to the limits by the appearance in August 1968 of the encyclical that was to shake the Church, *Humanae Vitae*. He cautioned calm. He coolly said that in this and all matters of faith and morals people should 'follow Peter'. He said that individual conscience properly formed was supreme, that the encyclical contained a rich theology of marriage not to be missed in all the controversy, and that 'he could not believe that contraception was the acid test of Christianity'. That summer a priest wrote to him and asked if it was all right if he grew a beard. 'As long as it is not against your conscience and that it is open to life', replied Derek.

On 3 June 1969 he celebrated the Silver Jubilee of his ordination to the priesthood. Bernard Fisher joined him. He met the clergy after Mass and spoke to them about priestly life and his hopes that their working together would develop over the years. At that Mass Father (later Canon) Nicholas France, ordained in June 1968, was present. Nick was to become like a son to him and his work in Portsmouth was associated with Nick from then on.

The decision to convene the extraordinary Synod of Bishops in 1969 seemed to be a direct result of the *Humanae Vitae* débâcle. It was on the theme of collegiality. It was the first Synod with 'circuli minori' language groups. The Pope was looking for solidarity with his encyclical and in some ways the Synod sought to close the ranks, restore confidence and unity of mind. The Synod meetings were to be a feature of Derek's life from that time on.

In July 1969, a request came from the Vatican Secretary of State, Cardinal Cicognani, that he attend the European Bishops' Symposium at Chur in Switzerland, representing the Holy See. It was a controversial meeting touching on the crisis about authority and celibacy. There emerged at the meeting the presence of a group of '*prêtres contestataires*', disenchanted and angry priests who threatened to blockade the bishops' meeting, even with violence, so deeply did they feel about the questions relating to authority. The report in the *Irish Times* some days later is very revealing:

> The cool, almost donnish voice of the Right Rev. Mgr Derek Worlock was an instructive contrast, during a hectic week at Chur, to the occasionally tense and strained utterances which marked the relationships between the bishops' meeting in the St Luzi seminary on the hill and the priests' meeting in the Volkhaus Hotel on the bank of the river. Monsignor Worlock, who has been a priest for twenty-five years and a bishop for almost four ... makes important statements in a deceptively mild manner and is, in fact, one of the most influential modern voices in the English hierarchy today.

The article quoted extensively his words about celibacy and priesthood following the difficult meeting in Chur. The occasion seems to have provided a platform for his views on the key considerations about the pastoral needs of the Church in Portsmouth diocese. Commenting on the question of priesthood in England and Wales he said 'The problem in England and Wales is far less that of the theological basis for the priesthood than of the manner in which it is being exercised'. As for *Humanae Vitae*, he told Pope Paul quite plainly that the loyalty of English Catholics was the reason for the pain. If they were disloyal they would feel no pain or compunction about papal teaching.

He envisaged that the way forward would lie in team work; not just in teams of priests but of clergy and lay people together, taking responsibility, under the dean and under the bishop, for the pastoral concerns of a given area. He always opposed an over-clericalized Church and saw the demise of clericalism to have its roots in the Second Vatican Council. In Portsmouth diocese he had established one five-priest team to care for the local student population, supplemented by a number of qualified lay people anxious to help.

The conference in Chur had thrown up two particular issues – clerical celibacy and political involvement on the part of priests. He was quite clear about these from the point of view of his own personal exercise of priesthood:

It hurts to hear celibacy talked about as if we were in some way sexually inadequate – even perverted. For me it is part of the basis of my personal relationship with God. It is also very closely related to the real spiritual brotherhood of priests ... and the relationship between the priest and the people he is trying to serve ... Having said that, I am quite prepared to believe that, in some parts of the world and at some stage in the future, it may be necessary for priesthood to be given to married men. Historically that is how it may happen.

This very issue did surface many times during his years in Portsmouth and Liverpool. When he went to Liverpool he was to find that the Movement for the Ordination of Married Men would be given a high profile and Father Michael Gaine remembers being a thorn in the Archbishop's side over this because clearly it was not a matter he felt free either to accept or to reject out of hand. A consensus had not been reached. He felt its time had not come, whereas Michael Gaine was convinced it was overdue.

The celibacy question undoubtedly played a part because Derek's own view was the traditional one that the priesthood either was celibate or it was not. He really felt that priests, young or not so young, would feel under unfair pressure from their married counterparts. To have a 'mixture' forming the priesthood was not something he could take on board. At the same time Derek fully endorsed the introduction of certain married Anglican clergy into the Catholic priesthood as it was 'the exception to the rule'.

He was to experience protest again soon after in a different context when he represented the Pontifical Laity Council at the World Council of Churches meeting in Canterbury, in August 1969. Here the issue was more about white supremacy and white racism in society. Many delegates present advocated violence as the only way to change a corrupt society and to combat the evils of militant atheism and communism. Once again he found his newsletter a useful medium for reporting on the matter:

It was interesting to see the line of approach [expounded by an African American professor of Political Science who called for violent destruction of an evil system] and the support it found from many parts of the world. For me the climax came when the same delegate led us in prayer. Might God forgive us for our complacency in accepting the fruits of White Racism and might we have understanding of one another's viewpoint when we find ourselves at opposite ends of a rifle barrel.

Experiences like Chur gave an opportunity to express his 'political' and pastoral view that in some countries priests might have been denied the opportunities which we had in Britain of close association in the parishes. This may have caused those priests to seek a more overt political stance on behalf of people in opposition to the authorities and the bishops. They did not have the same experience of meeting their bishops and of working with them in their everyday problems. This was a view he had learnt in practice in Stepney; he was not just quoting the theoretical tenets of the Vatican Council. He favoured greater consciousness of political problems but saw the rightful role of lay people, through unions and other organizations, to lie precisely in putting their political consciousness, and their faith, at the service of the community and society. Always it was the better service of the people and the more effective preaching of the Gospel which were the priorities.

When he took a keen interest in the setting up of the National Conference of Priests this was what guided and motivated him. He knew it was important for the Church that the Conference of Priests did not become a separate faction or pressure group in relation to the Bishops' Conference, but that they should work together, even though each had their identity and freedom to air and explore their own concerns. He wanted to remain close to the Conference of Priests, not to inhibit their discussions or vet their proposals but to avoid a repeat of occurrences at Chur and to present a united and strong image of the whole Church. Vatican II had stressed the need of a Church for all, inclusive of all, with a rich diversity of gifts.

He attended every annual meeting of the Priests' Conference after the first at Woodhall, Manchester in 1970, at which the bishops were not represented; it was a more or less informal attempt to start the foundations for the future Conference. In 1971 Cardinal Heenan asked Derek to attend the gathering in Liverpool, at Christ's College. He always recalled, with a pained look on his face, that at that gathering someone had declared 'I spy strangers' and he had felt vulnerable, uncertain whether or not to leave. He held his ground. From then on he slowly established himself as the trusted intermediary between the priests and the Bishops' Conference. He became the 'father figure' of conferences, always ready to advise or clarify some point. He thought of himself, with some justification, as 'the memory bank of the Bishops' Conference'. At the 1994 conference, in a homily at one of the Masses, he gave a personal, moving account of his battle with cancer, which visibly moved the priests and lay people present. More than any brilliant conference agenda or structure, the personal story, the personal touch, was what remained in the memory of the listener.

His skill as a communicator was becoming established. He had always used the media well in his efforts towards evangelization and recognized all too well the uses and abuses of radio and television. He had already become well known as a young priest and Monsignor at Westminster for his late night 'Epilogue' on the radio. With the advent of local radio he was even more suited. He immediately saw its potential for getting across the message of the Gospel effectively.

The Catholic Information Office was set up, through the Bishops' Conference, at the beginning of 1972 as part of the intended five-year review of the Conference structures. The need for a separate, properly constituted media department was recognized. People like Elspeth Orchard of the Laity Commission and Bob Walsh of Social Welfare were brought in to help form the committee which would be responsible to the Bishops' Conference.

Later Mgr George Leonard and Mgr Jim Hook became key figures in the Media Office secretariat, with the committee placed under the able and thorough Chairmanship of Bishop Hugh Lindsay. But the Media Office was a concern that Derek had come to see as his own. He was, rightly, proud of his media experience from the times of the press conferences in Rome. But it was irksome to those responsible to find decisions taken or policies adopted at the level of the Bishops' Conference which had not been the subject of consultation.

In the matter of local radio coverage and televised events Derek was out on his own. He had always admired and emulated the great media communicators like Richard Dimbleby. Sometimes he was literally 'out on his own'. One memorable occasion in Portsmouth Cathedral, when Mass was being televised, gave him, and the viewers, something more than was planned. As he processed up the aisle for Mass a woman came out of the congregation and took hold of his crozier with both hands, shouting aloud about the 'rod of Jesse'. Completely nonplussed, he simply left her holding the crozier and walked on, whilst his MC and secretary, Nick France, made his way, out of camera shot, to the deranged woman and retrieved the crozier just in time to pass it to him at the top of the aisle. Viewers probably thought it was a new liturgical rite.

In a broadcast for Radio Solent, on 26 January 1972, during the Week of Prayer for Christian Unity he used the example of blindness in relation to St Paul's experience on the road to Damascus and his conversion to Christian commitment. The radio, he was aware, put people in touch with others by means of voice and the spoken word, coming right into people's homes, touching their hearts as if spoken only to them. In this way the Lord had spoken to the heart of Saul in his blindness. It was a most effective piece of broadcasting.

In a long address he gave at a symposium on 'Urban Structure and Christian Strategy', he looked at the question of man and woman in the world today, the human predicament and the problem of belief in God. He drew on one of his favourite writers, Frank Sheed, to emphasize that the Christian belief allows no dichotomy between the flesh and the spirit, and spoke of the triple partnership of God, the individual and one's fellow human beings.

The social and human problems with which people were grappling in the 1960s and 1970s were things which the Church had to face and shed some light on, not from some external vantage point but from within. The many aspects of the Constitution on the Church in the Modern World – the 'Schema 13' that had so exercised the Council Fathers – had to be shown to be serious and relevant. If local Christian activity did not show this, what could? These principles were at the heart of Bishop Derek's work, he was driven and motivated by them, he enjoyed the challenge. Whether they liked it or not, clergy and laity were to take their full part in the Church.

As the Isle of Wight came under the Portsmouth diocese, he saw it as part of his pastoral responsibility. So when a three-day rock festival was held on the Isle of Wight in the summer of 1970, although it was not a Church event, he felt the Church must be present. Some surprise and criticism arose because of the high profile he gave it, and the decision to take a 15-strong team of counsellors, volunteers and clergy assembled from the diocese, with the help of the De La Salle Brothers. There, he and his team moved among the crowds of young people. On the first day they were totally ignored, they perhaps appeared as curious as the rest of those present. On the second day a few young people came up to them to ask directions to the toilets or to ask where they could buy stamps. On the third day they were approached by a few more for a discussion about belief in God or the meaning of the Church. He often recounted this story as an example of what he saw to be the true role of the Church in the world: Vatican II in action. The festival event typified what Derek Worlock meant by dialogue with people where they were, and about shedding the light of the Gospel on the world.

Around this time, certain priorities emerged. Some pastoral schemes and community projects had flourished, others had foundered. Even an industrious bishop, with the help of his priests and people, could not do everything, nor could he succeed all the time. In 1968, Father Nicholas France became an invaluable helper and friend. Father France, whom Derek had ordained, provided that element of consistency Derek needed, being prepared to work closely with him on a long-term basis. He wanted to know that he could rely on familiar, trusted colleagues, without having to adapt too frequently to moves of staff, or moves of home. Father Cormac Murphy-O'Connor had served him well and faithfully and was now moving on. Cormac modestly recalls 'He didn't really need a secretary, he was twice as good as me'.

Initiatives which had their origin in the Council and which Derek Worlock brought to fruition during the hectic years of pastoral development in the 1970s, included the ordination of the first permanent deacon for the diocese – Patrick Taylor. The restored order of the diaconate was to find a ready supporter in someone whose watchword had remained 'the better service of the people' and the practical charity of the Church. What he later came to refer to as 'the ministry of the towel', based on the Lord's actions at the Last Supper, summed up what was at the heart of the Church's ministerial purpose. But not all his initiatives worked out well, even if he thought they did. 'He made claims about things working admirably when the reality was they didn't live up to that', recalls Nick France.

However, there were tangible achievements and in the period of eight years from 1968 Bishop Derek Worlock oversaw the building and opening of eleven new churches and the re-ordering of the sanctuaries of practically every church in the diocese. Again the guidelines were clearly followed, the art was in striving to implement the spirit of Vatican II. Such an emotive issue as 'change' in the lay-out of churches, no less than new ideas in the celebration of the liturgy, provided a minefield through which he was constantly having to tread. What parishioners' forebears had sacrificed so much to build and preserve now seemed to some people to be in danger of being discarded by a 'radical' bishop. The way through called for the utmost tact and steady nerve.

The subject of liturgical renewal was not only a matter of conflict and seriousness. He loved to repeat, in later years, the story of the farm hand in Ireland who came to the priest to arrange his wedding. The parish priest informed him that there was now a new rite of the marriage ceremony. The man said he would do whatever the priest told him. On the day of the wedding the farmer, all dressed and ready, suddenly remembered that he had not fed the cattle that morning. Rolling his trousers up to the knees he strode off across the fields to see to the feeding and hurried straight back. Arriving rather late and breathless at the church, he went up the aisle where everyone was waiting. The priest reminded him that it would be the new rite for the wedding. At the top of the aisle, as his bride approached, the priest whispered in his ear 'Would you ever drop your trousers, Pat'. The man looked at him horrified and said 'I think I'd prefer the old rite, Father'.

For some time there had been a growing feeling in the diocese that their Bishop was 'only on loan to them'. When, in 1975, Cardinal Heenan died after a painful illness, the possibility of change in the diocese of Portsmouth became much more focused. He would not have welcomed a change, though it is generally considered that he was ambitious for Westminster. Whether he was suited for it was a matter of opinion. A decade in Portsmouth had enabled him to get to know the parishes, the people, the clergy and the members of other churches and civic bodies. New churches had been built, many priests and deacons had been ordained, whilst other priests had come through the valuable link with Cloyne diocese in Cork, Ireland.

Not quite so successful, however, was the scheme to bring priests from Malta and other countries. The link with the Church around the world was part of his thinking about the nature of the Church. It was for this reason that a connection was made between Portsmouth and the diocese of Bamenda in the Cameroon, West Africa. Some memorable visits there remained with him all his days, as *Give Me Your Hand* demonstrates. The meeting with the Fon (chief) and with the poor yet incredibly happy people of Africa, whose greatest joy was to hear the Good News, left an indelible impression which inspired many a sermon back home. Now he knew in practice, not just from Council statements, that the missionary life of the Church was essential if it was to keep looking outward in a spirit of evange-lization rather than navel-gazing. The legacy of recusancy had to be blended with a renewed sense of mission in the world.

However, with the death of the Cardinal at Westminster specula-tion was rife about a successor. Among the names being mentioned were Alan Clark, Derek Worlock, George Dwyer and Michael Hollings, although the latter was considered to be 'too radical' by some. Derek Worlock was nearly fifty-six, still relatively young, ener-getic and as enthusiastic as when he left Westminster, though some-what wiser and more mellowed by experience and bouts of ill health. His busy life had sometimes forced him into a state of exhaustion, and he would have to rest for a while. The annual holidays, with the Joseph family in Ireland or abroad, or sometimes in Cornwall with other friends, the Evans family at Falmouth, had been a good safe-guard against over-intensity, but somehow such holidays had become secondary to the tasks which were given, as ever, to the willing horse to do. Nick France says that after five years of working with Derek Worlock, he too became a workaholic like his boss!

However, holidays were generally a time to relax and Elaine Evans remembers one memorable holiday when they had been out fishing in Falmouth Bay for mackerel. They returned home that evening to find the kitchen tap had been left turned on all day and the whole of the ground floor was flooded. 'Derek was the first to take off his socks and shoes, roll up his trousers and start brushing the water out of the door.'

The See of Liverpool had also become vacant with the retirement of the ailing Archbishop George Andrew Beck. Archbishop Beck had worked courageously against ill health for eleven years in the arduous task of leading the largest Catholic population in the coun-try. Liverpool was a large urban sprawl with immense social pro-blems in the outer estates and overspill areas where new towns had grown up. Besides this, it was the English heartland of the Orange and the Green with a legacy of sectarian strife.

When Bishop Worlock came up to Upholland College in the north for a Bishops' Meeting in 1975, he no doubt eyed all this and won-dered in his own mind who would inherit that northern vastness, that maelstrom of religious and social problems. He would certainly have good reason to believe that the successor to John Carmel Heenan might well be sought in the direction of 'Pompey'. But it was not to be. Here there was another moment of disappointment in his life when the long-expected news came. 'It fell like a bomb-shell on my breakfast table', he told reporters. He was to go north to Liverpool and the Abbot of Ampleforth, Basil Hume, was to go south to Westminster. One friend, close to him, stated that Derek cried from disappointment. The translation to Liverpool, which felt, he said, like a divorce, was on 7 February 1976, and he had to travel to Liverpool to view his new diocese and assess his new responsibilities with a heavy heart. The reason why he was not selected for Westminster will probably never be fully known other than by the Vatican officials who take their secrets to the grave. Speculation has continued over the years: some believe that Derek was simply not a charismatic enough figure to lead Britain's two and a half million Catholics, but, then, Cardinal Hume is known more for his pastoral and spiritual qualities than for political leadership. Others say the Westminster clergy were very much opposed to the idea of the man they once feared as secretary to three Cardinals becoming their new Archbishop. A significant number of Westminster clergy are said to have written to the Apostolic Delegate, Bruno Heim, but they may not have all been against Derek Worlock, and could have simply been outlining their reasons for wanting someone different.

Many would have remembered him as the power behind the throne during the Griffin and Godfrey years. He had been viewed then as a very efficient secretary but authoritarian figure who was used to getting his own way. It was believed, for example, rightly or wrongly, that he had been instrumental in the removal from parishes of priests who were members of the Vernacular Society because, in preparation for the Vatican Council, the society had sent all its evidence directly to Rome instead of through Westminster channels.

Mgr David Norris, who worked with Derek at Archbishop's House and again for the Bishops' Conference, says that Derek was 'careful, efficient, but unpopular. He found it difficult to unbend – and was very reserved.' Others have hinted that there was also some opposition to Derek being appointed to Westminster from 'two or three bishops' who may have been concerned by his post-conciliar ideas, and there were others who specifically supported Basil Hume.

A 'handful of liberal Catholics' are said to have wanted someone more upper-class, who would move things on, an 'inspirational outsider'. Derek Worlock was considered as an establishment candidate of experience, but largely a bureaucrat, with a narrow clerical education and socialist tendencies. The former Apostolic Delegate Bruno

Heim says that the fact Derek had been secretary to Heenan and to Heenan's two predecessors and had run the diocese while they had been ill 'might have caused them [the priests of Westminster] not to want him'. Personally, he himself was on 'good terms with Worlock until he died'.

Bruno Heim conducted widespread consultation and hosted a number of dinners for prominent Catholics of the day, and is credited with having listened carefully to all opinions. Hugo Young recalls attending one of the dinners at Wimbledon with politician Shirley Williams and Mildred Neville from CIIR. He does not recall any particular name being mentioned that evening. Mildred Neville, however, claims that Basil Hume and the late Michael Hollings were both mentioned and that Bruno Heim showed interest in Hume. Some contend that the Abbot of Ampleforth had already been spotted but, because it would be an unusual appointment, Rome took some convincing.

There was support from the *Yorkshire Post*. Christopher Monckton at that time was the *Post*'s leader writer: he says that he knew Abbot Hume from the Yorkshire dinner party circuit and from attending retreats at Ampleforth and that there was 'awe and respect' for the Abbot who was seen as a 'holy man and an able administrator'. Bishop Gordon Wheeler might have been another name mentioned, but he was ill at the time. Monckton's leader supporting Basil Hume was sent by someone in London to the Apostolic Delegate. Others who are said to have supported the Abbot included Sir Miles Fitzalan-Howard the Duke of Norfolk, Sir William (now Lord) Rees-Mogg and Norman St John Stevas (now Lord St John of Fawsley). In Rome, the head of the Benedictines, Abbot Primate, now Archbishop, Rembert Weakland lent his support, as well as *The Times* newspaper and others.

The wisdom of the Vatican's final choice has not been questioned by any of those interviewed for this book and many have commented on just how Cardinal Basil Hume in Westminster and Archbishop Derek Worlock in Liverpool complemented each other and how much they were able to achieve as President and Vice-President of the Bishops' Conference. However, at the time, friends of Derek Worlock did consider it to be a 'slap in the face' for him to have been by-passed for the Westminster appointment.

In the pastoral letter entitled 'Keeping Going', with which Derek 'signed off' as Bishop of Portsmouth on the Second Sunday of Lent,

14 March 1976, he described how a schoolchild replied to a priest's question at a family Mass by saying that the word 'good-bye' meant 'keep going'. This unusual answer became his theme for taking leave of the people and clergy of Portsmouth diocese. He wrote:

> Perhaps that is the best message we can exchange today when, at the summons of Pope Paul, I must leave you now to take charge of the Archdiocese of Liverpool. I have always marvelled that the first apostles succeeded in travelling so far with the good news of Jesus Christ ... They were, as we say, travelling men. A bishop, as successor of the apostles, must be the same. For the last ten years I have travelled from parish to parish, trying to help you to live according to the Gospel. Now I am asked to leave you and travel to another part of the country, though with the same Gospel. I cannot disguise my sadness at leaving you. But as an apostle it is my task to 'keep going', never ceasing to take the message of the Gospel wherever it is most needed.

This letter, especially the sentence last quoted, tells us precisely what Derek Worlock's whole pastoral motivation consisted of. He went on in the letter to quote St Paul describing the priests and people he was about to take leave of as 'my joy and my crown'. He was leaving them the same mandate he had tried to follow himself when he became a bishop ten years earlier: 'My going cannot mark the end to the process of renewal for which the Church has called. You too must "keep going", persevering in faith and in bringing Christ's compassion and love to all around you.'

The thrust of the letter repeated one of his favourite themes of how relationships in the Church are served by structures, not the other way round. With an eye to his successor, he wrote 'I am confident that he will relish also that spirit of compassionate service, loyal devotion, orthodox teaching in renewal and responsible initiative and freedom within unity, which has been the mark of our diocese'. He was anxious that there be as little hurtful comment or unnecessary speculation as possible about who his successor would be, he asked for prayers for himself and the one who would follow him and for a spirit of collaboration in the consultation process that must follow.

There is a sense of regret and sadness in the business-like explanation of how 'On Tuesday next, 16 March, my authority is transferred to Liverpool. The Canons of the Portsmouth Chapter will meet that day and elect a Vicar Capitular who will have charge of the diocese until a new bishop is appointed by our Holy Father the Pope.'

Reflecting on the Portsmouth years one priest of the diocese wrote:

> By the time he left Portsmouth Diocese Derek Worlock had set us firmly on the road that would lead to Collaborative Ministry in a Church which has a sense of mission. He did have to face opposition and resistance from some people and some of the changes he introduced were not always appreciated.

A leading layman in the diocese who had worked closely with the bishop was John Doyle. At the end of the ten years Derek Worlock had spent in Portsmouth, John Doyle wrote this tribute:

> Imbued with the spirit of the Council, inured by two decades of work with three Primates of the Church, and with youth and vision, he was to make our diocese something of a model in terms of *aggiornamento*. Clergy and laity alike could scarcely have anticipated the thoroughness, efficiency and general pastoral care that was to be brought to the task. Change is invariably painful and it was no easy matter to create structures and to make people realize that these were not an end in themselves but destined to sanctify the people of God, to recognize their partnership with the bishop and to stimulate them in their daily lives.

Nick France reflects: 'He dragged us out of the past. He was at the forefront of new ideas, conciliar renewal – and raised our status as a diocese – it was unusual in the light of what went before.' Although not everything in Portsmouth continued after he left, some commissions survived and 'general expectations lived on'.

Adrian Hastings, in his *A History of English Christianity*, writes:

> He [Derek] had been an obvious choice for Westminster: absolutely at home in Rome, Worlock knew the Church's administration both there and in Britain like the back of his hand. He was in fact, indeed self-consciously so, the very model of the post-conciliar ecclesiastic.

Hastings goes on to say that while he 'lacked any touch of charisma he soon established in Liverpool a remarkable working relationship with David Sheppard'. Professor Hastings now believes that Derek was 'unfairly not loved' and proved himself at Liverpool to be most imaginative. 'His immense practicability served him well.'

CHAPTER ELEVEN

Going North

To do the impossible I must believe in the invisible.
(Archbishop Worlock, on taking possession
of the Archdiocese of Liverpool, 1976)

Although he was not born within the shadow of the Kop, or with an Everton scarf around his neck, the remarkable outcome of Derek Worlock's twenty years in the north were such that by the time they came to an end there was universal acceptance of Cardinal Hume's words of tribute: 'He made his home in Liverpool. He was concerned not only for the Catholic flock there but for Liverpool and all its people.' There was a tangible acknowledgement too of his remark in the panegyric at the funeral on 15 February 1996: 'Derek belonged to Liverpool.' This represented an achievement which was both a personal one for him and one that went very deep into the heart of the archdiocese and city he served so well for so long. The *Liverpool Daily Post* reporter, Ann Todd, put it another way: he had become 'an honorary Scouser'.

The Liverpool years were destined to be ones of great excitement and fulfilment, but ones of sorrow and trial as well. As he often said, 'Liverpool doesn't do things by half.' The call that was made upon him to join with the other Church and community leaders in bringing a Gospel of solidarity and compassion in times of deprivation and anguish, and a Gospel of shared joys in times of triumph and success, was something even his unique experience could not fully prepare him for.

A reflection written whilst on holiday in Cornwall in 1981 (published fifteen years later, in *The Tablet* of June 1996), about the changes in his own life, was more prophetic than he could have known at the time:

Even in the hidden years at Westminster, I was preparing (or being prepared) for my later role, which found fulfilment in the implementation of all the insights and recommendations of 'Lumen Gentium'. This may seem to be development rather than change, but it must at least be true that certain people, events and influences hastened and sharpened up the process.

The training he undoubtedly had for the role of fronting the process of renewal in England in the wake of Vatican II was providential. The Portsmouth years showed this supremely, but things moved on: a different generation and a new era were ushered in. The developments he was drawn into in Liverpool, willingly or unwillingly, from 1980 onwards, were things that took him by surprise and which no one could have been trained for.

Going north, though it would prove to be a move of great significance in the long run, was initially the cause of a great deal of heartache for him personally. It meant leaving his beloved Portsmouth and all the associations he had cherished from his time there, in places like Winchester, Alresford, Abingdon, Bournemouth, Southampton, and the Channel Islands. These may have become fonder in the memory as they slipped away. Now he was to swap Winchester for Warrington, Bournemouth for Bootle and the Channel Islands for the Isle of Man, to quote Canon Nick France. In turn, these places too were to have a special meaning for him in his subsequent ministry but at first they may not have seemed to him like a fair exchange. He described going north and leaving his former diocese as 'like a divorce'. Again, the man who was an advocate of change nevertheless found change of personal circumstances a hard bullet to bite.

There were some brighter considerations, though. He knew something of Liverpool from Cardinals Godrey and Heenan. His own father had, after all, been posted in charge of Ground Defence at Speke during the war and had lived in Hoylake. Bishop Sheppard, whom he had met, albeit fleetingly, in London days, had arrived in Liverpool six months earlier. Furthermore, he had made several visits to the archdiocese and the north-west and had friends or contacts in the YCW movement and the Laity Commission there. Pat Keegan had told him all about Hindly, Tom Casey from the Family Social Action Committee had gone with a group to Portsmouth to meet him when news of his appointment to Liverpool broke, and Philip Duffy had

travelled to Portsmouth with some of the Liturgy Committee in order
to discuss the plans for his forthcoming Installation. He had been
assured of a typically warm welcome. He had also been assured of
Liverpudlian humour: Monsignor Cyril Taylor and some other clergy
had come to see him at Portsmouth Cathedral and walked round the
raised sanctuary that had been built as part of the re-ordering. Cyril
Taylor stood looking over the edge of the step and remarked 'they
need a bloody safety-net down there'.

On 18 February 1976, four weeks before his official move to
Liverpool, he had gone there for the inevitable press conference
which was called to introduce him. Father Charles Lynch was then
the Press and Information Officer and helped to arrange it all. It was
held at the curial offices in Brownlow Hill and the archdiocesan
newspaper, the *Catholic Pictorial*, described the first impressions of
the new Archbishop-elect. 'He walked into the Board Room, a tall
distinguished man with an air of quiet dignity. In keeping with
modern practice he is a young bishop, but his youthful appearance
belies even his fifty-six years.'

He began the press conference by thanking his predecessor,
George Andrew Beck, for his welcome and for his courageous and
important work in the archdiocese, particularly his work for Catholic
schools. 'I know the warmth and the kindness and loyalty of the
people here', he told them, 'I have friends here. I am from the
South but I look forward to being able to make my home here and
working with the priests and the people in all that must be done.'

Some may have already glimpsed a steel fist in the velvet glove. He
set out his hopes about ecumenism straight away, expressing the
desire to work with Bishop Sheppard in maintaining the priorities
already established, building on the foundations already put in place
by Archbishop Beck and Archbishop Stuart Blanch. He announced
that he wanted to try to

> close the gap between religion and life, between what goes on in
> church and what goes on at work and at home; to make our Faith a
> living reality that can be a sign of hope to people in rather
> troubled times; and at the same time to secure justice and human
> dignity in the ordinary affairs of life.

Thus he set forth his statement of intent. It was a carefully balanced
appraisal of what he saw as his mission in his new archdiocese,
spelling out 'the double mandate from Pope Paul', as he called it.

He came with the firm belief that the Pope had given him the task of addressing people's social and material needs and ensuring that Liverpool, with its sectarian past, did not become 'another Belfast'. What a mandate!

The train which brought him from London on Sunday 14 March 1976 pulled in at 4.20 p.m. at Lime Street station and a large crowd of waving, smiling, hymn-singing people greeted his arrival. Whether he found their enthusiastic rendition of 'Faith of Our Fathers' encouraging or not is not clear but he smiled back at them all and the ice was broken. Perhaps from that moment he resolved to do what he had always done – immerse himself completely in the place where he found himself and give it his all.

One small child, in an attempt to get a better look, got his head caught in the railings and had to be freed by anxious parents! The new Archbishop waved to everyone and got into an open-topped car that took him away through the streets and to the Metropolitan Cathedral. There he was welcomed by the Administrator, Canon Michael O'Connor, and went to pray for guidance and strength in front of the Blessed Sacrament. He got an early insight into the extensive problems of the fabric of the Cathedral: a leaking roof and buckets strategically placed to catch the rainwater. Such was the extent of the problem that, twenty years later, the buckets were still in evidence to greet a new Archbishop, Patrick Kelly.

Driving through the city he may have reflected that in many respects the move north to Liverpool had brought him to a situation reminiscent of his earlier ministry at Stepney. There the derelict tenements, the streets torn apart by war, the problems of urban decay and poor housing, were all ingredients of a city and its surroundings which he was now seeing again. There was a difference, however. This time he would be part of a process of regeneration that was to see Liverpool and the region grow, find new hope during the 1980s and 1990s, and experience a gradual restoration of pride to Merseyside. Bringing back life to the waterfront, encouraging home-making in the city centre once again, these were priorities he would witness and contribute to.

The 'better service of people' and the needs of the city emerged once again on his agenda: he had no doubt at all that this was a constitutive part of the Gospel to which the Church must be committed, part of the mission of the whole People of God. The imaginative and at times courageous work of Derek Worlock and David

Sheppard was to lift things onto a higher level than before, but they were anxious to acknowledge the very real debt they owed to the previous Church leaders and the people themselves who were tired of religious bigotry.

Bishop David Sheppard says that ecumenical relations had already been established between himself and Archbishop George Andrew Beck. Although Archbishop Beck was not well, Bishop Sheppard can recall talking with him about the future of the Colleges of Education and about a somewhat difficult appointment of a former Catholic priest who had become an Anglican. He also remembers going to visit Archbishop Beck after he became ill, at St Joseph's, Upholland and later in the Lourdes Hospital. The friendship they developed had been an important foundation for ecumenical relations in Liverpool.

Whatever his private feelings, and whatever measure of disappointment he felt in not succeeding to Westminster but going north instead, Derek had to steel himself and give the new scene his whole attention. It was partly for this reason that he stayed away from any official visit back to his former diocese for the first few years. He feared treading on the toes of the new Bishop there, Anthony Emery. Though perhaps diplomatic, it was in some ways a needless deprivation and sacrifice, as Bishop Emery was a jovial and tolerant man who would have been understanding and welcoming.

One exception Derek made to this self-imposed policy was to go to the funeral of a man who had been one of his first lay trustees of the diocese, Sidney Quick. He had placed a lot of emphasis on having lay people act as trustees and share responsibility for decision-making in the Church. On that occasion he met some of his former priests and tentatively and shyly greeted his former 'pride and joy' – priests he knew and those he had ordained and worked with over the years. But he was aware that all this was no longer 'his' in the same way as before. After the funeral the clergy were all to go to a reception in the parish. Typically he wanted to make phone calls, which he did from the presbytery, and took a long time about it. Waiting outside, the parish priest, anxious to greet people at the reception, said 'Who does he think he is, the Prime Minister or something!'

Derek was careful, courteous, and always diplomatic. Almost before he set foot in Liverpool self-conscious Liverpudlians would ask him: 'What d'yer think of Li'pool?' Before he could answer, they told him:

'We're very warm people, very warm.' He quickly learnt not to answer the next crucial question – which football team did he support? He was smart enough to realize that, one way or another, his answer would split the city in two, or any parish congregation in half. So, for the first few years at least, he played safe and replied 'Southampton'. He could argue that it was hardly possible to develop any allegiance to the Merseyside teams so soon, and as both Liverpool FC and Everton FC were riding high in the League at the time, he was on safe ground supporting 'The Saints'. Perhaps the Everton fans will have forgiven him for later admitting his support for 'The Reds'.

From the cathedral he went to his residence at Archbishop's House, four miles south of the city centre, in Mossley Hill. It is unlikely that he got much rest that night. Who knows what anxiety and anguish mixed to fill his mind as he contemplated the challenge presented by his new responsibilities in the great archdiocese of 500,000 Catholics, the largest Catholic population in the country. He recognized that it was a place with long-standing traditions, loyalties that went deep, and a history of strong denominational and sectarian divisions. And, of course, it was not just the city of Liverpool he had come to serve but the territory of the Lancashire Martyrs too; it was necessary to remember the fiercely guarded independence of those who were born of the recusant families of the North. He was often to remind people that he himself came from a land of the martyrs, in Hampshire.

The house he was to occupy had been the home of Archbishop Beck, by then a very sick man, who had been in office for eleven years and had found a new home at St Joseph's, Upholland, the diocesan seminary and centre for pastoral formation. George Andrew was loved and respected for his humility and his learning. He had once been described by Richard Dimbleby as that 'rumbustious Bishop Beck', an influential figure in the world of Christian education, well-known at the Vatican Council where Derek had met him, and a leading member of the Bishops' Conference.

Archbishop Beck relinquished his position as Archbishop of Liverpool and handed over his crozier to his successor with dignity, confiding in Derek that in his experience the task of running the archdiocese was 'a killer'. He had, by the end of his life, fulfilled in no small measure the spiritual objective he had set himself and which he spelt out in his hand-over speech – to be a godly man, a manly man, a mortified man.

In Archbishop's House Derek had the help, for only a few weeks, of the nuns who had looked after George Andrew but who resolved to leave; the Order could no longer spare them for this work. This was a shock. He put great store by having a stable and workable 'family' around him as the necessary back-up for his work. He arrived back one day shortly after his arrival to be ticked off soundly for being late for dinner. Punctuality was not one of his virtues. Nor was patience. He could not countenance that kind of confrontation and knew that he would have to find some better arrangement soon. But he had the help of two people, Jean Jones, secretary by this time to three Archbishops of Liverpool, and Teresa Byrne. He eventually got some of the Faithful Companions of Jesus to come to staff the house, Sisters Mary John Somers, Loretta Keating and Mary Condron; later they were joined by Sister Emanuel Grant. Two priests in particular were on hand to help him in the household – Father Nick France, who had accompanied him from Portsmouth for a few days, and Father Anthony Dennick, who had been the Archbishop's secretary for seven years in Liverpool. It was important to him to have Nick France to help him bring a little of his Portsmouth home, the picture of the Madonna and Child, his paintings, photographs and mementos from Portsmouth, to provide a bridge with his former home.

With a good knowledge of the parishes, Father Tony Dennick was well placed to introduce Derek to the various parts of the archdiocese in those crucial first months. He paved the way for a series of pastoral visits to deaneries and parishes in a fact-finding exercise that enabled Derek to feel more at home. There were, however, some surprises in store. Tony Dennick was able to prepare him for the encounter with certain characters, not least among the clergy. On an early visit to a parish, one very wet night, they went round to call on the people in the parish club assembled to meet him. Stepping in out of the pouring rain a man greeted him with the words 'Grand Knight, Your Grace', to which Derek answered, looking at the heavens, 'You must be joking'. 'No, Your Grace', he replied, 'I *am* the Grand Knight.'

Tony Dennick remembers well those early days and Derek's desire to get to know the parishes. But in his enthusiasm the method chosen was, with hindsight, not the best. Mgr Dennick tells how every Sunday they made a tour of two or three parishes. 'I had to work out the Mass times', he says. They would arrive at one parish in time for the start of Mass, at another in time for the homily, and a third in time for him to speak at the end of Mass. 'It was quite a programme and not understood by most priests, who seemed to sense that there was some sneaking in – and I got the backlash – because it appeared that way.'

A pastoral letter was being read in the churches one Sunday: the Archbishop's first pastoral for Lent. Standing at the back of a church in Bootle, having gone there unannounced, he listened to the old priest speaking: the text was so emasculated and chopped according to the priest's own whim that it took some time to register that it really was the Lenten pastoral letter Derek had so painstakingly written. (Another version, which circulated, was that he took the text out of the priest's hand and said 'I'll read that properly', unaware that the priest was struggling with throat cancer.)

At the back of another church he took by surprise some children playing hopscotch in the porch during Mass. He was a bit taken aback but philosophical about it later, saying 'Well, at least they were there.'

The culture shock of going north expressed itself in a number of other ways. He found a group of Liverpool schoolgirls who got a fit of the giggles when he addressed them and, somewhat exasperated and disconcerted, he said to them: 'Come on, share the joke.' 'It's just that every time you speak', they explained, 'you sound just like the Duke of Edinburgh.' He was to find his rather smooth southern accent a problem many times. In Lourdes with the archdiocesan pilgrimage at the end of July of the first summer, he had explained the story of Lourdes in a sermon at the Grotto and at the end said 'And if you want the *barths* they're over there to the left'. Some people evidently looked mystified. Bishop Harris had to explain to the puzzled audience that what he meant was 'The *baths* are over *there.*'

Although accents and culture proved a problem, Derek knew that the Church was big and Catholic enough to accommodate everyone. On the day following his arrival in the archdiocese, he made an official visit to the Lord Mayor. He was delighted to find that Councillor Owen Doyle was a Catholic, a product of the YCW and active in his own parish. On his rounds he discovered that four of the Mayors of local boroughs were Catholic, and products of YCW. The days of a Catholic political party in Liverpool were long gone. The times when Councillor Longbottom, an Orangeman, had clashed with Archbishop Richard Downey had not disappeared from local legend, and Downey's famous remark, after a narrow defeat over an issue in the Council chamber, that it was better to win by a short head than to be beaten by a long bottom, was still remembered. The tradition of Catholic social action and commitment to parochial activity would be a vital part of the co-operation the archbishop was hoping for. He made the development of Family and Social Action a priority in his Liverpool years.

Before getting to know the pastoral needs there were some canonical requirements to fulfill. On 16 March he met the Cathedral Chapter of Canons to present the Bull of Appointment. Bishop Harris and Bishop Gray were the Auxiliary Bishops who had done much to oversee the archdiocese during Archbishop Beck's illness. The correct procedure and official 'swearing-in' complete, he was able to begin to get to know those priests with whom he would now be working and discuss the plans which he wanted to implement in the archdiocese. Collaboration had always been a key factor for him but he would soon know that although Liverpool liked 'a boss' it disliked 'a bully' and that the respect and trust of priests and people alike would have to be won gradually when it came to pastoral policy. Though he believed in delegation and the principle of collegiality learnt at the Vatican Council, the practice of these concepts called for flexibility and effort on both sides. He was determined to try.

Critics say that Derek arrived in Liverpool an 'emotionally bruised and wounded man' and that he already had a pastoral plan worked out for Westminster and merely changed the name to Liverpool. Whether that is true or not, the people who had provided such a great welcome for him at the railway station now gave him a tremendous reception by their presence at the Metropolitan Cathedral for the Installation ceremony, five days later on 19 March, the feast of St Joseph, patron of the archdiocese and of the universal Church, which was held at 7.00 p.m. Granada Television covered the event. The fruit of Philip Duffy's visit to Portsmouth was a specially composed setting of 'Sacerdos et Pontifex'. Philip and his brother Terry had had some misgivings about the Archbishop's alleged taste in music. He had a reputation for liking folk Masses, perhaps because of stories of the visit to the Isle of Wight pop festival or his avant-garde ideas about the liturgy.

Instead, they were to find in him not only a personal friend and ally but a reforming spirit where the life of the Cathedral was concerned. He had been to the Cathedral with Cardinal Heenan for the opening ceremony in 1967. Now when he spoke to the Administrator about 'our Cathedral' it was no longer a distant problem for someone else to oversee. He was told that the building was 'in the wrong place, it leaks and nobody comes to it anyway'. He set about dispelling the gloom and predicted a brighter future for this futuristic edifice, legacy of Cardinal Heenan's desire for 'A Cathedral in our time'. He did not underestimate the repair problems but he did not want to sit back and watch the rain come in! The Cathedral was to become one of his unresolved problems: though he took the decision to launch an appeal for the Cathedral and agreed to the necessary work being done, he did not live to see it completed.

One thing he was resolved not to do, when he arrived in Liverpool, was to allow the cathedral to be shut down for repair. That would have put people off altogether and it would have been impossible to build up attendance again, especially with people living a distance from it. He lifted the moratorium on spending and asked that the embellishment of the side chapels be resumed. As if to prove the point, he welcomed to his home, shortly before Christmas one year, members of Cardinal Griffin's family who had offered to donate money for the re-ordering of a side chapel in memory of the late Cardinal. The Chapel of the Oils was chosen – dedicated to St George and the English Martyrs. Robin McGhie designed a back cloth depicting the various uses of the oils. In a moving little address to the family – there were twenty of them present including the Cardinal's sister, Katherina – he spoke of how he had kept the cloth that had bound his hands after the Cardinal had anointed them at his ordination. He told how he had carried the holy oils in his pocket for almost seven years and finally had to administer the anointing to the Cardinal on his death bed that night in 1956 at Polzeath. He had carried the link with Cardinal Griffin, to whom he said he owed so much, through to his new archdiocese by way of that chapel. It was a typical gesture.

But outside and beyond the Cathedral the concerns of the archdiocese had to be addressed quickly. People were looking for a lead, an inspiration which Archbishop Beck had been unable to provide during the past year or so. Derek himself was ever anxious to make his mark, to prove a success and to set about the renewal with the same zeal as he had had in Portsmouth. He wanted to focus especially in the early days on the morale of the priests, lay participation, Christian unity and liturgical renewal.

A difficult aspect of the situation facing him from his first days in the north, was the 'procession', as he once referred to it, of priests coming to his house, or even ringing him up, to say they were leaving the priesthood. He found this heart-breaking. The low morale of some clergy would affect others, he was sure of that. He was secure in his own priesthood but the loss of priests made him edgy and anxious to stem the tide. Cardinal Heenan had seen defections as related principally to lust and selfishness, and let people go gladly on that basis. One Liverpool priest, Fr Kevin Kelly, says that Derek found it difficult to take on board that a priest would retire from the ministry to get married: 'he was kind to priests who left, but could not empathize with them.'

For Derek it was different. The idea of giving up priesthood was something he could not assimilate, for him it was such an inestimable gift and privilege, a call there inside him from the age of three. He had compassion, however, and at the same time tried to hang on to all who came to say goodbye. In many instances, it was a *fait accompli*, priests were just coming out of courtesy to say farewell; they had made a mistake, they wanted to marry, or the stress was too much. He took each on its merits and tenaciously kept hold if he thought there was even the slimmest chance of someone changing his mind. Support was vital. At the very end of his life, when he was dying in hospital, a senior priest and valued friend left the priesthood to get married; it was undoubtedly a blow to him. What made it slightly easier was that the priest had sufficient trust and respect for him and came personally to tell him of his decision, though anxious about the effect on him in his serious condition. True to the principles he had always tried to follow, there were no recriminations, no condemnation. Despite the real shock and sadness, there was room left to try to accept the decision, even if he could not understand it fully.

A further shock was the high number of clergy funerals in the first year or two of his time in Liverpool. He joked that he might have to appoint an episcopal vicar for funerals the way things were going. It was in the course of celebrating these funeral Masses that one of his great strengths emerged; his ability to say something that encapsulated the person's life, to catch the character by some phrase or description, and find exactly the right Scripture text with which to sum up that person's ministry. The quip about a vicar for clergy funerals hid the truth that such funerals were his domain and no one else's. Many were glad about that. Some, however, found the 'I' dimension came in too much, especially when he talked about how he had touched some priest's life. He tried hard to personalize things, perhaps too much, but even so his efforts were often taken to be boasting.

Within a few days of settling in, therefore, he set out on a fact-finding tour of the archdiocese, consulting the priests and the people in the deaneries and parishes, seeing what structures were already in place. He intended to spend a year doing this in preparation for a pastoral plan to be presented to the archdiocese in due course – which tells against the suggestion that he had one already prepared! The plan was not to be just about 'churchy' things, but also about people's everyday problems. In his New Year's Message for 1977 he referred to the pastoral plan, hoping it would provide a service to the people and 'assist in revitalizing the areas of Church and local society which need this spiritual deepening in face of today's problems'. Conscious of the emphasis there had been in the 1974 Synod of Bishops on Evangelization, he wanted the archdiocese to look outwards not inwards. 'I hope we shall not lose sight of those parts of the world where injustice and sadness and hardships exist today to an extent exceeding anything within our own experience here.' In saying this, he cited Northern Ireland, parts of Africa he had visited himself and the people of Latin America. He hoped that the redevelopment planned for cities like Liverpool would not be 'at the expense of other parts of the world less fortunate than ourselves'.

The initial round of deanery meetings had its ups and downs. Some people resisted him because he spelt change, disruption, innovation. Others were only anxious to show him that they were already ahead of the field in all these ways, though many parish and deanery structures were paper exercises. Even the Archdiocesan Pastoral Council was a rather unrepresentative and too large group of people chosen for their 'expertise'. He wanted to change this from a merely consultative body to a more executive one based on parish needs and composed of people from different positions representative of the parish. 'True representation is elusive' he admitted, 'but an effort is needed at least.'

He learnt rapidly that solutions could not be imposed and that people would dig their heels in if they felt threatened. In places such as Chorley and Leyland there were even those who objected strongly to the idea of a pastoral letter signed by the Archbishop of

Liverpool. They could, however, offer no feasible alternative when he asked them for suggestions. Critics say he concentrated too much on the inner city of Liverpool at the expense of such places as Wigan, Leigh and Warrington.

To help start a process of discussion, to get people to meet and talk to each other about the Church, in some cases for the first time, he introduced the Twelve Apostles Scheme. It was along the lines of a similar project he had initiated in Portsmouth diocese. The objective was to get each parish to form Twelve Apostles and let that be the launch pad for further ideas and joint pastoral action. He arranged for hundreds of set of tapes and booklets to be sent to the parishes. Some years later many of these packages were still lying unopened behind presbytery sofas, but the scheme did enjoy modest success.

As in Portsmouth he was keen to meet the clergy as soon as possible and arranged for them to come to Christ's College, as it was then called, in Woolton. The priests had mixed reactions: some feared changes; other, mostly younger, priests were pleased that they had someone who was interested in them and wanted them to be part of things. The Archbishop spoke to them about his hopes and plans for the diocese.

Bishop Vincent Nichols was one of the young priests and remembers another meeting, when he was sitting in a corner of the dining room at Cathedral House listening to the new Archbishop and suddenly being 'stunned' by hearing Derek mention his name. Derek's memory for names was phenomenal.

After one of these early meetings, some of the younger ones came to see Derek to ask him what they could do for him. One of those was Mgr John Devine. It was a good sign that a rapport was building up particularly among the younger section of the clergy and it was a great encouragement to him. John Devine remembers the genuine delight when they knew Derek Worlock was coming to Liverpool. 'His name had come up, but people said he would go to Westminster, so we were delighted when he came here.'

But there were genuine obstacles to surmount and the accusation of interference was still around. He put great store by the relationship of priest to bishop. John Devine, who was the representative of the younger priests on the National Conference of Priests, remembers having regular meetings with Derek. 'I think he found it easier to relate to younger men than his peers. Everything he did was the implementation of the Vatican Council. He was serious about it and a lot of the older priests found it a bit threatening. The older Irish ones were suspicious of a quintessential Englishman and a Southerner to boot.'

The national and international tasks he had accrued over the years since Westminster were not shed despite his busy schedule in Liverpool. He and Cardinal Hume were asked to lead the delegation for the Synod of Bishops in Rome in September 1977. It was on the subject of catechetics. Derek noted the change in Pope Paul VI. He had aged and looked tired: small wonder – he had just celebrated his eightieth birthday.

Josephine Clemson, head of RE at St Edmund Arrowsmith School, who had written some booklets for RE in schools, joined the group that went to Rome. The Synod had not met since 1974 and was now to be a three-yearly event instead of two-yearly. The task which Paul VI faced in collating all the Synod deliberations and propositions into a document as good as *Evangelii Nuntiandi* was in fact completed by Karol Wojtyła, the future John Paul II. The document, *Catechesi Tradendae*, restored the status of traditional Catholic social teaching as part of the corpus of cate-chesis in the Church.

Meanwhile, the workload on behalf of the Bishops' Conference continued unabated, and did so until illness later forced Derek to take a back seat. He was known for looking carefully at the detail of a text or document, and foreseeing problems before they arose. A classic case was his negotiations with the Inland Revenue over covenants. Vin Nichols recalls:

> In one sense, it was Derek at his best. The Inland Revenue having been through the charities came to the Catholic Church and said they would like to deal with covenants nationally, not diocese by diocese. It was the first serious case. The Inland Revenue never suggested there was anything malicious.

Derek was asked to head the negotiations with the Inland Revenue and 'did so with a combination of sensitivity and contacts with people in the business world, and politicians and in a way where they would end up friends'.

Similarly later, he was called on again when the question of priests' income tax arose and again the tax authorities wanted to deal with the Church nationally as a corporation, instead of through individual dioceses. It was, however, work which illness prevented him from finishing.

These concerns, however, lay in the future: they were to be part of the more intense and complicated life that overtook him at the end of his years in Liverpool. For the time being, it was to be the issue of ecumenism that occupied his mind.

CHAPTER TWELVE

'Into a Deeper Communion'

Collaboration and trust were to be key factors in the work for Church
Unity on Merseyside and way beyond Merseyside. Very soon after he
had arrived at Archbishop's House, in Green Lane, Liverpool, a
special visitor rang the door bell. Bishop Sheppard was on the step,
with the gift of a bottle of wine, anxious to establish from the
beginning a friendship which would in time prove to be one of the
most enduring and inspiring of Christian partnerships. The Church
Leaders' Group which had been formed, and which met regularly,
benefited from remaining unchanged in its membership for a period
of nearly ten years.

The two bishops had previously met as frequent presenters of the
Epilogue on television, and several years later at Lambeth at the
suggestion of Archbishop Michael Ramsey. As we have seen,
Archbishop Ramsey, who had invited Derek to dinner at Lambeth
when he completed his service as secretary at Archbishop's House in
1964, thought that he should meet David, who was then, like Derek,
beginning his ministry in the East End. But their meeting had been
too brief to give any hint of the wonderful and vital 'double act'
which was now to capture the imagination and lead people on to
new levels of ecumenical endeavour. In Liverpool they met as two
men intent on understanding each other, albeit quite different in
character and background, and with the vision to see that their
partnership could be a powerful symbol and effective source of a
deep Christian fellowship within the local Churches.

They could not foresee that they would sometimes be referred to
as 'the ecumenical pantomime horse' – a phrase of Derek's that
perhaps owed something to his interest in the stage – or as 'Fish
and Chips'. The explanation of this latter phrase was added as the
folk-lore developed, so that it was said to refer to the fact that they
were always together, seldom out of the newspaper and to be taken

with a pinch of salt (as Bishop Ronald Brown put it). Derek came to dislike the phrase and it became quite inappropriate later when, from 1986, the partnership included Dr John Newton, the Methodist District Chairman and Moderator of the Free Churches, with whom they formed 'The Liverpool Three'.

The partnership, however, was not without its critics in both the Anglican and Catholic Churches. Among the Catholics there were those who felt time was spent on ecumenical collaboration at the expense of giving support to priests in poor parishes fighting against incessant vandalism, crime, and falling Mass attendances. David Sheppard says that at the beginning of the growing relationship he took advice from within his own Church: 'I was told "Do be careful, don't rock the boat, things are fairly calm" – I decided I wouldn't take any notice.'

The complementarity of the two Bishops in their role as leaders was such that they captured the imagination at a time when heroes were in short supply and the religious divide seemed as wide as ever. Grace Sheppard thought of Derek as the hawk and David the dove. In situations, political or delicate, both were needed. David himself recognized that Derek was a shrewd and able negotiator who would spur him on to try something on behalf of both of them. That was the strength of the partnership.

Endeavours for Christian Unity which they and their Free Church colleagues, especially Norwyn Denny and John Williamson, strove to exercise from the beginning, were based upon a firm start already made by their predecessors, Bishop Stuart Blanch and Archbishop George Andrew Beck. David Sheppard recalls:

> My appointment was made in January 1975 and my secretary had put some telegrams on my desk, the top one of which was from Archbishop Beck. I realized that ecumenical partnership, which had mattered to me before, would be much more important now, given Liverpool's history.

There were the beginnings of trust and friendship over the issues relating to the proposed ecumenical training college for teachers and in the visits David made to Upholland, and later to the Lourdes Hospital, to see George Andrew. A new era would see more steps taken to strengthen friendship and commitment which would reach their high point in the signing of a Covenant of Unity by the six Merseyside Church leaders. It was this 'Call to Partnership', on

Pentecost Sunday, 26 May 1985, which took them, and the local Church communities generally, into a new mode of working and praying together. The Anglican Cathedral was the setting and it is worth recording here the content of that Covenant because it signified that the commitment to unity among the Churches was not simply the outcome of personal friendship between Church leaders but a movement from the people, expressed in their own local covenants and representing the point that many had reached on the pilgrim road to unity. The Covenant sealed the future shape of the pilgrimage in a way that was not dependent on the few but built on the majority; it would not be imposed unsolicited and it would transcend personalities or future changes of leadership.

The wording of the Covenant is as follows:

Almighty God, you call your Church to witness to the love of Jesus for all people; and you send your Church into the world filled with the power of your Spirit; bind us together now as partners with you and with one another in the task entrusted to us, that obedient to your command we may proclaim the Good News, and make disciples of all the nations. We ask this through him who came to save us all, even Jesus Christ our Lord. Amen.

The prayer is a good example of the collaborative effort to produce a statement, an invitation to the Churches and all religious traditions that would challenge them to act for unity without being either a threat or merely empty words. The experience gained by the Churches of Liverpool and the region, as well as the Church leaders' own need for support – for a network of co-operation – helped to bring into being the Merseyside and Region Churches Ecumenical Assembly (MARCEA), and other local groupings.

The development of such bodies around the country made it possible to contemplate the setting up of new ecumenical structures for the whole of England, Scotland and Wales. Churches Together In England, in Scotland and in Wales, and the wider Council of Churches for Britain and Ireland, which superseded the British Council of Churches, made it possible for Catholics to play a full and effective part in the national structures. The contribution which Archbishop Worlock made to these reforms was widely recognized, even though he would not live to see the new ideas in action beyond the first few years of their existence. In this we might compare him a little to Pope John XXIII, his great hero, who inspired and encouraged the Vatican Council but did not live to see it mature into the influential and effective force for renewal that it became. Derek saw new ecumenical bodies, or 'instruments' as they were called, offering a more inclusive context for moving forward together along converging (not parallel) lines, until all should meet in Christ.

Vin Nichols was working with Derek during what he describes as

> some difficult but interesting processes – such as the way in which the British Council of Churches agreed to end its life and Churches Together in England and Wales and ACTS in Scotland emerged. At certain crucial meetings Derek found ways through by telling jokes and had everyone in fits of laughter. It eased the tension, when for many people in the talks the real problem was the presence of the Roman Catholics – but he had achieved success.

He also recalls Derek telling him when talking about the rules for ecumenism 'Don't make the mistake of bargaining and always make people laugh'.

David Sheppard was emphatic that structures without prayer and reflection would never suffice. The very first Holy Week, after Derek Worlock's arrival in March 1976, was grasped as an opportunity to 'meet at the foot of the Cross', as he termed it, not for a business agenda but to talk together about the heart of the faith. This happened each Good Friday from then on in some form or other. One year they met in the church at Hough Green, Widnes, to meditate on the Stations of the Cross which were part of a new church building there shared by Catholics and Anglicans alike.

The experience of praying and thinking about the faith was the essential antidote to an over-academic approach to their ministry. Certainly there were frequent 'catch-up' sessions, at each other's homes or through long conversations on the phone on Sunday nights to keep abreast of the countless items of concern. But these were considered futile without the reflective side of things. A favourite insight, which Derek often repeated, was that expressed by Pope John Paul II in an address to the European Bishops' Conference:

> We need heralds of the Gospel who are experts in humanity, who have shared to the full the joys and hopes, the anguish and the sadnesses of our day, but who are at the same time contemplatives in love with God.

By the time the Liverpool years had come to an end for Derek Worlock, these sentiments had been truly lived and tested.

Many times in the years which followed 'The Liverpool Three' travelled the length and breadth of the country preaching the message of 'Churches Together'. The title had become the new symbol for the ecumenical process. On one occasion their destination was Devon. The churches there were wanting to make a covenant too. The main service was held in Exeter Cathedral but there was a shorter service and meeting with local Church leaders the evening before. To Derek's utter dismay his luggage had not been taken off the plane which had brought them to Exeter. The loss of his purple cassock and all the other things that made up his usual travel kit was a worry to him all evening. The situation was lightened by some pleasantries about whether ecumenism among Church leaders stretched as far as lending each other their robes or not. The Bishop of Exeter could provide a purple cassock almost as good as any Catholic one, but there was nothing for it but for all Church leaders to dress down and wear suits. It was not something Archbishop Derek felt comfortable about but there was no alternative. The evening Service went off well and no one commented on the suits. The Free Church minister was happier anyway. The problem of correct dress had been rightly overcome by the more important question of the sign of unity.

That night Derek stayed near Exeter with some friends, Stafford and Mima, the Earl and Countess of Iddesleigh. Their warm hospitality and a laugh about the missing cassock smoothed away any remaining niggles, and the following morning, the luggage restored, the service to launch Churches Together in Devon went off with all the dignity and success he had wished. The incident had united those concerned more than any amount of planned ecumenism could have done.

As people expected, ecumenism was at the top of the agenda when Derek Worlock arrived in his new archdiocese. It had become so through the Portsmouth years. The mutual trust and understanding which developed were something that needed the outside agency of God's grace for it to happen in the way it did. To arrive ultimately at a position where each Church leader could confidently speak for all the others, in matters like housing, unemployment and community relations, was the target they aimed for. In some instances it did happen. David Sheppard recalls that fairly soon after Derek's arrival, they stood in Derek's drawing room at Green Lane and said to each other 'Our predecessors were good friends, let us hope we shall be that in private, but let us look for some imaginative public things which can push the ecumenical partnership forward'.

Later, when the city looked to its leaders to give words of direction and consolation at times of tragedy, it did not matter which of the main Church leaders spoke, it was known that he spoke for the others. The efforts made during the late 1970s and early 1980s found a tremendous endorsement in the applause given to the Pope in May 1982 as he entered Liverpool's Anglican Cathedral and walked down its central aisle. Cardinal Hume was quoted later as saying that it remained with him as the most earnest and insistent prayer for unity he had ever heard. Pope John Paul II's statement that the movement for Christian unity was 'not just a matter of the intellect but also of the affections', was something that Derek and many others built on for a long time afterwards in their continuing efforts.

Of course, it would be over-optimistic to imagine that the 'Mersey Miracle', as it came to be known, put an end to all sectarianism forever all over the region. Many problems remained, some new ones arose, paradoxically as a result of friendlier relations which irritated the extremists at both ends of the spectrum. There were other voices that said the 'Mersey Miracle' was overstated because sectarianism was on the wane anyhow because of sheer indifference and apathy on religious matters. This is perhaps no more accurate than the one that said the partnership between the two bishops solved everything. It was, and still is, a much more complex matter than either of these positions. Liverpool Auxiliary Bishop Vincent Malone commented that it was an extraordinary thing for Derek, a Vatican II Catholic, and David, an evangelical in the Church of England, to form such a relationship. 'One would not have expected too much harmony but in fact they found a lot of common ground', he obs-erves. In doing so they gave permission, as it were, to others to do the same.

It was not just differences in background and Churchmanship but the matter of family and life-style which had to be accommodated and understood in this remarkable partnership. David's wife, Grace, and his daughter, Jenny, eventually became part of Derek's extended family but that had to be worked at. The commitment to celibacy for Catholic priests was never in doubt in Derek Worlock's mind though it was frequently challenged over the years by references to 'family life'. He was rock solid about the matter; it was part of the fabric of his life and ministry. He told people that celibacy freed you for the uninterrupted service of God and the Church. Yet it was clear that many priests and bishops had, like David Sheppard, made marriage an integral part of their vocation, and that their work for the Church was just as hard and just as dedicated, if not more so in some cases.

Grace Sheppard, who, like David, became a close friend because she shared Derek's readiness to listen to different viewpoints, or different mind sets, felt that Derek sometimes envied the intimacy and comfort of a family, especially in the dark and demanding days when tragedy or illness accentuated the feeling of loneliness. She knew also that he had made the archdiocese his family in a genuine sense, and took his point that there was a valuable, indefinable bond between celibate clergy that could not be achieved among married clergy. David Sheppard says that Derek, towards the end of his life, talked to him about the cost of celibacy. During Derek's illness he says things were 'more on the surface'. It was not because Derek was less strong mentally, but because he was more vulnerable and acknowledged that. 'I would like to think he had learned a little bit from us about taking more time off and relaxing more', says David Sheppard.

Derek was said to have had difficulty in his relationship with women, but Grace Sheppard says she felt comfortable with him, possibly because he did not see her as a threat in any way. But she was always conscious of her position in the threesome as David's wife. She says there was a 'deep mutual respect' and after his cancer was diagnosed, there was empathy because of her own fight against the disease. Grace recalls his dry sense of humour as well as his serious nature which she says 'found echoes' in herself. Pat Sampson also had a good relationship with Derek: 'People say Derek couldn't cope with women, but I was able to uphold a good friendship and always found him terribly kind.' Pat Jones, Anne Casey and Elaine Evans are among other women who enjoyed his friendship and trust and remained his life-long friends.

There were many occasions when he talked about the positive aspects of celibacy. On pilgrimage with young people Derek said that he was glad to have been and to continue to be a virgin, and hoped it wasn't construed as selfishness or even frigidity, but he could recognize the way marriage had helped his colleagues in other Churches to have a mature approach to sexuality and a warmth in the exercise of their own ministry. On a programme for Yorkshire

Television he was caught out. The presenter finished the interview and then asked a final question which was kept on film: 'Archbishop, have you ever been in love?' Taken aback, he explained what he thought being in love meant but in the end answered 'No'. Afterwards he was angry with himself. He reflected: 'I should have said yes – in love with Christ, in love with the Church, that would have been a better answer.'

Whatever might have been the strengths and the weaknesses in the pastoral strategy in the years which followed, it will always be recognized by the majority of people in the Church that Derek Worlock's greatest legacy was probably his contribution to ecumenism in England. Bold steps had to be taken in regard to social problems as well as theological ones to achieve this legacy. He believed there could be no genuine progress on the road to ecclesial reunion if people's everyday needs and concerns were not being met by the Churches together. The crucial ingredient was that the search for greater unity was for the 'better service of the people' in every sense, as it always had been. Vincent Nichols talks of Derek's double commitment to both ecumenism and the role of the Pope. But loyalty and commitment to papal authority, he points out, in 'no way weakened that to ecumenism'.

In a place like Liverpool those needs were always obvious. It was often said that Liverpool wore its heart on its sleeve. Almost from day one, the two bishops worked together with many others to face the social problems and to try to show that the 'gap between religion and real life' was not unbridgeable. David recognized Derek Worlock essentially as a 'bridge-builder' and a man who really believed that few obstacles were insurmountable provided the Churches worked together.

The support of the Church Leaders' Group was first sought by the Dunlop factory workers, who asked that they march with them to protest about redundancies that would ensue from closure. Derek, believing that the time had come when one of the Church leaders in Merseyside could speak for all others, told the shop stewards who had come to his house that he would march and so would the others. It was not the first time that his optimism made problems for others but in the end such gestures proved to be vitally important for the community and for the Churches' credibility too. On this occasion David Sheppard recalls he had a Diocesan Synod arranged and had to leave half-way through the meeting in order to join Derek on the march. 'But I actually think it was very important for us that people saw that human need, like unemployment, sometimes comes before churchy things', he commented.

In the Dunlop march Derek, Norwyn Denny and some of the workers were wearing heavy Russian hats against the cold weather so that photographs gave the impression of a rally in Red Square. Dunlop represented one of the first of many calls for Church solidarity in matters of injustice. After an early visit to the Ford Car Plant at Halewood, Derek came back with stories about 'Robbie' the robot. It was 'Robbie' because it was robbing people of their jobs. When a prolonged dustmen's strike left an estimated twelve hundred tons of rubbish on the streets the Church leaders warned that political capital must not be made out of people's livelihood. Thousands of jobs were being lost in the region, with a succession of factory closures announced at the end of the week on what came to be known as 'Black Friday'. The 'winter of discontent', in 1978, kept more than the Church leaders busy.

When Mrs Thatcher became Prime Minister in 1979, Merseyside was high on the media agenda. It took a while to persuade her to visit the area. Most people on Merseyside had little sympathy for government policy and no doubt the feelings were mutual. Derek shared the City Council's view that the image of the region was unfairly tarnished. A meeting with Margaret Thatcher did take place and she referred to the poor record of the workforce at the docks. Her remarks centred on the assertion that whenever there was a strike the Merseyside dockers were the first out and the last back. Jim Fitzpatrick, the Director of Mersey Docks and Harbour Board, corrected this immediately. He asserted that they might sometimes be the first out but they were also the first back. The statistics he gave were shown to be accurate and although no public retraction was made as he had wished, no statements of that kind were made again without careful checking.

In the many disputes and conflicts which erupted in the world of work during the late 1970s and early 1980s, the spirit of *Gaudium et Spes* (the Vatican II document on the Church in the World Today) was Derek Worlock's guiding light.

Today a strike may still be a necessary, though final resort in the defence of workers' rights and fulfilment of their just demands. As soon as possible, however, ways should be sought to resume negotiations and the dialogue of reconciliation. The importance of dialogue in industry and commerce is a process of collaboration in which the representatives of work-force and management form a working partnership. *(Gaudium et Spes,* no. 68)

In applying the Council teaching to the situations he found in the city of Liverpool Derek Worlock tried to spread the belief, which he often repeated in articles for various publications, that Trade Unions can be a corrective to the abuses of private property and excessive private enterprise, whilst the company or management side becomes a true Trade Union when it brings a fair profit for all its members.

After the sad and painful spectacle of the street riots in Liverpool's Toxteth area in 1981, when hundreds of police and citizens were injured, Mrs Thatcher again arrived, by car in the early morning. Outside Liverpool Town Hall where she met city leaders and Bishop Michael Henshall (the Bishop of Warrington, representing Bishop David), Derek Worlock and other representatives of the community, a large and hostile crowd had quickly gathered and were chanting 'Maggie, Maggie, Maggie – out! out! out!' With this in the background she asked, frowning, 'Why such hatred?' It was difficult to know where to begin. Centuries of racial and religious prejudice, the deep roots of anger dating from the days of slavery, lack of job opportunities, poor housing: the list was long.

On that occasion Derek offered a phrase: 'reconciliation not recrimination' was called for at such a time. Bishop Henshall, whose contribution to drafting a suitable and helpful statement from the Churches during the period of the riots was much appreciated, mentioned the word 'compassion' and Mrs Thatcher frowned – it was not one of her words, she replied.

It is certainly possible to see the fruits of what the Churches and city did in the aftermath of the Toxteth riots. A more enlightened method of 'community policing' and the setting up of a Liverpool 8 Law Centre were among the initiatives that led to a greater opportunity for redress of injustices in the community. Yet bitter feelings and fear remained and the deeper issues remained unresolved. Not a few clergy and local people felt that solutions were attempted which were condescending and were, in any case, too little too late. Respected and experienced priests such as Peter Morgan, Austin Smith and Neville Black genuinely and understandably felt that people like Derek Worlock and David Sheppard, though they had walked the streets of Toxteth and met community leaders in the role of honest broker between the people and the police, had at the end of the day gone home and got on with other things. But the Bishops could not be there all the time anyway and they did experience some hair-raising moments such as when they were pinned against a wall by a police van. Some say the amount of time they spent in Toxteth was exaggerated and that when people complained they did not have access to the Archbishop it was merely presumed he was in Toxteth.

The courageous steps which had to be taken, and quickly, towards religious co-operation could not ignore the deeply in-grained differences and fears that existed in the community, nor bypass the sincerely held beliefs of people in an area still divided politically and on religious lines. Care had to be taken to move at such a pace, and in such a way, that all would be able to move forward in due course. But there was a tendency in Derek to believe that things would not slide back – part of an optimism that was a naive one at times. When he lay dying in hospital in 1996 a prolonged dispute at the docks broke out. He was really far too weak to give his mind to it but he sensed and protested that the Churches were not acting. In fact they were, but at different levels and not in the way he might have chosen. He followed the developments on the news and felt the Churches were dragging their feet, but his usual critical judgement and discernment were by then not equal to the complexities of the situation. Nicholas Frayling, Rector of Liverpool Parish Church and a friend, visited Derek in hospital and remembers him asking 'What are we going to do about the poor dockers? Get the ecumenical leaders together.'

Bishop David, for his part, drew his convictions from his pastoral experience in London, and from his view of the Church of England as a 'bridge' Church that historically tried to keep together the diverse social and ecclesial elements in the community. He saw a particular role for the Church of England in keeping the Free Churches and the Catholic Church together, keeping the means of communication and dialogue open. These roles as bridge and as gate-keeper, however, were given a new direction and strength where doctrinal matters were concerned through ARCIC, the Anglican–Roman Catholic International Commission, and through the many other inter-Church talks and processes. Irrelevant as they may have seemed to the majority of people, even Christian people, they were an essential aspect of the move forward in relationships.

Archbishop Derek's experience of pastoral care came from the people of Stepney. He had surprised Edwyn Young, the Anglican Rector there, by defiantly walking with him down the middle of the street. He brought with him to the north the desire to apply Catholic social teaching, which he had seen Cardinal Griffin put into practice and which he learnt as a young priest with his 'Team', to the daily lives of people, and he had that clear double mandate from Pope Paul VI to ensure that the social needs were addressed and that Liverpool did not become another Belfast in its sectarian divisions.

Together, the two bishops, supported by the leaders of the other main Churches, found a strength and a confidence through each other which would have been diluted otherwise, and they gave the lead to others by working jointly in everything which, conscience permitting, could be done in unison. The word 'together' was to prove the key word. Diverse gifts when blended form a formidably strong bond. David Sheppard describes himself as painting in 'broad brush strokes', perhaps with bolder ideas, working on a large canvas on which Derek added the small brush work, the small print.

Derek used to jib David about not forgetting to take his 'suit of shining armour' when going in to see Government Ministers or argue a case with officials at Whitehall on behalf of people in Liverpool. He would often suggest that David should bat first because he could be sure of a positive start – some straight sixes – and it gave him time to ponder before breaking in. Whereas his own approach was more subtle, more cautious in many ways, planning ahead the next moves, anticipating the next questions, Derek took enormous courage from David. Waiting in the wings, off-stage in the studio for *Wogan*, they prayed together, and chivvied each other along to get the adrenalin flowing and the spirits high. They got to know each other so well, that there were occasions when they were able to read each other's minds and one 'would make the speech for the other'.

The imaginative use of events which were already planned was a hallmark of the way the Churches furthered the cause of unity. In the summer of 1977, a visit by Her Majesty the Queen to Liverpool was arranged, as part of her Silver Jubilee celebrations. The visit involved her official presence at both the Anglican and Roman Catholic Cathedrals and care was taken in the planning to show the co-operation that was possible and desirable for such an event between the religious denominations. The use of the two cathedrals in this even-handed way was to become a part of the way things were done ecumenically in the city. It was especially significant at the time of the papal visit some years later. When the Queen made a further visit to Merseyside, Derek and David got their heads together to see how they could make maximum use of the Queen's kind offer to be at their service for the afternoon in any way they wished to suggest.

The time the Queen spent on Merseyside was, as with so many of her official visits, a means of giving pleasure to thousands of people. The loyalty and pride which Derek's family had always taken in the Royal Family were strong in him too. He felt happy for Liverpool. He recalled an awkward moment or two, though. The sun was shining through the stained glass windows of the Metropolitan Cathedral where Her Majesty and Prince Phillip sat, in two specially prepared seats, in the sanctuary. The Queen turned to Derek and remarked on the variety of coloured glass. He explained it was the work of John Piper. 'I suppose', she said, 'that as the sun goes round the colour inside the building changes.' Ignoring the implication about the sun moving he replied 'Yes, ma'am, and if your congregation go red in the face and then purple in the face it's not due to anything you said but to the fact that you have preached for too long'. The Queen was very amused. At the end of the afternoon, as the royal party was leaving, he overheard a conversation behind him about whether the Queen's outfit that day was 'cerise' or 'light cherry'. A Scouse voice rose audibly from the crowd as she passed and declared 'Look she's got 'er orange on'.

The desire of the Churches to plan and act together was also given early expression on a youth pilgrimage to Taizé in 1978, when Archbishop Worlock and Bishop Sheppard, Norwyn Denny, the Methodist Chairman, other Free Church and Salvation Army leaders, led fifty young people and youth workers of various denominations on a journey of faith and shared Christian activity. The community at Taizé provided a good context in which to explore together the different priorities and understandings which young people had, to see how much they could share in joint action and prayer and what fundamental distinctions there were in their religious beliefs.

In Taizé extraordinary things happened. The Catholic group were from working-class families and found the informality and casualness of meal times – the piece of wet cake slopped onto a plastic dish – almost insulting. They hadn't come there to be treated like that and expected something different. The Protestant group comprised young people from a more middle-class background and did not see any insult but rather an adventure. They thought of it more as an experiment in living a different life-style for a time. The cultural differences ran deeply through all that happened in that week. It was the coming together of diverse backgrounds, priorities, insights that helped the whole disparate group to gel.

It meant that the Church leaders, apart from helping to explain to the young people the differences in the doctrinal beliefs they each held, had little to do except express the points of unity and celebrate them. After a week together the group of youngsters wanted to plan and celebrate a joint liturgy. Should it be Mass, a Communion service, a Bible service? It was decided to make it all of these. The preparation of the Scriptures and of the Eucharist was difficult but perfectly possible given the will to persevere. Everything was celebrated jointly, as one group, showing the level of unity that had been reached. But the Church leaders had to think of people at home, in the parishes, the diocese, in Rome! It had to be painfully but firmly explained that there could be no shared Eucharistic prayer and consecration, no inter-communion as far as Catholics were concerned. That was where the skill of youth leaders like Father Harnett and Richard Wiggins was important; the understanding and trust the Church leaders had adopted at home helped them to guide the young people through the difficulty of that moment away from home.

There were to be similar pilgrimages to Iona and Lindisfarne (Holy Island), Rome and Assisi. The confrontation over the issue of inter-communion, despite the patient explanation of it, posed a problem. Everyone sat together in a circle in the church at Iona. The assumption that the rough home-made bread and wine could be passed around by everyone when the time came, each to his or her neighbour on the bench, put certain people into an embarrassing situation. Rather than advance the understanding of unity it highlighted the gulf in an unfortunate and unhelpful way. Afterwards Derek commented that there was 'some picking up of pieces' to be done – literally and psychologically.

Issues of a similar kind arose again in the subsequent Youth Pilgrimages which the Church leaders undertook. Each of these pilgrimages had its own character but behind each was the objective of looking at questions of faith and life outside the usual environment in places where the young people could reflect freely and openly with the Church leaders and youth workers. Looking at the traditions of Christianity before the Reformation, and moving behind controversies to the earlier common spiritual heritage they shared, became more sharply focused for everybody in such settings.

David Sheppard describes that first pilgrimage to Taizé as 'very precious'. He says that it also helped enormously on the ecumenical scene to have the same persons in the Catholic, Anglican, URC, Methodist and Baptist Churches in office for ten years and enabled a 'very trusting relationship to grow.' He tells how Norwyn Denny came to him on the first pilgrimage to ask him what Derek would think about something. 'I think he also did the same to Derek, the other way round – and the others were very supportive. The Methodist chairman said "You speak for us, you go ahead".'

The trip to Rome was more of a challenge. The Roman Catholic ambience might have understandably posed a threat to some if the Church leaders had not shown their own courage in accepting the challenge. It was away from the normal environment, and young people and Church leaders alike could get a perspective on their needs and reflect on the issues involved. In the hills above Rome, at the villa of the English College, Palazzola, near Albano, the mixed group were able to look closely at what exactly were the differences between them, gain a better insight into the Roman scene and history, and enjoy both the recreations offered by the villa's swimming pool and its ancient monastic character. Derek knew the place well, though he had not been a student in Rome and had not walked around the villa for some years. He invited David to walk with him to inspect the cricket pitch. It was a field covered in a carpet of thick grass and wild flowers; David was amused to find, eventually, the concrete strip in the middle which would serve as a wicket in summer. It must have seemed a long way from the County Ground at Sussex.

At a special audience with the Holy Father, organized by Derek with his inside knowledge of procedures and people in the Vatican, many of the young people were in tears. It was not just the Roman Catholic contingent. In the awesome atmosphere of the Vatican Palace, the wonder of their meeting a man who, though head of state and leader of the world's Catholics, spoke to them as a human being and a kind of father who wanted only their commitment, their happiness and the gift of true unity, overwhelmed everyone.

The papal audience, far from being a threat, proved to be the turning-point in the pilgrimage, as all recognized that the myth of Roman bureaucracy could be dispelled by human exchange between people of different religious persuasions. The young Methodists made a point of visiting the local Methodist Centre and the Anglican church too. On arriving at the Methodist church just opposite Castel San Angelo, dwarfed, like everything else by the bulk of St Peter's Basilica, they found the door locked. Any awkwardness was soon dispelled by the singing of Wesleyan hymns, with everyone joining in. Dr John Newton's face was wreathed in smiles.

Later, in Assisi, they encountered a spirituality which was available to all as the spirit of St Francis – 'Il Poverello', the Poor Man – captured the imagination, and the peaceful green expanse of the Umbrian plain at sunset mellowed the mood. The issues of poverty and simplicity were obviously a key part of the experience in Assisi. They contrasted tellingly with the grandeur and pomp of some aspects of Rome. One young person remarked that Assisi had made the whole trip worthwhile but admitted that, whilst there, she could think of little else but the meeting with the Pope and his gentle simplicity.

By chance, or by providence, Assisi was to be the place where Derek, and David and Grace Sheppard would find further common ground, on holiday. A memorable visit to the beach at Forte dei Marmi, a place where the white marble quarries from which Michelangelo took his material form a backdrop to the blue Mediterranean and golden sand of Italy's coast, followed by a few days in St Francis' birthplace, helped to seal a friendship in a unique way. Here Grace discovered that she and Derek shared a liking for figs and she found some in Assisi *en route* to a restaurant for lunch. Later she grew tiny figs in pots on her verandah back home in Liverpool and was able to take some of them to Derek when he was in hospital.

Events like the Youth Pilgrimages, by no means easy or free of painful questions, where people were learning to examine and articulate their beliefs – especially regarding the Eucharist – were an effective means of evangelization. Such pilgrimages were to be a hallmark of the Christian partnership in Merseyside. They challenged people, not in order to cast doubt on doctrinal differences where these were genuine, but to find possible ways forward for greater sharing. People wanted an end to sectarianism, but wanting was not enough. Imagination and action had to play a part if it was to happen.

The interest in the commercial and business life of the region, and the regeneration of the area and of people's lives, became as one piece with the 'churchy' aspects of ecumenism, as Derek called it. In this, both Bishop David and Archbishop Derek made a significant contribution from the beginning. Derek became a member of the Merseyside Enterprise Forum which looked at the question of the regeneration of jobs in the wake of new technology. This gave links to the Chamber of Commerce and other bodies within the city of Liverpool and further afield. He helped to produce a number of reports relating to the economy and prospects of Merseyside in the light of technological advances. There were shades here of his days with the Cardinal just after the war, when such matters first became a major issue for the Church.

A government-led study of the problems of inner city areas in 1977 the occasion for the Churches to really get together on a single issue that was not just a 'Catholic', 'Anglican', or 'Baptist' issue, but a people's issue. Sensing that here was a chance for symbolic action together, Derek exclaimed that if the Churches could not send one report, signed by all the Church leaders, to the relevant Government Department, 'then we are all wasting our time'. Bishop Sheppard says:

> Derek really took the initiative with that and said if we can't all speak with one voice we are going to send in different answers. I think it was Norwyn Denny who again said 'Well, if you and Derek can agree a text, you do that for us'. We burned the midnight oil preparing it.

On one occasion in London Derek met Prince Philip, who, having heard of the work he was doing, said to him 'Archbishop, you've got it all wrong, surely new technology creates jobs rather than destroys them?' The discussion got a bit heated and neither would give way. They agreed to differ, at least in so far as Derek was convinced that if some jobs were created many more were lost for ever and so was people's dignity. The Ford 'robot' had shown that. Prince Philip had clearly forgotten the matter when they next met formally at Corpus Christi College, Cambridge. There both David and Derek were proud to receive an Honorary Doctorate in Divinity, Prince Philip presenting the certificate. To Derek's amusement this involved receiving a blessing, in Latin, from the Prince.

The exodus of people, especially the young, from the north-west in search of work in London and the south-east was something of a hobby-horse for him from a very early stage as Archbishop. He became particularly eloquent and animated on the subject of the 'Tebbit Express'. Norman Tebbit was Minister for Employment at the time: hence the nickname for the trains specially brought into service to carry many Liverpool hopefuls to London and the south-east in search of work. They left Lime Street on Monday mornings and came back home on Friday evenings, successful or otherwise in their quest for jobs.

The infamous remark had recently been made by Mr Tebbit that people should do what his father had done: namely, got on his bike and looked for work. Derek later commented that many people had got on their bikes but had come back, having sold the bike, without finding a job.

When Norman Tebbit visited the city to address the local Anglican Synod, and was not greeted with a wave of enthusiasm – especially when he said, after a long debate, 'You have told me nothing new' – the Church leaders took him out for a meal. Some home truths were called for. It had not been an easy ride for him at the Synod, so deep were the feelings about unemployment and opportunities, and during the conversation afterwards he thumped the table in some frustration, as the point was made to him that people in Liverpool felt very strongly indeed about the issues involved. 'But *I* speak with passion', he remonstrated. Derek replied, as quick as a flash, 'Well, when you also speak with *com*passion you must come back'.

Bishop Sheppard later chaired the Board for Social Responsibility of the Church of England. He was able to call upon his experience with his earlier engagement in the 'Faith in the City' initiative and its report, commissioned by the Archbishop of Canterbury, Robert Runcie. It took a hard look at the social and spiritual needs of urban priority areas, not just in Liverpool but around the whole country. But more locally, he and Archbishop Worlock focused such involvement further when they founded and chaired the 'Michaelmas Group'.

It was so named because the group first met on the two bishops' initiative in Derek's home on Michaelmas Day at the end of September 1984. The group comprised twenty or more of the top businessmen of the city. They met regularly at breakfast time, to discuss ways of bringing industry back to Liverpool and the region. It was to be a forum where senior decision-makers in the city could meet and talk about the Merseyside agenda in trust and security.

After Merseyside County Council was abolished and the open forum for strategic debate disappeared, Michaelmas became more of an enabling group working behind the scenes.

Roger Morris, secretary to the group and secretary of a group of charitable trusts in Mersey-side, sees the group as having set out to provide Bishop Sheppard and Archbishop Worlock with quality discussion, enabling them to speak for a wider group of people in Merseyside, especially about their social needs. Other subjects as well, such as the Mersey Barrage proposal, were discussed in the forum.

The group was particularly active during the time of the Militants on the City Council. The two Bishops are said to have been the only ones to have had the Cabinet phone number during this time and they visited all major political parties and prepared papers for discussion in the group. During the time of the city's financial crisis, when the city came to the verge of bankruptcy and power was divided up, Bishop David and Archbishop Derek worked through the Michaelmas Group to bring in advisers to see what could be done. In a well-publicized joint letter to *The Times*, headed 'The tragedy of our city', they wrote: 'Before the eyes of the rest of the nation, Liverpool is tearing itself to pieces ... a city renowned for its spirit and solidarity in face of danger.'

In many of the major events affecting Liverpool the two Church leaders worked quietly in the background, with sometimes only the knowledge of Michaelmas. The Merseyside Docks and Harbour employment dispute, which became particularly bitter, is one such example where behind-the-scenes attempts were made to talk to the parties involved.

Roger Morris believes that the group helped the Church leaders to see problems from a different perspective. After meeting and working with the Archbishop once a month for a ten-year period, he became very impressed with the way he had of doing things and how he knew the correct procedures. He viewed him as a very balanced person.

> He was obviously a spiritual person and able to present needs and long-term objectives in a most balanced way. He could always see what was politically possible and was one of the best draughtsmen I have ever seen. He prepared well, could summarize what had been said and was a master of detail. He didn't just take everything in – he was nearly in a class by himself!

Aware that some people found Archbishop Derek unapproachable because of his formality, Roger Morris strongly rejects any suggestion that he didn't have a sense of humour and recalls occasions in the Michaelmas Group where the Archbishop deliberately lowered the temperature in some heated debate, by making a self-deprecating remark. Roger also rejects any suggestion that the relationship between the two Bishops was ever over the top, but he was aware of what he describes as a 'curious schizophrenia' about the relationship in Church circles, particularly Anglican and Catholic. On the one hand, there was a tremendous sense of pride that something was happening ecumenically, and would not have happened without them, but then, on the other, some of their flock regretted that.

Some commented that the Bishops spent too much time on public affairs and not enough on the pastoral needs of their own churches. Roger Morris believes the pair worked hard both in a national and local setting, but did not always get the credit for what was achieved locally. He recalls the pattern was that they discussed with others in the Michaelmas Group what they wanted to do and how to achieve it. 'Mostly I think it was Derek Worlock who saw the agenda and was determined to work for it.' But it was together with David Sheppard that they took up the challenge. 'If there was a report of a confidential meeting with someone in government, the Archbishop almost always gave the report and said "We were hoping to see X and we did!"'

One issue on which Derek did not get the full support he was looking for, was that of Church schools. He was most anxious about the relationship between Church schools and State funding, but found not many shared his concerns. Bishop John Rawsthorne recalls that the reorganization of Catholic High Schools in Liverpool was a contentious issue.

At one time we had forty-two schools and we came down to fifteen in one go. Some had only a hundred youngsters and that was repeated throughout the diocese. Every time there was a school closure it brought unhappiness, anger, feelings of desertion. He [Derek] always bore the brunt of those feelings, but he tried to be realistic.

The Episcopal Vicar for Finance and Development, Monsignor Michael McKenna, points out that the Archbishop committed £12 million to Catholic education in ten years and that all the refurbishment of schools was paid for without any debt. The battles of 1944 over Catholic schools had not been forgotten by Derek.

There were many other issues that Derek raised in the Michaelmas Group, and together with Bishop David they grappled with the relationship between poverty, unemployment and human dignity. Roger Morris also recalls the Archbishop's interest in health care generally, but adds that after his diagnosis and surgery, he began pressing for specific things relating to health care. Discussions with senior business people and managers could concern a mixture of things, but whatever the subject, the Archbishop was considered their equal. 'He had such a quick mind and he had the power', adds Roger. Everyone was aware of how powerful the Church lobby could be. He was sometimes also detached, yet compassionate when the need arose: this is how Roger Morris remembers working with the Archbishop.

At the time of the Zeebrugge disaster, when the ferry *Spirit of Free Enterprise* went down, Roger Morris had gone to visit the Archbishop with some documents.

> He was in relaxed clothes watching a rugby match when there was some news from Zeebrugge. He stopped and turned to me and said 'this is something you probably need to watch' – because of my shipping interests. He was not impassive over what had happened, but he was not shocked by the tragedy. He had been hardened by experience. He was interested and compassionate but not overwhelmed by it.

Derek maintained his interest in the concerns of the Michaelmas Group right up to the last year of his life. He gave his time, and diminishing energy in the last months before his illness, to the Churches' Enquiry into Unemployment and the Future of Work. This involved frequent meetings in London amidst an already busy schedule, but he saw this not just as a gesture of concern to unemployed people but as an integral part of preaching the Gospel, which had always been the underlying motivation of his work as a bishop. The theological and social analyses of the problem of unemployment were, for him, two sides of one coin. As ever, his involvement in this was made possible by the encouragement of Bishop Sheppard, who chaired the early sessions of the group.

Close partnership with the people with 'clout' had to go hand in hand with some battles, always painful, which had to be fought alongside the people of Liverpool in their struggle to remain in the area and to have decent housing and opportunities. He knew they were on-going concerns because, again, they were about people, not statistics that could be ticked off as 'dealt with'. A well-known example of this was the Eldonian Village project in which the people of the Vauxhall area, just north of the centre of Liverpool, were fighting for the right not to be dispersed around the city when their workplace, the Tate and Lyle sugar refinery, was closed down. The local people wanted to stay as one community and have a say in their own destiny. Once again, as in Stepney days, Archbishop Derek came to be something of a rallying point for the local people. He vowed to stand with them, 'wearing cope and mitre in the street if necessary', against the pressure of the City Council which at that time had a Militant leadership and which wanted control of the housing programme.

This act of solidarity and courage convinced those who had at first been sceptical that the Archbishop was on the side of the people and the disadvantaged. He had proved that he wanted them to stay as a community as much as they did. The Church was seen to stand with them against unjust pressure to leave. Standing with the people – wearing cope and mitre or not – earned him tremendous respect.

It was soon after coming to Liverpool that he drew up his scheme for closing some churches and amalgamating the parishes with others. His plan was for a rationalization of the parishes around a reduced number of churches and schools which would then be served by a team ministry. Eldon Street and the Vauxhall community came right into the firing line.

The down-to-earth, no-nonsense people of Vauxhall, many of whom were descendants of Irish Catholic immigrants, had other ideas, as Tony McGann vividly recalls. He remembers some of the older priests also being devastated by the new Archbishop's ideas for their deanery and a public meeting was called. Tony spoke about unity in the parishes, tradition and community. 'The "Arch"', he says, 'took a lot of bashing. They didn't want his reorganization and told him so. I stood up, and the *Catholic Pictorial* photographer caught me pointing my finger at him. There was a lot of battling and the Archbishop was regarded as Public Enemy Number One.' He recalls that

Some priests wouldn't move and some resigned. We said that once a presbytery goes and the priest goes, the people are not going to be bothered about religion. He [the Archbishop] told us that it was not just about going to church. There were no jobs and communities were being broken up and people were living in slums. We said 'you split the Church up and there will be no community'.

But the antagonism was short-lived. Tony McGann recalls that at that time the Vauxhall residents were fighting the Church and the City Council; both were the enemy. After plans were announced to demolish the high-rise flats and disperse the people, 'The Eldonians' came into being and launched the fight for the right to keep the community together. The local church at Eldon Street gave them their name. Jim Dunne, who was involved in the rationalization plan for the diocese, recalls 'In one sense the local residents managed to fight the Church and were then able to take on the political system'.

The Militants came into power in the city and the residents were told they would all have to move, that the flats would be bulldozed and municipal housing would be built on the land. A decisive moment had come. The Archbishop stepped in. 'He was the first to put his shoulder behind us', Tony McGann recalls, 'and humbly said to the Council "I will stand shoulder to shoulder with these people in these streets if you try to move them".' There was incredulity that an Archbishop who had been the apparent adversary of their hopes, fighting for reorganization of the parishes, should now be fighting with them in support of their plans to find an effective way forward.

Eventually the Eldonians won the right to develop their own housing project, but only after Archbishop Derek and Bishop David had made several journeys to London to talk to the Housing Minister. A £7 million grant was awarded to the project which Tony McGann believes was awarded through the intervention of the two Bishops. The Eldonian Village began to take shape and the old religious rivalry was gradually being forgotten. Previously, in this staunchly Catholic area, buildings had been daubed with slogans and there had been sectarian strife with the leaders of the Orange Lodge in Netherfield Road. But now 'The Mersey Miracle' had been worked. After the two Bishops had walked the newly-built streets in their full purple together, a joint ecumenical service was held that brought together the Catholic and Protestant communities in joint recognition of what had been achieved. As a ceremony was held to mark the naming of two streets, Archbishop Worlock Close and

Bishop Sheppard Court, sectarianism seemed to be a thing of the past. It was not as simple as that but the achievement was a real one nonetheless: the psychological barriers had been breached and the Eldonian Village material proof of the fact that together a community could be re-built. The slogan 'We did it better together' arose from that and formed the inspiration for the next ten years. The battle-cry 'Better Together' caught the imagination in a way that many joint sermons could not have done.

It was an essential part of their success that both Bishops were able to use the media in all its forms to further the Christian message. It was not just their appearance in the papers and frequently on radio and television, but the fact that they worked behind the scenes in the structures of the media, with bodies like the Catholic Media Trust and CRAC, helping with research or advice in regard to programme accuracy and content, finance and personnel. When interviewed or appearing together, as for instance on *Wogan, Panorama* or *Question Time,* they were able to complement each other's contribution. Again, it was an example of strength in unity. Bishop David says that he learned a 'huge amount about dealing with the Press from Derek'. When a Press statement was to be made, they each prepared their own statement and then agreed a joint statement. David remembers Derek as being a 'great chiseller of getting phrases right and thinking about how things would be picked up by the media'.

Personal friendship and unity became strengthened through such projects. The two Bishops also had to face points of disagreement, but their friendship stood the test. There were those who did not want David rocking the boat of the Established Church, there were Catholics who intensely disliked the Worlock–Sheppard liaison. There were times when some issues were, in the eyes of certain people, fudged and blurred by what they saw as wishy-washy ecumenism. David openly said that he could envisage certain instances where abortion was preferable to bringing the foetus to full term. The Catholic position could never countenance this, yet that did not force Derek to the conclusion that David's view was to be publicly condemned. Would silence mean consent therefore? Derek's stance was one of protection and 'total respect for life from the womb to the tomb', he told David Alton, his own MP. But he sensed that public condemnations, especially of people whose integrity he accepted completely, would only serve to close the door on future collaboration, a door that had been painstakingly and slowly opened by both sides. Each side knew perfectly well what moral laws and beliefs the other held fast to; progress did need not to be blocked by open confrontation. But Liverpool priest Francis Marsden questions whether there were some subjects 'too touchy' to be brought up in an ecumenical setting. He remembers an occasion when there was an ecumenical panel made up of Catholic, Anglican, Methodist, Baptist, United Reformed and Salvation Army representatives. He put a question to the panel asking what was the chance of some agreement being reached on 'Some of the moral issues which divide the denominations, such as embryo experimentation, abortion, homosexual acts, remarriage after divorce'. Francis says to his amazement his question was pulled out first by Derek, but then he 'doctored it, by missing out the troublesome phrase "abortion and homosexuality"'. Such contentious moral issues proved a challenge to ecumenical progress.

David and Grace Sheppard both remember well the support Derek gave them on another occasion when there was some adverse publicity about David in the local press. David was away at the time, and Grace was particularly grateful to receive a phone call of support and understanding from Derek. When the Church leaders met socially on summer evenings or round the table at Christmas, or when Derek spent New Year's Eve quietly at the home of David and Grace, discussing the year that had passed, the bond of family grew strong. With them he had less reason to be looking over his shoulder or having to close ranks as he might sometimes when among fellow Catholics. He could be more himself.

CHAPTER THIRTEEN

His Liverpool Home

Let nothing trouble you, let nothing frighten you: whoever has
God lacks nothing. God alone is enough.

(St Theresa of Avila)

Between 1980 and 1982 three extraordinary events took place which
brought Derek Worlock and his fellow Church leaders on Merseyside
into a prominent position in the life of the city and the nation. In a
real sense the three events were linked. They certainly constituted the
most active and extraordinary period of the Archbishop's years in
Liverpool and established him in his Liverpool home. They represented the busiest period of his long ministry, apart, perhaps, from
the days of the Vatican Council. The consequences of these three
events were among the most far-reaching of all the events he was
involved in during his long and distinguished career.

In September 1977, the National Conference of Priests had proposed that a National Pastoral Congress be held to bring together the
people, religious and clergy of the country in a representative way to
discuss key issues in the life of the Church. Such a concept had
slowly begun to find favour during the 1970s and the writing of a
document *A Time for Building*, in which Bishop Victor Guazzelli had
played a central role, strengthened the call for a national gathering of
Catholics. The bishops endorsed the idea and began to find ways of
bringing it about that would give a spiritual fillip to the whole
Catholic community. Archbishop Worlock was asked to coordinate
the planning, with the help of Bishop David Konstant and Bishop
Leo McCartie; it was a small step to the choosing of Liverpool for
the venue. Perhaps the choice was looked at cynically by some, but
Liverpool's central location would have been clear had they looked at
a map of Britain and Ireland. The deciding factors were certainly the
wish of the Archbishop to have it on his home ground and the fact

that he was the link between the Conference of Priests and the Bishops' Conference.

He and Cardinal Hume were anxious to have the Congress accepted in Rome – by the Congregation for Clergy and the Council for the Laity in particular. It was emphasized that it would be a one-off event, not the setting-up of a permanent Council, which Rome would not approve of, and that representatives of the Council for the Laity in Rome would be invited to be observers at the Congress. In the approach to Rome Cardinal Hume was the essential front-runner, whilst Derek provided the back-up. As with so much that happened in the ensuing three years, their combined negotiations provided impetus sufficient to get the Congress accepted and to launch the whole enterprise in Liverpool. By the end of 1979 all the finer details were in place. Now local people, the heroes of Liverpool, had to find the beds, the good-will and the energy needed to make a dream come true.

Derek Worlock saw the Congress as having some striking similarities with the Vatican Council. The planning was all important, and the follow-up would be even more crucial. He was closely involved in the Congress at every step. His role was to greet all the delegates as they arrived by coach, and to visit each of the sectors where they were meeting in groups. The sectors were schools around the Liverpool area, each sector having a co-ordinator or president, and secretary. The method, which Gerald Priestland, commenting in the Press, called an attempt at 'divide and rule' on the part of the bishops, was to begin in small groups, move into sector groups after day two, and eventually to come together as a Congress, at Liverpool Philharmonic Hall, to compose some resolutions.

From the beginning, everything hinged on getting everyone assembled for the opening ceremony in the Cathedral. How to have everyone in place in time for that, and how to house everyone adequately in the homes of Merseyside people were the two great logistical nightmares of the Congress, though in the event they were achieved; in a nice ecumenical gesture, seven delegates found a home with Bishop David Sheppard and his wife Grace. Michael Sampson had been asked to chair the organizing committee in Liverpool. For him it meant nine hectic months of working closely with Father Tom Sheppard, National Secretary of the Congress, and his assistant, Father Sam Erskine. It also called for close co-operation with Archbishop Derek himself. Inevitably there were differences of opinion at times, especially as the approach of the Congress increased tension. The Archbishop foresaw that the only way of getting even the most tardy delegates there on time, with coaches and trains coming from every part of the country, was to lay on a fleet of taxis from Lime Street station to the Cathedral. Despite concern about the cost of this exceeding their budget, he got his way, as he usually did. The expense was secondary to the need for everyone to be there on time to give the Congress the best possible start. Michael Sampson agrees that 'Without the taxis we would have been 300 people short at the opening of the Congress'. Julian Filochowski, Director of CAFOD, remembers that before the Congress some said that it would undermine the bishops and pointed to the trouble in The Netherlands. Archbishop Murphy – one of the sceptics, he recalls, said 'We will have the tail wagging the dog'. But by the end of the Congress he was one of the many impressed by the praying and real sharing of faith as a community. Murphy is said to have commented that the Congress had 're-arranged' his ignorance.

Julian remembers the Congress as 'sending shivers down my spine', it was so awe-inspiring. Bishop Nichols believes the planning and execution of the Congress were one of Derek's greatest achievements. 'He steered it away from the potential of causing rifts and won the support of every bishop for the Congress document *The Easter People*'.

However, unlike the practicalities of the organization, which were handled superbly, the implementation of these findings of the Congress had one weakness. Many of the findings of the delegates were endorsed by the bishops and incorporated in *The Easter People* which formed the centre of the bishops' response, and which is still widely quoted to this day. But like the Congress itself, the good things which emerged from the bishops' response were to take a long time to filter through to every level of the Church. The inherent difficulty was that the Congress recommendations had no binding force in the parishes, and their success relied on the understanding and acceptance, or otherwise, of the local parish communities and the priests.

The Easter People was acknowledged as a fine document. It was put together in a flat over the garage attached to Archbishop's House in Liverpool. So Derek Worlock had first-hand involvement in the whole process of the Congress from its inception to its final response document. He himself believed he could use that document for ten years in his teaching and preaching. Drafting and perfecting documents were his strong points, as the Vatican Council had shown, and he was clear in his own mind that this document was thoroughly in line with the Council and was a kind of local application of it. The difficulty again was the gap between the written word and its practical realization in the parishes or deaneries. But Kevin Muir of the YCW and Laity Commission says there was no consultation with a group of lay people about *The Easter People* as it was being written and that the detailed reports and proposals of the working groups were never published. A little booklet entitled *The Acts of the Pastoral Congress in Liverpool 1980* was, however, published, but for some reason has been forgotten and never received widespread publicity.

The National Pastoral Congress, for all its shortcomings in practice – and they were human shortcomings rather than structural ones – was the most ambitious of all the projects in which Archbishop Derek was involved. As with everything, for him it became all-consuming, but the length of preparation was greater than anything else he had been involved with, except the Vatican Council itself. The liturgies celebrated for the whole Congress gathered at the Cathedral and led by the Cardinal and by the Archbishop were events which will always remain in the memories of those who took part. They were probably the events which gave the Congress its spiritual thrust and the imaginative drive that was needed if it was not to become just a talking shop for the vociferous minority. There are those who say that whatever was achieved in 1980 has not been properly followed up or developed. Vincent Nichols contends that the Congress substantially changed the life of the Catholic Church in England and Wales and 'showed a way of doing things and how priests, people and bishops could sit down together and talk'.

At the National Pastoral Congress 'The English Catholic laity had never before been so out-going', Adrian Hastings writes. They had never been 'so central to the life of the nation, so rich with distinguished people in the ranks'. This might now be seen as an exaggerated and premature statement but it says something of the mood and status of the Catholic Church in the wake of the Congress.

Although the Congress was very much a qualified success and its effects may not have been as enduring as was hoped, arising from it came the desire and the decision to invite the Pope to Britain to endorse what had taken place: Cardinal Hume and Archbishop Worlock took the invitation to him personally in Rome.

Even before the detailed planning of the first ever papal visit to

Great Britain could begin, and whilst lessons were being carefully learnt from the Pope's historic and wonderful visit to the Republic of Ireland, rioting broke out on the streets of Toxteth, Liverpool. What became known as the Toxteth riots engaged the Church leaders in a strenuous and heart-breaking time of reconciliation and rebuilding. Community and police liaison had to be carefully restructured, and a sense of confidence restored in the community, especially the black community which suffered most. It led the two men into deep waters of negotiation and discussion with local community leaders, local government and central government with many different initiatives arising from the ashes of the streets of Liverpool 8. This is well described in *Better Together*.

Not only the rioting but the unexpected turn of events in Argentina in conflict over the Falkland Islands jeopardized the proposed papal visit. There were long weeks of delicate negotiation required here too if the visit of the Pope was to go ahead. It was part of this period that Derek Worlock referred to as 'The week that never was', by which he meant that it was an unreal time that completely engrossed him, the Cardinal, and many others (including their counterparts in Argentina) in an attempt to salvage the visit.

The Liverpool part of the Pope's visit was a late-comer on the agenda. That he came to Liverpool at all was largely thanks to the efforts of Archbishop Derek, though the decision was not popular or diplomatic with those who had been planning only one visit to the north-west. Walking through the 'rehearsal' in the Anglican Cathedral with Archbishop Paul Marcinkus, the inevitable question of timings arose. Marcinkus was playing devil's advocate and asked the Dean, Edward Patey, what would people think if it was announced the next day that the Pope had cancelled his visit to Liverpool because of lack of time. 'Quite frankly', Edward answered, 'they would not believe you.' Nothing more was said on the subject.

In the event, the whole visit, a pastoral visit, followed sensitively by a visit to Argentina, did go ahead and was a triumph for everyone involved. The visit brought benefits not only to the Catholic community but to many of the other Churches in Britain too when they welcomed the Pope in a spirit of brotherhood and common mission. The Pope came into the city of Liverpool via Toxteth, the Archbishop explaining the scene and recent history to him, and visited the Anglican Cathedral first before taking his pilgrim route along

Hope Street to the Roman Catholic Cathedral. It was an historic day of reconciliation and new hope.

At the end of the visit to the Anglican Cathedral Derek thanked the Pope for endorsing what the Liverpool Church leaders had tried to do, and told him of the friendship and collaboration between himself and David Sheppard. The Pope, in reply, remarked to Archbishop Derek that 'ecumenism is not just of the intellect but also of the affections'. He recognized that friendship and human respect were the basis of everything else, and the fact that symbolic gestures of closer unity between the Churches had no meaning if the underlying respect was not genuine.

Because of a mix-up in the otherwise impeccable planning of the event, the other Merseyside Church leaders, unable to avail themselves of the privilege of the Popemobile, were without transport to the Catholic Cathedral and had to commandeer a passing ambulance to get through the throng in Hope Street. This did nothing, however, to damage the spirit of partnership among them. It seemed like a dream to everyone when Archbishop Worlock, in a voice breaking with emotion, welcomed Pope John Paul to the very heart of his Liverpool home.

The combined strength which came from the success of the papal visit proved to be a further stepping-stone for a number of joint endeavours in the years that followed. Not least among these was the reorganization of the Colleges of Higher Education in Liverpool. A federation of Catholic and Anglican Colleges was established where once there had been separate institutions.

Symbolism played a big part in the ecumenical affairs of Liverpool and the whole area. The development of the Liverpool Institute of Higher Education (LIHE), for example, had a symbolic importance. The two bishops knew that the federation of two teacher training colleges in Liverpool – one Anglican, the other Catholic – would be a powerful symbol of ecumenism in the city, a real external sign of partnership between two traditions. Furthermore, such an amalgamation would put in place a relationship for future teachers, the moulders of society, that would build in a better understanding and ecumenical spirit. It also had a pragmatic advantage in that any Government cuts or rationalization of higher education would be less likely for an institution that had the backing and involvement of both Churches.

The training college run by the Sisters of Notre Dame, at a prime site at the end of Liverpool's Hope Street, agreed to sell the site and move to the more modern site and building of Christ's College in Woolton. The Anglican teachers' training college at Stand Park Road, Woolton, was adjacent to both elements of the Catholic college and negotiations began, under the influence of the two Bishops as joint chairmen of governors, to form a federation of the three colleges. In all the protracted negotiations that took place over a decade Derek was admired greatly for what Bishop Malone describes as his ability 'to combine vision with detail'. He was able to assimilate long and detailed documents and master all the implications of a complicated matter. His tenacity helped to see the process through to what became the Liverpool Institute of Higher Education and then its successor, Liverpool Hope University College. The inclusion of the word Hope was very deliberately a reflection of the theme which Derek and David had made their own: encapsulated in the title of their book, but more importantly put into practice with regard to the life and unity of Liverpool and the region.

The negotiations were not without their difficulties, as it was not just the coming together of two buildings but the joining of two traditions and communities which was at stake. Bishop Vincent Malone was very involved in the meetings and recalls that during the phase of discussions involving the amalgamation of Christ's College and Notre Dame College his was the only dissenting voice on one particular point. A vote was taken and it went in the Archbishop's favour. But later, after the meeting, Derek told Bishop Malone that he had been quite right but that 'we couldn't have done that' for reasons which he then went on to explain. This approach was fairly frequently found at meetings, and some have gone so far as to suggest that Derek was a 'one-man decision-making machine'.

At the Archbishop's Council meetings, which were held every three weeks, few members interrupted or contradicted him when in he was in full flow. The democratic decision-making process he often advocated was not so often evident in practice and he would often push through, even filibuster, a decision. The trouble was, though the process was not good, the reasoning and veracity of what he was arguing were seldom in doubt. This headstrong approach upset some people, though no one remembers any deliberate attempt to hurt or shout down. There was courtesy there. He knew how far things had come, battles won and lost, hard-fought positions achieved – he was conscious of the strategy and the legacy of former days, like the 1940s and 1950s, to win the Church's respect. This made him determined not to lose ground. The indirectly damaging effect on others was not always recognized by him, or if it was he chose to make it quite secondary. As chairman at meetings this process was all the more reinforced because of the characteristic feeling of being 'under siege' at times and needing to bluster his way through. But most of what he said, with a few exceptions, was well thought-out beforehand. Some also say he could be persuaded to change his mind about something if the reasons were sound. Bishop Nichols recalls one occasion when he did exactly that over the closure of St Patrick's, Park Place – one of Liverpool's oldest churches.

Today, Liverpool Hope University College strives to build on the legacy which the two bishops and their colleagues and helpers strove to provide. The Rector, Simon Lee, named the library the Sheppard Worlock Library after their partnership. In the wider context of the country as a whole they were also key partners in the search for new ecumenical structures, or instruments, which would reflect more accurately where things were – reconciled in many ways but not yet one. Neither of the two bishops believed in uniformity as a prerequisite of unity, but had learnt to cherish the sincerely held beliefs and traditions of different Churches. This meant respecting the rules too. The key to the movement forward was not in bypassing the Church's laws but in a better understanding of them.

It was for this reason that Derek intervened when, at the Nottingham Conference to prepare the way for the new ecumenical instruments, the proposal was made that all the delegates at the conference join in one united service rather than celebrate in their own traditional manner. This, he felt, was the first mistake to avoid if we were all to learn truth from one another and all come to meet, eventually, in Christ by the recognition of each other's liturgical and spiritual practice. Back at home the mixture of imaginative steps forward and adherence to Church rules was applied in the new situations like Hough Green and Warrington. These new areas called for sharing and common witness and new shared churches were built. When it was rightly pointed out that a single, shared tabernacle was not a legitimate or helpful expression of where the two denominations were, the two bishops used their authority to explain the reasons for separate compartments within the tabernacle, clearly distinguished. It was not just a warning against a breach of the rules but an accurate statement of the reality of Church, as it is now.

In all their years of friendship, Grace Sheppard says she only received the Eucharist once from Archbishop Worlock and that happened through difficult circumstances. She had gone to the Blessed Sacrament Shrine in Clayton Square and sat in the congregation next to a Liverpool housewife. They had chatted before Mass began. When it came to Communion, Grace said she knew she could not receive Communion and sat tight in her seat. The woman next to her got up and said 'Come on'. Grace told her the reason for not going forward and the woman became distressed and said 'You must'. 'I was torn between her distress and embarrassing Derek. I got up with a prayer to God saying, "Please, I know and feel this is right to go with her".' Later, she explained the circumstances to Derek and said she hoped she had not embarrassed him. He had understood her dilemma.

Derek tried hard to weave into a unity the disparate concerns and demands of an extremely busy schedule. The mission to the Church abroad was as important as care of the people at home, the unfamiliar as important as the familiar. As soon as he had time to assess the missionary situation pertaining to the archdiocese, he set out on a journey to Latin America in 1979 – the first of a series of such visits. On one such visit to South America he caught a bug which resulted in coeliac disease (an inability to digest wheat gluten) and he later became involved in protracted debates with the Vatican over whether gluten-free hosts could be used for Communion by coeliac sufferers. Despite this unfortunate incident, he generally derived enormous pleasure from the journeys and the meetings he held there and found it very stimulating to see the work of his priests at first hand among the poorest of the poor.

Returning from this first visit he set up what came to be known as the LAMP Project (Liverpool Archdiocesan Missionary Project), according to which there would be six Liverpool priests at any one time working in Latin America, under the guidance of the Boston-based Society of St James, for a period of six years. This way, those who returned could give the Church at home the benefit of their missionary experience, and new blood was fed into the work each time another priest went out. It was always emphasized that this was part of the solidarity with brothers and sisters in South America and not a patronizing imposition of the ideas of one part of the Church upon another.

Critics in Liverpool who felt they were being neglected in favour of his trips abroad came up with a parody of LAMP – SWAMP – the South West Lancashire Archdiocesan Missionary Project, with a plan for the Archbishop to spend a week in each of their parishes! Some even ventured to say that they saw less of their Archbishop than the priests did in South America.

He made a visit to South Africa in April 1989, just before apartheid and the unjust imprisonment of Nelson Mandela were brought to an end. This visit, with Bishop Sheppard and his wife Grace, the Director of CAFOD, Julian Filochowski, and the Chaplain, was a profound experience not just of the injustices of poverty but the institutionalized violence which had spread throughout that land. Julian says the bishops were welcomed not 'because they were a double act, but because of the hope and encouragement they gave to budding ecumenism'.

The two Liverpool bishops spoke eloquently at the Anglican Synod held in Cape Town shortly before leaving for home after an exhausting and harrowing eighteen days. They took the same message undiluted to the people there as they took everywhere, concerning the strength that is to be found in a united witness, built on friendship and acceptance and founded on the person of Christ, not on human expediency. This message was never an attempt to force their own views on others but just to say 'This is the way we have tried to go about it and this is our experience'. 'They had first-hand experience of going to very courageous places and wherever they went they spoke with feeling and hope in the townships, in the Eastern Cape, in Pretoria and Johannesburg', Julian Filochowski recalls. They were deeply sensitive to the different situations in which people were placed, and realistic about what could be achieved.

Many visits to Northern Ireland shared this same sensitivity and brought considerable strength to those embattled by the Troubles there. The symbolism was not lost either when David turned down an invitation from Archbishop Robin Eames to go to Northern Ireland for the anniversary of the Enniskillen bomb, on the grounds that Derek had not also been invited in an equal capacity. This took courage and its effect on Derek was very profound.

These long visits abroad and the ecumenical activities at home did nothing to diminish his continuing joint commitments to the Catholic Church in Rome. The meeting of the Synod of Bishops would not have been the same without his presence and involvement. In scenes reminiscent of the Vatican Council, if on a smaller scale, he would invariably be drawn in to help with the drafting of Synod Documents, working into the early hours with a small group of bishops and trekking back to the English College to complete the work even at that time in the morning, to meet the deadlines. He brought the same kind of commitment to his work for the Council for the Laity and the Committee for the Family, at their annual meetings in Rome. Even when a new set of names for these committees was proposed, his great friend and collaborator on the Council for the Laity, Pope John Paul II, demanded the retention of his services as a Consultor.

It seemed that Derek Worlock's priestly and episcopal ministry was inextricably bound up with the Eternal City and many wondered why he had not been called upon to head one of the Vatican Congre-gations for the Laity or Clergy. But it is understood in Rome that he had made it quite clear that he was not seeking such a post. Cormac Murphy-O'Connor recalls hearing him say ' "If the Pope personally said he wanted me to go, I would go", but otherwise he did not want to settle in Rome'. He had to undertake some very different missions to Rome, when the papal visit to Britain was in doubt, or when he led all the northern Catholic Bishops on their *ad limina* visit every five years, armed with well-prepared reports on their dioceses. One skill that eluded him all his life was a fluency in Italian and other foreign languages, though he inherited a little of his mother's facility for French. This perhaps prevented him from being drawn still further into the Vatican inner workings. He would not have welcomed so complete a detachment from the work he loved – the daily pastoral round of a bishop among his people. 'He was so thoroughly English that a bit of him would have been a fish out of water, but he would have been effective', says Cormac.

The daily round in Liverpool was a frantic one. Each Sunday if there was no civic or other occasion, he would visit the parishes of the large archdiocese. Geographically it was not as large as Portsmouth, where he had frequently a two-hour journey to make, but with 220 parishes, many convents, numerous schools, religious houses, individual homes, places of work, places where people were cared for and the local government offices and voluntary organizations, his diary was always completely full. It came as a surprise to some to find that he was most at home sitting in the middle of an infant school class talking with them about the Gospel stories. At the end of his life he was to remark that he loved children. He had caught the infectious sense of fun and simple attitude of his great mentor Cardinal Griffin in his ability to relate to the little ones.

He always thought of 1984 as an *annus mirabilis* for Liverpool. This was the year of the International Garden Festival which was held in Liverpool on former wasteland by the Mersey where a rubbish dump had previously been the only feature. Thus 1984 was for Liverpool not the dire year predicted by George Orwell, but a year of success, flowers and optimism. There were developments at this time that, though they represented a great deal of hard work behind the scenes were showcases for a more vibrant, hope-filled Liverpool. The Flower Festival, the Tall Ships Regatta and the floodlighting of public buildings, including the two Cathedrals, seemed to be rich symbols of a city on the up and up, a city with pride in itself restored once more.

Derek always attached great importance to the value of education for adults as well as for children. He had fought hard for the Northern Institute at Upholland, and had shown great skill and diplomacy in defending the choice of some of the speakers, who had attracted powerful criticism. He did not, however, foresee the furore that was to come later from concerned teachers, parents and priests over 'Weaving the Web', a national religious programme for secondary school pupils. It must have been a bitter pill for him to swallow when one of his own priests, Francis Marsden, criticized the programme after Mass on Education Sunday in 1991. Fr Marsden spoke out after, he says, two years of unsuccessful attempts at dialogue with the Archdiocesan Centre for Religious Education. The programme, he still believes, is a 'major sell-out of Catholic schools and doctrine', and was imposed without widespread consultation among the clergy. At that time he was Chaplain to a school in Huyton. Within days of his public criticism he was reprimanded for 'attacking a bishops' document' and made to promise he would not speak publicly in the future. Forbidden to speak he resorted to writing, and prepared notes for a booklet published by Parents Concern entitled *Weaving a Web of Confusion*. Together with other published material, it led to an outcry.

Francis Marsden was called to Green Lane to explain himself. He says Derek was cool but courteous and handed him four pages of critique of his text. He was told he was not to accept any engagements to speak about his book or write anything further without Derek's permission. Within a week he was also moved from the school chaplaincy. Having extolled the principles of dialogue and consultation all his life since the Council days, the whole episode made some believe that the Archbishop had suppressed 'genuine theological debate because it did not suit his vision of the Church'.

At the opposite end of the theological spectrum, Fr Kevin Kelly also at times found himself reprimanded for his liberal views. He remembers the occasion when he wrote an article for *The Times* concerning the removal of Charles Curran from the Catholic University in Washington. After the article was published, he sent a copy to the Cardinal and to Archbishop Derek. The result was a phone call saying he should not have sent the article to *The Times*.

After the *annus mirabilis* of 1984, however, a very different mood descended on the city and seemed, for a while at least, to drive away the optimism that had been growing. An event at the end of May 1985, as tragic as it was unexpected, had many serious repercussions for several cities, not least for Liverpool and its people. On Wednesday 29 May, in the Heysel Football Stadium in Brussels, violence broke out among the supporters of the rival teams, Juventus of Italy and Liverpool FC. The fighting led to a wall collapsing and an ensuing crush which caused loss of life and many injuries. Derek was driving across London when the tragedy was announced on the radio. He was horrified. His reaction was to feel that the image of Liverpool, just recovering from the effects of the 1981 Toxteth riots, was about to be besmirched yet again.

After the horror of what happened it was clear that people needed to air their grief and to turn to God for both consolation and in a spirit of repentance. To be together was what mattered; Derek sensed this. It was necessary to quickly bring the healing process before God, to take the opportunity to remind people of their need of God at such a time. A Mass was quickly arranged in the Metropolitan Cathedral, two days after the events in Brussels. To a packed and subdued congregation he said:

> It is with a whole flood of emotions that we come together this evening following the tragic and terrible events in Brussels last Wednesday. If I use the word 'flood' it is because perhaps the tears of very deep sorrow are still upon the cheeks of the people of this city. To mourn the dead is a Christian virtue; whatever else is said about us in these days, Liverpool always had a big and generous heart.

The priority had been to show a corporate act of sorrow, not an expression of guilt. The people of Turin and Brussels were remembered in prayer. The Church leaders knew that there was enough guilt, false or otherwise, overlaid on Liverpool. The questions about who was to blame and what should be the reparation could wait for the outcome of the inquiry. Healing and reconciliation were the themes that needed to be aired first. This would call for a civic gesture as well as a religious one. 'Whatever collective responsibility may be ours for the tragedy', the Archbishop declared, 'must be publicly acknowledged in due course.' There was a feeling of genuine sympathy for the members of Liverpool Football Club because they had been magnificent ambassadors for the city and for the game. Their record in Europe had been exemplary over a period of twenty years. If some fans were in any way responsible for the tragic events, they represented a rogue element, extremists who had nothing to do with the game of football. 'We must try to put an end to the hooliganism which has had such tragic results', he told a silent Cathedral congregation, 'we must stand together at this difficult time. We shall need each other if we are to give renewed meaning to our Liverpool pride.' He seemed to find the words that articulated the feelings in people's hearts at that moment.

The deeper issues that were exposed by the tragedy were given greater focus as the days went by. It was said, not for the first time, that Liverpool wore its heart on its sleeve, that it was excessively self-indulgent in grief and introspective in guilt. The world's Press homed in on the scene to exploit all the bad things that could be found to say about the city. The spotlight which was turned on Liverpool at the time cruelly exposed the many problems that did indeed exist but were not of the people's making – unemployment, poor housing and general economic depression.

When the representatives of Liverpool City Council decided to make a visit to Turin to take a word of apology to a city which had lost some of its young people, it was a natural thing for the councillors to ask the Church leaders to accompany them. For this reason the visit became a civic and a religious one, with a meeting of the officials of the two cities and a Mass in the cathedral at Turin. David Sheppard aptly described it as 'like a family visit after a bereavement'. What was said was not the important thing, it was the fact that they had gone there. David Sheppard recalls the service vividly. He says all the Militant leaders, many of whom had not been in a church for a long time, were present. Derek celebrated and he had been asked to give the address and kept thinking about this most unusual group of people. Then came the sign of peace and the Militants were 'embracing this large Italian crowd'. Derek carried with him ever afterwards a key ring with the Juventus emblem on it, a permanent reminder of the sad events of Heysel in which he had felt the sorrow personally.

Derek mused on the fact that 'both Dereks' (Worlock and Hatton) were there in Turin, present at Mass in that lofty Cathedral. Religious and political leadership had blended, controversies and differences at home suspended for a time in that joint moment of sorrow and compassion. Derek Hatton and John Hamilton, then Leader of Liverpool City Council, had led the civic reception but its true purpose and nature were greater than any political act. The unity of the city of Liverpool, as much as the solace of the people of Turin and Brussels, was focused in that memorable visit.

Derek Worlock always felt that the troubles visited on the city by the Militant spell in power were only troubles that were coming anyway and given a dramatic turn of speed and shape by the people in power in the City Council. The Archbishop's loyalty to the powers that be at Whitehall, his desire for peace, his respect for genuine local leaders and their legitimate claims for justice, made it an awkward tightrope for him to walk. David Sheppard describes a year when no Government Minister came to Liverpool. Some say there was a vacuum in the leadership of the city and that the two bishops, Derek and David, filled that gap. They certainly kept communications alive between Westminster and Liverpool by talking to both city leaders and Government Ministers. Neil Kinnock claimed, after the 1985 Labour Party Conference in Bournemouth, that it was the joint letter by the two bishops in *The Times* that fired him up to denounce Militant. Flattered though they may have been, it was not their primary intention to isolate Militant politically but to draw attention to the plight of Liverpool and to call for a corporate effort at solving it.

Derek had first called on Derek Hatton at home on a hot summer's day, to find him not in one of his immaculate suits, but sunbathing in a pair of swimming trunks in the back garden. Recalling this broke the ice whenever they met later in times that were more strained. 'Heysel', as it was simply referred to in the years that followed, became not only a word that stood for tragedy and sorrow,

221

but a symbol also of unity and co-operation between hitherto un-likely allies in the city of Liverpool.

At the next home game at Anfield the two bishops tried to call for a minute's silence before the match. It was kept, but barely. The attempt to lead the singing of 'Abide with Me' failed because of an over-zealous crowd. When there was criticism for this Derek said in defence of the fans that they had sung their anthem, 'You'll Never Walk Alone', and that was enough. The other reason was that the PA system had broken down and the bishops had only a police mega-phone to make themselves heard above the crowd.

Four years later, Anfield football ground was to be once again the scene of an outpouring of grief and a focus of unity for thousands of people. It seemed unbelievable that so soon after the Heysel Stadium tragedy, another should strike football. Although the circumstances were entirely different the shock waves were no less deeply felt. This time the scene of the disaster was nearer home, at the Hillsborough ground of Sheffield Wednesday FC. Out of a cloudless blue sky, on Saturday 15 April 1989, came a tragedy that rocked Liverpool, the country and the world. In all, ninety-six people, mostly young men and women, died as the result of overcrowding in the Leppings Lane terrace.

The whole country was plunged into shock. The Archbishop went to the Hallamshire Hospital the next morning with John Newton and Michael Henshall to visit the injured and bereaved. Bishop Sheppard was away on the island of Barra but arranged to fly back on a Sea King helicopter arranged by his chaplain. The priority, as with the Heysel disaster, was to 'be there' where the people were hurting, where the needs were most acute. Bishop David was able to return in time for the Mass in the Metropolitan Cathedral on the Sunday evening, a Mass arranged at short notice so that people could come together and grieve together.

Eye-witnesses at Hillsborough spoke of a sense of unreality, of a strange silence in the crowd in the presence of death, of numbness and shock. Many were just in a trance for days afterwards. At the Hallamshire Hospital too, it was like being in an unreal world. The horror of what had happened registered only slowly on the mind, the nature of it was unprecedented, the scale of it too much to take in. So many people in the football ground that day felt that what they were seeing before their eyes was indeed a bad dream.

The report which Lord Justice Taylor issued after the event talked of 730 people complaining of injuries sustained in the crush, broken ribs and damaged chests, fractures and bruises. Thirty-six people were injured outside the ground. Trevor Hicks, who lost two daughters in the tragedy, spoke of the way Archbishop Worlock had impressed him by his honest answer to the question that he posed. The question in his mind that dreadful day, when their deaths had been confirmed, had been: where had Sarah and Vicki gone, where were they now? Derek Worlock's answer moved him. It was neither arrogant nor insensitive. 'We do not know', he said, 'It's a mystery.' Believing in God, believing in heaven did not make the pain go away, or lessen the reality of the suffering. It did not work like that. Trevor Hicks believed that this approach helped him to cope. The Church was simply trying to be there amidst the suffering.

It was Derek Worlock's visit to the hospital in Sheffield that enabled him to get an insight into the tragedy and find the words that would help people to come to terms with it. In the car coming back he wrote his homily for the Mass which had been planned for Sunday. More than eight thousand people were at the Cathedral, inside and outside the building. Many had walked there in order to be together, to grieve together. Derek spoke, in a subdued but confident way, of the people he had seen in the hospital, the courage and dignity of the bereaved, the dedication of the nurses and doctors treating the injured fans, the solidarity that showed itself in face of common adversity. He said of those who had died, quite simply, 'they are with God'. Nothing more could be done. It was a time for trust rather than anger but the anger and the shock were real and could not be suppressed. David Sheppard recalls the many funerals that Derek went to, all of those in Catholic parishes. 'I would never have done that. I think he had a great sense of the bishop being there, and wanting to be beside people.'

An official Service of Remembrance was held in the Anglican Cathedral two weeks later. Once again, in different circumstances, Hope Street and the two Cathedrals had become powerful symbols of a unity which was too deep to be expressed in words. The moving address given by Dr John Newton spoke of the work of grieving that had to be done before the new hope could spring up again, and the anthem of Liverpool led by the Cathedral Choir and sung by all present lent an indescribable poignancy to the occasion. The message was clear, that the victims of Hillsborough, their relatives and friends did not walk alone but walked with God in some mysterious aspect of his great plan. Liverpool had said goodbye to those God had taken.

Archbishop Worlock had to say many good-byes before his own, to people who had travelled a road with him in a special way. He felt the parting of each one very keenly, as if part of himself had gone with those to whom he said farewell. November 1986 saw the loss of someone whose friendship since Westminster days had meant much to him, Maureen Joseph. Her husband Henry rang in the early hours of 24 November to tell him of her death after a long illness. When he heard the news he lay awake for a long time, his mind coursing over the many occasions shared together, at Vernon Road, on holiday in Ireland or on the continent, the many family celebrations at which he had been present and of which she had been the matriarch.

At that time the then Apostolic Pro-Nuncio Archbishop Luigi Barbarito, the Pope's representative in London, was staying at Archbishop's House during a tour he was making of the dioceses. His secretary at the time, Kieron Conry, asked in the morning if all was well, as a call had just come through for the Nuncio from Wimbledon. At breakfast it was a matter of who spoke first. The Nuncio had just lost his mother and Derek one of his dearest friends. It was a sad breakfast but they discussed the value of the gift of faith at such times.

On 28 November Derek drove down to Birmingham for Maureen's funeral. It was really like losing his mother all over again. In his funeral sermon he said of her that she 'brought the sparkling, ever-present gift of her faith to all who knew her'. He spoke of how she made her faith shine out in her home, with her family, in her love for her grandchildren, in her early working days in Birmingham as a nurse and in her faithful attendance at Mass. It was a sad but some-how strangely happy occasion in the Oratory Church in Edgbaston, where she had frequently attended Mass and where she had arranged the flowers and kept the church clean.

In 1990 the two bishops, Derek and David, produced *With Christ in the Wilderness*, a book of Lenten meditations. Pat Jones, who had helped in post-National Pastoral Congress work in 1980, came to their assistance with a section on notes and questions for discussion groups. This book was successful; many people wrote to Derek later to say they had a copy and it was their daily reading for Lent.

In 1990 he again had to say goodbye to one of his dearest friends. At the beginning of May Derek heard that Bernard Fisher had died. His passing really felt like the end of an era; with the loss of his great friend from schooldays, Derek felt part of himself had died. 'The

Fish' had been parish priest at Alresford in Hampshire for four very happy years. It had been a consolation to Derek that Bernard had come home from the States, after a ten-year voluntary exile there, and found a niche in a parish back in Hampshire, the area which had meant so much to both of them for many years. The people of Alresford had loved him and mourned his death after his all too brief time with them. Whilst in the United States, in the parish of Mount Carmel, Ridgewood, New Jersey, Bernard had suffered a severe heart attack. He had found wonderful care and support from the clergy and parishioners there during that crisis and indeed throughout his years there. Yet Derek was convinced, especially after the heart attack, that his friend should be back home as soon as possible. He had spent a week of the previous year's holiday in Ridgewood with Bernard, with the intention of persuading him to return to England.

Despite the busy schedule which he always had, especially in May, he set off to Winchester for Fr Fisher's funeral, on 9 May. The Mass, at which he preached, was at St Peter's Church, and afterwards he went to St James' Cemetery where Bernard was laid to rest – in the same cemetery in which were Derek's parents and others of his family. With Bernard's passing a life-long friendship was ended and many memories of former times shared together from college days, through ordination and then in Portsmouth and in Alresford, must have come flooding into Derek's mind.

At the funeral Mass he referred predominantly to Bernard Fisher's expert knowledge of St Thomas More, who had been his motivation and his example in everything he did, from his teenage days. He was an acknowledged authority on Thomas More, and had found many opportunities to lecture on him when in the States, as well as in England. The spirituality of More was his mainstay and he had inspired many in an understanding of the saint. Derek was able to say, in his moving tribute to his friend at the Requiem Mass, that he would now be meeting merrily in heaven the saint who had been such a inspiration to him.

May 1993 saw the sudden death of Bishop Kevin O'Connor. He had, since 1979, been a faithful and popular Auxiliary Bishop in Liverpool, and since the death of Bishop Tony Hitchen in 1988 had taken on the unlikely role of troubleshooter. Calm, level-headed and pastoral, he brought many gifts to the service of the archdiocese. Very different in background and style from Derek, he transcended any difference by his humble and gentle approach to things. He got things done, even if it took time. He was especially good with the sick, retired clergy, and those in need or trouble. Derek did not always express the appreciation he felt, and was often critical of Kevin's style, but deep down he knew he owed him a great debt, not least for the understanding he showed when Derek himself was very ill. Kevin O'Connor and Tony Hitchen were both highly regarded and had a particularly good relationship with the clergy, and their deaths were a great shock and source of sadness to everyone in the archdiocese.

At the beginning of September 1994 Derek attended the annual meeting of the National Conference of Priests (NCP). He had scarcely missed a meeting in over twenty-one years. His first experience of it had not been the happiest: he had been asked to go by Cardinal Heenan as an observer for the Bishops' Conference, but the priests had not been ready to include observers of this kind. From that early difficult experience he had, over the years, become a close friend and helper of the Conference as it developed, and his expertise and commitment were once again the things which won him a lasting respect. He had become a trusted and most highly valued link between the priests and the bishops through the NCP.

But the 1994 meeting was to be his last. He was invited to preach at Mass. The original theme allocated was that of going out to spread the Gospel throughout the world and he quipped that his present problems of mobility made the choice of theme somewhat ironic. Instead he opted to speak about his cancer and how he coped with it. His theme became an emphasis on the importance of keeping going, the old theme he had so consistently expounded all his life. He spoke of the need to *want* to continue, of *wanting* to go on. He spoke too of how letters and greetings from well-wishers had helped him on the road to recovery. He told the priests about a 'get well' letter he had received from an Ulster Protestant and another from a man in prison. He was someone doing a long sentence for selling drugs, someone he had known in Liverpool. The man had written 'I don't know if your God listens to prayers from people like me but I want you to know that if he does there's a prayer in there for you'. Of all the letters he received – over a thousand – that was the one that touched him most, all the more since it was so totally unexpected.

Some of the priests listening to this now frail, rather sad figure would have recalled the much fitter and more vibrant man of earlier years. His sense of fun came through at the end of such conferences, as he always had a party piece to offer, exercising his talent for limericks and songs based on the deliberations of the conference, or on the delegates, quite mercilessly at times. The most extraordinary party piece, for this rather shy person, was his 'submarine trick'. A chosen victim would be called out and made to lie on the floor whilst Derek would recount some maritime story. The person's jacket would be put over him as he lay there and at a suitable moment in the story the contents of a full pint of beer would be poured down the sleeve

There had been many occasions for fun in the past, times like his jubilee or birthday, or one of the many academic and civic honours heaped upon him during his time in Liverpool. He delighted in organizing parties and carefully including his relatives, friends and fellow priests not only in the celebration of Mass but in wonderful meals afterwards.

His golden jubilee as a priest, in 1994, was combined with a remarkable initiative: a year-long period of reflection, study and celebration on the theme 'In Communion with Christ'. Organized by the members of the Pastoral Formation Team in the archdiocese, it was arranged so that everyone could look at a number of themes, notably priesthood, scriptural understanding, Christian Unity, religious life and reconciliation of the alienated and the poor. The year was stretched to eighteen months, in the tradition of Holy Years. There were never any half-measures for Derek Worlock. It was as if he was reaching back right into the distance of his early ministry – the ideal of the YCW and The Grail, liturgy groups and family groups, 'The Team' and the Lay Apostolate, the great themes of the Vatican Council, the parish and deanery projects, the women's organizations, the collegiality of the Synods, The Twelve Apostles Scheme, the National Pastoral Congress, young people's needs, religious life, the training of priests, the world of work, the work for Christian Unity. In fact all the themes of his past life and long ministry came together in this final plan, this final project, a summary of all his life's projects. He knew in his heart of hearts that it was to be the finale and that is why he planned it so well.

The real significance of this, his last major diocesan initiative before illness took him permanently from the scene, lay in the fact that it did not need his immediate presence to make it happen. The structures and the spirit of lay people's participation in the life of the

Church had been established. Loath as he was to let go, the ultimate achievement was to be found in doing just that. His inability to see the project through in person, for reasons he could not have changed, meant that the work he had tried to do must now be left to others. This was true of some of the social projects for which the 'hurt city' of Liverpool cried out. It was true of the more obviously 'churchy' things as well. When, amidst scenes so like those of Stepney, the local community in Vauxhall Road, Liverpool, had demanded their right to stay as a community and rebuild their lives together, two bishops backed them in a way that will never be forgotten. It was an example of the Church taking the part of the vulnerable, as in the days of Cardinal Manning in Westminster decades earlier.

CHAPTER FOURTEEN

The Long Good-bye

So steady all weary hands and trembling limbs.

(Hebrews 12:12)

Part One

Derek Worlock's former secretary and chaplain Canon Nicholas France, in an article for the Catholic Press in February 1996, observed that at the end of his life the Archbishop 'had his bags packed and was waiting at the station, but the train did not arrive'. It was an apt description of a travelling man.

The process of saying good-bye was to be a long and difficult one, spread over a period of four years. Preaching one of his last sermons, at the Centenary Mass for Westminster Cathedral in June 1995, he spoke about Sir Harold Wilson, who had died not long before and who for many years had lived opposite the cathedral in Ambrosden Avenue. In a memorable phrase he described seeing him gazing from his window in the last years of his life, as if taking his leave in 'the long good-bye of Alzheimer's'. It was to prove something of a prophetic utterance about his own last, prolonged illness.

Parting was always a sweet sorrow for Derek Worlock, as when he had parted with his closest priest-friend Bernard Fisher, and his own parents. They were buried in St James's cemetery with Archbishop John Henry King, with the mother of Richard Challoner, and with many of the priests once connected with the history of the area from Penal times to more recent years. That little burial ground, itself a history book of recusancy, full of associations with Catholic courage and resilience, was like a microcosm of his own ministry and the Church in which he had been brought up.

Standing in St James's cemetery surrounded by his memories, he had felt the strain which the experience of loss and the pressures of office over the years had put on him. Physically it showed itself in breathlessness and weakness in the legs and a constant clearing of the throat when he was speaking. He knew that he no longer had the energy he used to have, and the powers of recovery, the ability to bounce back, had deserted him.

The experience of illness and suffering is a subjective thing. Those called on to accompany someone through such experiences will know the difficulty of trying to describe or make it intelligible to others. That Archbishop Derek Worlock's final illness became as real a part of his long ministry as any other phase in his life was due to the fact that it became a public concern; many people were called upon to accompany him through it, to share it with him in different ways, and many others supported him in the solidarity of prayer. It was not only in his health and strength that he called for collaboration but in weakness too.

In his autobiography, *Not The Whole Truth*, Cardinal Heenan began by recalling that his tribute to one of his predecessors, Cardinal Hinsley, had quite deliberately started with a description of Hinsley's final days. He explained that he chose to do so because it would tell us more about the man than we would learn from observing the baby in its cradle: 'All babies look much the same anyway, and we cannot tell from looking at them what sort of person is going to emerge in later life.' In contrast, we have chosen to trace the journey from the beginning and to consider the precious gift of suffering, which is itself a sharing in Christ's ministry, as the final demand from God – the final act that reveals the human character and determines the human vocation.

Some people decided prematurely that Archbishop Worlock's public contribution to the Church had ended by the summer of 1992; there were some important acts of Christian witness after that date. People were right, however, to identify June 1992 as a turning point, when irreversible changes in his health occurred and a slow decline set in. We choose that point in his life at which to begin an account of what might be called his final ministry, significant because it was a ministry of suffering. For some it was the beginning of a time of alienation when there appeared to be a drop in morale, when leadership was taken away and direction was lost, when 'he seemed to drag the whole archdiocese down with him into his own dying process', as one priest put it. For others the Archbishop's final years of life gave a new appreciation of his humanity and his achievements.

On Monday 29 June 1992, at one of the busiest times in the year, the summer break still some way off and the days long and demanding, signs of serious illness began to appear. He was returning from Salford to Liverpool, having taken part in a celebration of Mass for the feast of St Peter and St Paul to mark the Golden Jubilee in Salford Cathedral of Bishop Geoffrey Burke. Salford diocese, led by Bishop Patrick Kelly (later to succeed Derek Worlock as Archbishop of Liverpool), had celebrated the occasion with a wonderful Mass and a reception. It had been a fine summer evening but not over-warm, and Derek had felt quite chilly when he was leaving. He seemed relaxed and calm. Without warning, walking to his car to go home, he began to haemorrhage heavily from the nose. His handkerchief was soaked in blood. Although he was shaken and felt weak, he did not appear unduly anxious. He remained calm and arrived home about an hour later. Nose-bleeds had occurred before; they usually signalled a drop in blood pressure and did not last long.

When he arrived back in Liverpool, the doctor was not called in as the bleeding had cleared up and things seemed to be improving. The following days were busy ones with a service for the covenanting of churches at Ainsdale, a visitation of the parish of St Joan in Bootle, and the ordinations of two priests, Paul Maher and Neil Ritchie, arranged for Saturday 4 July and Saturday 11 July, in Formby and St Helens. All went ahead as planned, but the pressure of long ceremonies was getting too much. A further haemorrhage occurred after the ordination on 11 July and more followed during the night. In spite of that he set off for Swanwick in Derbyshire next day to give a public lecture on the subject of 'The Gospel as Public Truth'. The lecture was at 8 p.m. but he wanted to drive back and be in his own bed, which meant getting back at midnight. The next week continued with interviews and meetings in Liverpool but he was in poor shape. The following Friday, he was up in the night with more nose-bleeds and there seemed to be no choice but to go down to casualty at the Royal Liverpool Hospital, but although several X-rays were taken they were said to show nothing. Somehow he knew differently. His fears were mounting, but he did not at that stage believe that there was anything seriously wrong.

Shortly before this, the Pope had been admitted to the Gemelli Hospital in Rome for an operation on what the Vatican described as a benign tumour in the colon, and the Archdiocesan Press Officer, Peter Heneghan, was keeping Archbishop's House informed of the latest bulletins, which were unusually detailed and graphic for Vatican Press Office releases. Peter could tell Derek was not himself, possibly very ill, though his interest was in the Pope's condition. That night, 18 July, the Archbishop complained of feeling unwell and more inconclusive X-rays were taken at casualty in the Royal Hospital, the examination lasting to the early hours of Sunday 19 July, as the bleeding had started again. Dr Conal Gallagher was called in. Con decided that it was time for specialist advice and suggested he should see Mr Ray Donnelly, the surgeon and director at the Cardio-Thoracic Unit in Liverpool's Broadgreen Hospital. Con Gallagher called the Donnelly household after 11 o'clock on Sunday night and Mrs Donnelly answered the phone. She noted the lateness of the hour and asked if it could wait till morning. Derek said to Con 'Tell them it's the Archbishop'. She passed on the message to her husband, whose response was that he would see him first thing in the morning.

By means of a little subterfuge to avoid publicity, he entered Broadgreen Hospital next day without fuss and Ray Donnelly performed some tests. The trouble was eventually attributed to a tumour in the left lung which would require surgery. Ray Donnelly came personally, on the Monday evening, to inform him.

Had there been any previous warning? he asked. Derek explained about the breathlessness and the haemorrhages. He had never related these symptoms to the disease he was now known to be harbouring. The large tumour had not manifested itself in any other way until then. Although he had been a smoker in much earlier days, he had not smoked a cigarette for thirty years, so the cancer was not attributed to smoking in his case. The surgeon explained it was possible that 'passive smoking' might have played a part, as it had done with his other famous patient, Roy Castle, but no precise cause could be found; it could only be speculated that it involved an unspecified combination of factors.

Ray Donnelly explained that the incidence of lung cancer in the Merseyside area was higher than in any other part of the country. The Archbishop now felt he had become one of the 'statistics' – he so disliked that word but it was apt. It was scarcely any consolation to be in company with a large number of fellow victims, but, as Ray Donnelly pointed out, it gave Derek a certain sense of solidarity with fellow-sufferers and he agreed with that. He found himself cast in a role of leadership he had never envisaged and one he would rather not have had, yet in a strange and unexpected way it brought him closer to people.

As further tests were taken in the days that followed, a major operation looked more and more likely. After consultation it was agreed that he should be admitted to Liverpool's Broadgreen Hospital at the end of the following week, on 24 July, with a view to exploratory surgery. Rumours were beginning to filter through the corridors of Radio Merseyside and the *Post and Echo* building, possibly further afield too. It became a problem to ward off the attentions of the Press. Here the services of Father Paul Thomson, who at that time was Editor of the *Catholic Pictorial*, and Press Officer Peter Heneghan, proved invaluable. Peter had realized that something was seriously wrong and anticipated difficulties with over-zealous and partially informed newspaper reporters. Archbishop Worlock was always high-profile news in Liverpool and his poor health had been a source of speculation for a long time. The hint that he might be seriously or terminally ill ran like quicksilver through the Press and developed into a clamour of enquiries. The Archbishop himself wanted things kept very quiet; when the time came to issue a statement he would do so. A phrase of the doctor's about 'renal colic' had been picked up and that proved to satisfy the so-far insatiable curiosity in the media and provided an effective smokescreen for a while.

The surgeon had patiently and sensitively explained to him that if the explorations showed an advanced state of the disease he would not take any further steps but would merely make him comfortable for whatever time remained. If the left lung alone were affected, this would be removed. Meanwhile there were to be further tests, and more visits from the doctor. In fact, Con Gallagher, during the week leading up to admission into hospital, brilliantly exercised the art of providing just enough privacy and just enough company to help him through that stressful time.

No one could have remained unmoved after having received news of cancer. The Archbishop showed his usual courage and resilience but the shockwaves had hit him hard and the emotional turmoil was obvious in his face. He declared he was putting his trust in God, and in the doctors. He would await the outcome and let things take their course.

There were still things to be done. He had agreed to give an address on Tuesday 21 July at the ceremony to mark the conferment of Grace Sheppard's Honorary Degree from John Moores University. Despite the dreadful news he had been given, he was determined to go ahead without a word, so as to keep it an unspoilt day for Grace and her friends and family. The only concession he made was that he spared himself the long procession and arranged with the Vice-Chancellor, Peter Toyne, that he should make an informal entrance, after proceedings were under way, from the side door of Liverpool Cathedral where the occasion was being held. Peter Toyne kindly agreed and he walked in as unobtrusively as he could, with the aid of a walking stick.

Both Grace and David Sheppard knew that Derek had been to hospital but were unaware of the diagnosis at that stage. They sensed something of the gravity of the news when he came into the Cathedral that day; they could read him well. It was an occasion for courage on all sides and Derek gave his touching tribute of congra-tulations to Grace whilst she later spoke of her own long battle with illness and referred to the virtue of bravery, knowing, perhaps, the significance of the word that particular day.

David and Derek had met at the Metropolitan Cathedral the previous Sunday for a televised service for the Granada Telethon and he had told David about the hospital appointment. This fund-raising project was something they had been involved with for some time, helping with the distribution of grants from the fund to local charities. David was talking to Peter Heneghan in Cathedral House before the outside broadcast began. They were both avid cricket fans, often exchanging comments about recent matches, and David was in full spate reminiscing about one of his innings for Sussex, recalling the detail of every ball. Derek, seeing them there, remarked 'Good grief, are you two at it again!' and went off down the corridor leaving them lost for words. His humour and sense of timing had not abandoned him, even amidst all the anxiety he was experiencing.

Later, in the full glare of the TV cameras his pallor and strain were portrayed for all to see. The press rumours were flying more than ever. There were further enquiries that evening, the 'renal colic' line was wearing thin and the pressure to say something was growing. Further delay would only lead to more problems, and although the brave performance at the Honorary Degree ceremony had puzzled the reporters, they now assumed that there was a story in the offing.

The annual archdiocesan pilgrimage to Lourdes was soon to take place. Derek Worlock had always taken a particular pride and plea-sure each year in accompanying the hundreds of pilgrims from the Archdiocese of Liverpool. He had been to Lourdes forty-three times, but it soon became obvious that 1992 was one year in which he would not be able to attend. He believed sincerely in the possibility of cure, but he also knew that it was foolhardy to go anywhere, even there, against medical advice. So it became a difficult question as to how the news of the Archbishop's health should be broken to the archdiocese and to the press. The inner circle of clergy and friends became particularly protective, but people had to be told. Peter Heneghan put out the statement that Derek himself had prepared with Ray Donnelly, and which he insisted was not to be published until he had gone into hospital.

He feared questions at the door so it was decided to issue a statement on Friday 24 July to say: 'It is announced from Archbishop's House, Liverpool, that Archbishop Worlock this afternoon entered the Cardio-Thoracic Centre, Liverpool, for investigation of a lung condition which may require surgery.' As the Press Officer put it, when the successful operation was completed on 25 July, 'the uncertainty and drama of the previous days came to a close and the road to recovery could begin'. The press at last seemed to get the message that the Archbishop was a human being with feelings after all and needed now to be left in peace for a while. The surgeon had said that there was a fairly good chance of making a full recovery if the cancer was confined, but, he told him, the surgery would leave him weak and he would have to be prepared for the fact that he might not want to resume work again. With some surprise the Archbishop responded unequivocally and immediately 'Oh, I'll certainly want to'. That desire was everything in the process of recovery during the months which were to follow.

One of his chief concerns was that his voice would be affected by the operation and he would no longer be able to preach or speak in public. Other things he could cope with, but what if his speech was taken away? The voice was weakened by the operation, though he was greatly relieved when it returned to normal some days later, with just a little huskiness left permanently in the throat. Being unable to speak and communicate would be for him the ultimate deprivation in life. After all, his whole life had been about preaching and teaching.

By what can only be described as sheer determination, and with the help of excellent nursing care, he came back from the operation and its after-effects to resume his working life. The operation had revealed that the tumour was at the centre of the lobes of the left lung and this meant that it had been impossible to remove only part of the lung. The brighter news was that the cancer was not discern-ible elsewhere in the body. There were inevitably restrictions and difficulties in breathing. The nurse in the room providing intensive care was Sister Bernadette Doyle; 'Bernie', as she was called, was a precious life-line in his most agitated moments.

After a few difficult days and nights, beset, when sleep did come, by disturbing nightmares, he slowly began to look and feel more optimistic. The nightmares were attributed to the effects of the anaesthetic and the wrong sort of sedatives. When asked about the nightmares that so distressed him, he said that it was like going through a 'dark night of the soul'. He remarked 'Let's just say, the devil is a dirty beast', and would say no more.

The sense of relief that the operation had gone well gradually gave way to a marked impatience. He desperately wanted to be back on his feet as soon as possible, he wanted to prove his own prediction right about getting back to work again and he wanted to leave hospital for a phase of convalescence with an alacrity that surprised everyone. It could not be so rapid. What he wanted to dispel above all were the 'prophecies of doom' about his condition. It was mostly his own interpretation, not the result of anything the doctors and nurses had said. He sometimes thought of visitors as 'Job's comforters' but there was nothing but words of encouragement. Nor did he seem to derive any particular comfort from those who insisted on praying the rosary with him. Prayer did not come easily and he admitted it freely, but felt guilty about it, saying 'everyone expects more from the Archbishop'.

The expertise and kindness of the staff at the Audrey Leigh Wing of Broadgreen Hospital could not be faulted. Bernie Doyle, and a young trainee doctor, Stanos, from Greece, won his special gratitude for the expert care, attention and reassurance they gave him. He needed that, especially through the long and difficult nights. At home it was more problematical. The weeks which followed the operation put a great strain on everyone in the household. A 24-hour rota of nurses had to be organized and there were many broken nights when it seemed like everyone in the house was being called to attend him. The problem was that every three or four days there was a different night-nurse on duty, a new face and a new approach to get used to. That kind of constant change was something he found extremely difficult to adapt to. He could not bear being alone at night: even the strongest pills seemed to afford only a short period of sleep, and he was worrying about the course of treatment he still had to have as a follow-up to the operation.

In fulfilment of his own confident forecast, he succeeded in getting back to work some weeks later, but with greatly diminished energy. An intensive course of chemotherapy at home was prescribed to complete the treatment: a 'belt and braces' approach. This introduced him to a man who was to become one of his most trusted and respected friends in the last years of his life, Dr Peter Clarke. Dr Clarke, head of the Oncology Department at Clatterbridge Hospital, on the Wirral, not far from Liverpool, became much more to him than an oncologist. He visited him in hospital to explain the procedure and implications of chemotherapy. He soon found that his famous patient wanted to know everything – how would he feel, what would he be able to do during treatment, how long would it last, would he have any sickness, would he lose his remaining hair? Questioning was a vital part of trying to come to terms with the situation. Peter Clarke was experienced and recognized this. Yet Derek knew that some questions could not be answered, that there were imponderables. Dr Clarke told him he intended to do everything he could, within reason, to cure him of his cancer. This was what he wanted to hear. He knew where he stood and what the target was. From that time he put his full confidence in Peter Clarke, though he knew perfectly well that, even with belt and braces, there were no guarantees.

The long course of treatment, administered at home in his own room at Archbishop's House, consisted of five successive mornings of an intravenous drip each week for the duration of one month, followed by a break and then a repeat of the process. This was to last for four months in all. Naturally it made him weary, though he struggled to keep some sort of work-load going. A print on his bedroom wall of Christ on the Cross by Salvador Dali was an inspiration and helped to put his own suffering into perspective. Surprisingly, even in such circumstances he still managed a few hours' work each day at his desk and went out on a reduced number of engagements around the archdiocese.

The chemotherapy resulted in the loss of most of his hair, but he had no illusions about the fact that, as he said, 'There was not much there to lose anyway'. At first it had been a concern to him and he felt self-conscious about it, but in fact this aspect of the treatment, although embarrassing, became the least important.

Meanwhile, he had to take a course of expensive tablets to counter-act feelings of nausea. The tablets, which cost £10 each, helped, but his appetite played strange tricks on him and, among other things, he lost the simple enjoyment of drinking tea; his taste for certain foods was lost for a while too. As food had never really featured high on his list of priorities, and he was already restricted in what he could eat because of his coeliac condition (which made him allergic to wheat flour), the problem of eating raised few extra worries for him. It was, on the other hand, a constant problem for the nuns who looked after him. They arranged the necessary diet, and people brought in various types of food for him to try, but he had little interest in all of that. Of much greater concern to him was how he would get back into the public round of duties. In the back of his mind there was the growing recognition that he was not going to be able to resume work as before, he was going to be a changed man with a changed life-style.

Despite this he decided to make a series of visits by car to pres-byteries around the archdiocese, to the surprise of many of the priests who had surmised, wrongly, that they were unlikely to see their Archbishop again. The assumption of most people was he would not recover. At first, these visits were impromptu, like the visits he had made to churches when he first arrived in Liverpool, sixteen years before. On arriving at a presbytery he suggested that the priest come out and sit with him in the car so that they could talk. Later he began to let them know of his visits in advance. Often he found the priest was living upstairs and, as climbing stairs was out of the question, he got to know what it was like 'to sit amidst office equipment and cardboard boxes stored in downstairs waiting rooms'. Hospitality was offered but nearly always declined; he simply wanted it to be seen that he was not finished yet and that his first and last concern was for the priests.

Meanwhile the treatment was continuing. A crisis point came, half-way through the course of chemotherapy. He experienced a panic attack, one morning when he woke up, at the thought of yet another few hours tied to that drip with a needle in his arm. He felt he was already bursting with the various chemicals they were putting into him, and he just felt that he wanted to shout 'Enough is enough!' It was an understandable reaction. Peter Clarke came, talked it through and persuaded him to carry on with the treatment, pointing out that its effectiveness depended on its continuity and completion.

He became very thin, very spare and drawn in the face, but he was undaunted in his resolve to get fit again. It was an even harder road from then on, a road that would enable him to reach the milestone of his Golden Jubilee as a priest, and many other achievements as well, but at great cost.

A semblance of normality came as the months went by. The unpleasant treatment was over just before Christmas 1994, which was celebrated, if not with great alacrity at least with great relief. He always loved big Cathedral ceremonies and he put a lot of work into the Midnight Mass at the Cathedral, which was to be televised by the BBC; it would demonstrate to the millions of viewers that Archbishop Worlock was 'back on the scene' again. There would be no more chemotherapy. The Christmas holiday gave time for respite. The busy daily round was gradually resumed and his confidence grew visibly with the passing months. Although his determination was undiminished, there had to be many concessions to his weakened state. It was a source of frustration that several times during 1993 and 1994 he was forced to cancel engagements because of being unwell. The doctor had urged him to cut back and many of the normal aspects of his work were beyond him anyway. He hated cancelling things, however, because he was loathe to admit or succumb to weakness.

A lot of time in the months which followed was devoted to the writing of another joint book, with Bishop Sheppard. The book was to be his last one and the choice of title was not accidental. Both bishops agreed that it should be called *With Hope in our Hearts*. The purpose and content of the book were inspired by the developments in ecumenical partnership since 1989 and the experiences such as the Hillsborough tragedy in which he had been so closely involved. It was a sort of final testimony of their time as Church leaders in Liverpool. As time went by, he felt satisfied that he was defying the predictions and 'putting up the averages' as far as statistics for cancer in the region were concerned. At the same time he felt that he lacked the energy and perseverance needed for the book, that it was not adding significantly to the last one. But again the symbolic value of the collaborative effort and the need to exorcize certain events which had taken place made the project worthwhile. The need to write was still strong in him. It also provided an occupation he could cope with when a more active role was out of the question.

With Hope in our Hearts was published in 1994. It was rewarding to see it in print and know that he could still produce the goods, still give a tangible effect to his ministry. Though his pace of life was far slower, more cautious, the months of recovery led him into a time of resumed activity around the archdiocese, and he was already looking forward to celebrating a milestone in his career – the Golden Jubilee of his ordination to the priesthood. A guest list was beginning to form in his mind.

As so often occurs when making plans, the unexpected happens. A phone call came on the morning of 5 May 1993, from Father John McGuire, the principal Port Chaplain, to say that Bishop Kevin O'Connor had died suddenly during the night, at a conference of the Apostleship of the Sea in Fleetwood. At the funeral Derek found himself saying farewell to a man who might well have been expected to succeed him.

Afterwards he took a delayed and badly-needed week's holiday in Ireland. It had been some time in the planning and he had been wanting to go back to Kerry where he had spent memorable holidays in years gone by. The west of Ireland had been the place he often visited with Cardinal Griffin and with Archbishop John Murphy, the place where he had first met the Joseph family in the days when the Butler Arms in Waterville had been a regular venue. There he had made many friends, played tennis, gone swimming in the sea. There he had once joined in the fun at the hotel, dressing up as an old woman, with a tooth blacked out and wearing an old frock and shawl borrowed from a local woman. Everyone had enjoyed the joke of the old lady as she sat in the corner, explaining to passers-by that she couldn't get up till she got her frock back.

In Ireland too he had fond memories of ordinations and sad ones of priests' funerals. He had once accompanied one of the Portsmouth priests back to the man's home in Ireland and had been surprised when the priest suddenly stopped the car as they neared the family farm, and asked if he would like to 'meet the childer'. They went into a field and the priest began to make a series of odd whistling noises. Expecting to see the nieces and nephews running towards them in response to this, he saw instead a group of cows come over the hill. There was much to learn about Ireland.

But on this, the last trip there, he stayed in the Dunloe Castle Hotel from where he could see across, when the mist lifted, to the Dunloe Gap and the mountains. Although there had been changes and many more hotels and guest houses had been built in recent years, especially with the development of the airports at Kerry and Knock, he was able to relive some of the times which had meant so much in his earlier days. He toured the Ring, visiting Killarney, Killorglin, Tralee, Rathmore and Ballyferreter before driving up to Charleville via Limerick city. His journeys, even on holiday, always had a purpose other than relaxation. After visiting the convent at Bruff to see the Sisters who had once looked after Archbishop's House in Liverpool, he decided to visit the graves of three priests at the cemetery in Charleville.

The three Wray brothers, Joe, Dan and Jack, had been part of a large and very close Irish family. They had been special to him. Two had served as priests in the Portsmouth diocese, as part of the loan arrangement with the diocese of Cloyne, and when Joe and Dan Wray died he had gone across to Ireland to bury them. At that time they were among the first to be buried at the cemetery in Charleville. Now all those years later, the cemetery was full and he could not pinpoint the whereabouts of their graves. He spent half an hour, in pouring rain, searching until he found them; three brothers, brothers in blood and in priesthood, buried side by side. That meant a lot to him and it was as if he felt he owed a final word of gratitude to them for their help and their priestly witness.

In September he took a short holiday in Cornwall to try to pep himself up for the resumption of work in the autumn. By then no one doubted his resolve to get back into things, and his great friends Elaine and Tommy Tucker helped his recovery with some tender loving care. By the following Easter, plans for the Golden Jubilee were well in hand. There was to be a Mass in the Cathedral and a dinner in the Crypt Hall for 400 people. The number of potential guests kept increasing as he thought of people who had been part of those fifty years in some special way. By the time the dinner was booked with the caterers, there were 600 on the list. He was concerned about his health: things had not been too good and he was feeling unwell as 3 June approached. From somewhere he found the reserves of energy to do all that he had hoped, and enjoyed a magnificent celebration and reunion with many clergy, friends and colleagues not only from the archdiocese but from the other Churches too. Looking around the vast gathering in the Hall that night it was as if every aspect, every phase of his fifty years in the priesthood, sat there before him – Winchester, Westminster, Kensington, Portsmouth, Liverpool and Rome were all represented.

The idea then forming in his mind was to make a tour of all those places. He wanted to take a nostalgic trip back over the scenes of his earlier ministry and had received a number of invitations. He set off for four days of visits that took him to St Edmund's at Ware, Westminster Cathedral for Mass at the tombs of the three Cardinals he had once worked with, a brief look at the familiar and the new at St Mary and St Michael, Stepney, out to The Grail community at Pinner and a visit to Southampton and Winchester. He was back on 9 June in time to celebrate the Golden Jubilee of a senior priest in the archdiocese, in Wigan. Not surprisingly he had, however, worn himself out. In his efforts to fit everything in he had run himself into the ground. There was no strength there to shake off an attack of shingles that painfully affected his right eye, and the skin irritation was excruciating as the infection developed over the space of ten days. He consulted the surgeon, anxious about his general condition, but all seemed to be well and the treatment for shingles would just have to take its course.

Plans were under way to build a centre in Liverpool for research into the reasons for the high rate of cancer in the north-west. Derek agreed to become the Vice-President of the Lung Cancer Fund which was spearheaded by the surgeon who looked after him, Ray Donnelly. Whilst not wanting to become a kind of 'exhibit' as a cancer victim he was prepared and willing to give his name to something which was so obviously a good cause. The example of Roy Castle, whose plight as a cancer sufferer and whose bravery up till the time of his death that summer had caught the country's imagination, acted as a spur to Derek Worlock in his determination to go on.

A measure of his recovery was the fact that by the following spring he felt well enough to accept an invitation from Cardinal Hume to preach the sermon for the centenary of the foundation of the Cathedral in Westminster. He was flattered to be asked. The Cardinal knew what the Cathedral had meant to him. Three full years on from the lung operation he felt sufficiently confident to address his mind to the event and pull together the strands of all his years of priestly experience to try to do justice to the historic occasion.

Derek travelled down to London for the Mass on 29 June 1995. The sermon was widely acclaimed, even drawing the compliment from one reporter as 'being comparable with Monsignor Ronald Knox at his best', which pleased him more than anything else. He was also pleased that his friend Cormac Rigby was helping to provide the radio commentary.

Derek had laboured hard and long over the sermon, working at his standing-desk which was a more comfortable position for the painful arthritis in his neck. He researched the history of the Cathedral and drew on his own personal experience of the years in Westminster. It was a triumph, not only for the memorable phrase about Harold Wilson already quoted, but as a *tour de force* in relation to the Cathedral and the Catholic history that surrounded it. It had obviously been a thrill and an honour for him to stand in that famous pulpit before a large and appreciative congregation, but it marked the beginning of the end of his long battle for recovery from illness.

On 4 July 1995 his private worry about the return of the cancer began to be realized. He stopped in Peterborough that evening, *en route* to Walsingham for the National Pilgrimage of the Union of Catholic Mothers. For one awful moment in his hotel room he could not remember the purpose of his journey. Where was he going, what was he meant to do? It was a fleeting but frightening experience; he had always been so self-assured and confident in all his activities, and now for the first time he seemed to have lost control.

It was a hot July, and extremely busy: there were numerous long ceremonies, much travelling to do and many meetings to attend. As always, these required preparation. The pilgrimage in Walsingham went off without further problems, though he was not himself and looked pale and uneasy throughout. This was not particularly remarkable, as people had, for a long time, become used to seeing him looking frail. He carried out his part in the proceedings faithfully, taking a short-cut by car for the Holy Mile, and was utterly exhausted at the end.

A few days later, he summoned up all his strength to go to the Metropolitan Cathedral for the farewell service for Dr John Newton, who was retiring as Methodist District Chairman for Merseyside and leaving Liverpool to live in Bristol. John Newton and his wife Rachel had become trusted colleagues and dear friends, whilst John's success in forming the famous 'trio' with David Sheppard and Derek himself had been a cause of gratitude and satisfaction to Derek personally. His Christian friendship and collaboration had been a source of grace and one of special significance in Derek Worlock's life.

The people present in the Cathedral on that very warm evening saw a frail man, with the walking stick that had become his trade-mark, looking a little lost and clearly under strain. Yet he gave his heartfelt tribute to Doctor Newton, a typical few words that captured particular facets of his colleague's character. He entered fully into the service of thanksgiving for Christian ministry. He rested a little during that week and took part in several other engagements and services, including an ordination, to which he had looked forward for many years and was absolutely determined not to miss.

It was the first of two ordination ceremonies arranged for the middle of July and was to take place at Our Lady of Mount Carmel Church, in Toxteth. He considered this to have particular symbolic importance as it was to be the first ordination of a Toxteth-born man and because the area needed a boost to morale, since in the preceding weeks a vicious and hateful family feud had grown up in the area and there was much drug-related crime. For many years he had taken a special interest in Kenny Hyde, the young Toxteth man who was now to kneel before him to receive the gift of priesthood.

Kenny had trained for six years leading up to this momentous day. He no doubt hoped that the Archbishop, whose ill-health was now generally a cause of concern, would be well enough to ordain him, the more so as illness had prevented him ordaining him to the diaconate twelve months earlier. All the reasons to celebrate this occasion, whilst increasing Derek's determination, led to considerable strain. An edginess had set in and a grim determination, as if he knew he was fighting some inevitable, inexplicable calamity that lay ahead. Somehow he rose to the challenge. The occasion of the ordination was a wonderful culmination of so many hopes.

The second of the ordinations was on 16 July. There had been a further significant decline in his health and he now looked very drawn. This Mass was to be his last public engagement as Archbishop of Liverpool. The ordinand was Paul Rowan, a student at the English College in Rome and a native of Warrington. In Warrington too there had been a good deal of suffering in the aftermath of the IRA bombing and a great deal of healing had to take place. Once again it seemed that Providence was taking a hand in bringing about an opportunity for grace through the ordination of a new priest and for encouragement where there had been strife. These things were never mere coincidences to Archbishop Worlock.

Whilst celebrating that Mass he found it almost impossible to concentrate and looked weary and lost throughout the ceremony. Those nearby would have noticed this with some concern, although the precaution had been taken of having Bishop John Rawsthorne standing by. Almost every sentence in the Missal had to be pointed out to him in case he faltered or omitted words. It was horribly reminiscent of the way Cardinal Griffin had been during his illness, forty years before. Inevitably, the next day's trip to London for a meeting had to be cancelled, as by then he was in a state of total collapse.

For two weeks he lay in bed at home; the strength had gone from his legs and he had several falls attempting to get around unaided. Dr Con Gallagher discussed the possibility of hospital, but he resisted. Somehow he felt he might just shake this off in time, as he had done so often in the past. This time it was different. The illness that had gripped him was mortal. After some days of indecision, arrangements were made for him to enter the Lourdes Hospital in Mossley Hill on 31 July, when it became all too apparent that the household could no longer care for him adequately. Among the worrying symptoms he was experiencing was a loss of memory. He knew this; there were times of lucidity and times of confusion. Realizing that he was not thinking straight or talking sense was a painful experience and a frightening one. It was a sad sight to see him struggle to the waiting car that took him to the Lourdes Hospital. He would not return to his home in Green Lane again.

Part Two

You are not required to complete the task,
yet you are not free to withdraw from it either.

(*The Ethics of the Fathers*)

From 31 July 1995 there began a long and extraordinary six months in hospital. There was an immediate stream of visitors, cards and gifts of flowers from well-wishers, and a great wave of prayer throughout the archdiocese and the country, whilst those who nursed and attended to his medical needs during that time attested to the remarkable ministry he was able to exercise from his sickbed. One nurse remarked that it was a pity she had not known him in his health and strength if he could achieve so much in his weakness. In some respects the last months of his life were the most effective and influential of a distinguished career.

The weeks of illness also brought out less attractive traits in his character. Above all perhaps he displayed an increasing impatience with himself and with other people. In the overwhelming need he had to fill every day, every moment of his waking hours with some definite task and purpose, he found the limitations of his situation and the frustrations of hospital routine a terrible bind: he hated aimlessness. The insecurity that came from being left alone grew into an obsession about company, the doctors' attention and the ministrations of the staff.

To fill his day from early morning until late at night had always been his way. All his life there was a programme to follow; now it was taken away. Now that he had been divested of the cares and demands of office, his whole *raison d'être* had gone. But what he felt most keenly was the loss of freedom. It was more than the loss of freedom in itself, it was the imposition of another set of requirements inherent in the hospital timetable – the being controlled by someone else's priorities – which he resented more than any other aspect of his illness. Until then, for the most part, he had found his consolation and support in the setting of his own agenda and his considerable powers of self-determination. Now this was all gone.

He had a great sense of the futility and helplessness of being in hospital. All he wanted was to get on with the job he had been given to do and see it through to the end. Learning to let go was a painful lesson for him. Although this made him a demanding patient, even he had to admit the great forbearance of the nursing staff, who during the long busy days and the long vigils of the night cared for his every need. When the response to the call-button was not as quick as he wished, his intense frustration showed and communicated itself to those around him. From his earliest days of childhood he had craved attention in illness and had always been a poor patient.

Some of this was understandable. The outlook was bleak, his prospects of recovery were very slight and amidst all the encouraging words from the specialist and the nurses, he knew, deep down, that the strength that had gone from his legs would not return again. It was probably this realization that forced him into a state of depression for a time. In the first weeks in hospital he was in a totally demoralized state. So much so that a fortnight of his life around that time was entirely lost. He had no recollection of certain events, of things that had been said or of people who had come to see him. There was good reason to think that he was giving up his hold on life and that the former tenacious spirit had deserted him.

The heat wave, which had begun in June, continued unabated into August. He complained that the room was stifling and he felt claustrophobic. After some trial and error in search of another room, somewhere cooler and quieter was found: Room 6 on Unit 1 became his 'home' from that time on. Once there, he seemed to make up his mind that this was where he would stay. The room became his world, his kingdom to control, his prison cell. He seemed quite decided, almost resigned about it, and he knew in his heart that he was not going to go home again. Perhaps he was aware of the nature of his illness and, typically, had set his mind on how he could use the situation to the best advantage. He was quite resolved to make the most of the unpromising situation and continue his priestly ministry in another form. In the early weeks one central feature was missing – he found it almost impossible to pray and that left him feeling guilty, which added to his sense of helplessness.

Among the many visitors to the hospital were his friends David and Grace Sheppard. Their support was now more vital to him than ever before. They were truly friends in need and in their presence he could sound off some of his irritations in a way that he felt had to be disguised from others, especially his own priests. Cardinal Basil Hume and Archbishop Luigi Barbarito, the Apostolic Nuncio, were among many bishops, priests and friends who made their way to see him. No one found the visits easy. Was it a matter of saying goodbye or was that to say the wrong thing? No one knew the exact nature of his condition anyway and he did not appear to be a man about to die.

Family also played a part. There were occasional phone calls to his sister Patricia, who was not well enough to travel, and visits from his nephew John Hayward – who as a doctor saw in him the classic signs of depression – and John's wife Penny. His nephew, as well as his cousins Freddie and Anna, Michael and Ann Worlock, and Audrey Vinnicombe, tried to bolster his flagging spirits and had their own not very hopeful opinions about his state of health. They certainly felt that the depression was itself a barrier to any sort of recovery or quality of life. But any attempt to snap him out of it or talk him through it served merely to cause him to dismiss well-meant efforts as 'gloom and doom'. In the weeks and months which were to follow, some of the clergy and friends who had been so loyal and of such good service to him in Liverpool, were diligent in coming to see him to try to cheer him up: the Sampsons, the Josephs and the Winkleys, Allan and Barbara Wright, Julian Filochowski, Pat Jones,

Robina Rafferty and Anne Casey. The Winkley family travelled up from London to pray with him at his bedside. All represented different phases, different aspects of his life and his ministry over many years and they showed themselves good friends at what was his time of greatest need.

As his loss of memory and inability to talk coherently were continuing factors, it was decided to take a brain scan. This was taken at the Royal Hospital in the middle of August and revealed the presence of a solitary deposit in the middle of the brain, a secondary tumour which was quite inoperable. It meant that he had only a short time to live – perhaps a few months. On that depressing day he returned to the Lourdes Hospital dejected, but at no time did he despair. There was always hope and there was still work for him to do. He had sensed that the news was going to be bad and claimed, as he left the Royal Hospital, that the diagnosis was not a surprise to him.

As the brain scan had revealed the problem, further body scans were considered superfluous and would only have involved further stress. He was told by his oncologist, Peter Clarke, that with a course of radiotherapy which would require five visits to Clatterbridge Hospital, on the Wirral, and with regular doses of steroids, he could expect to recover some strength and perhaps get back on his feet again. The choice was given to stay at Clatterbridge for the whole course of treatment or travel the twenty miles there and back each day. He had no hesitation. To be resident at Clatterbridge would take him away from the ministrations of his own clergy. 'I've nothing against Shrewsbury', he told Peter Clarke, 'but I want to be among my own priests.' Some people might see this as a foible, but it was a matter of the insecurity he felt at that time and the need to stay in what had become familiar surroundings.

He took the more exhausting option of the daily drive to Clatterbridge. The treatment was administered quickly and efficiently and after the initial session he came out joking about the music – 'Pie Jesu' – which had been played in the treatment room. There was a sense of something being done, some purpose had been put back into his life, but whatever benefits were hoped for, he fully recognized that, barring some miracle, there would be only a temporary remission. It was sufficient incentive, however, to enable him in time to turn his thoughts to a new kind of ministry, one which was unexpectedly to benefit many people.

The promised amelioration was slow in coming, but gradually his memory improved and he could once again remember names and events, he could think and talk with greater clarity and so confidence grew again. It was an enormous consolation to a man whose life had been motivated by the need to communicate, who had always prided himself on his ability with words. Though still quite unable to walk unaided, and once more losing his hair, these things ceased to be an issue. All he wanted now was to be able to receive visitors, to carry out a ministry of healing and reconciliation with those whom he felt he had in some way affronted; he needed to be at peace with them and insisted that the names of each visitor were written down in a book.

But he was not at peace with himself. The ministry of reconciliation and affirmation to the priests who came to see him and to hospital staff alike was a continuation of the priesthood he would not relinquish. His constant refrain was 'You never stop being a priest' – he was determined to prove it. The nurses soon came to appreciate the special qualities of their unusual patient: he would talk to them about their families, their work, their worries and their hopes and astonished them by remembering all about each of them. Part of it was a desperate testing of his own powers of memory; he needed to know he could still achieve it. Everyone who got to know him at that time learnt to respect him, recognizing his vulnerability. Some came to love him too, somehow managing to ride above the irritation he caused with his constant demand for attention and the insistent pressing of the call-button day and night.

There followed a prolonged remission, which the physician assigned to care for him, Dr Brian Walker, described as 'a plateau'. Amidst all the frustrations of his confined hospital room, a time of grace and the opportunity to prepare himself for the end had been granted him. Meanwhile the procession of visitors continued to find its way to his door. People often went away with the feeling that it was they who had been ministered to by him and not the other way round.

The Rector of Liverpool Parish Church, Canon Frayling, has a memory that will remain with him all his days. He had visited the Lourdes Hospital just before departing for Normandy and promised Derek he would pray to St Thérèse for him at the convent in Lisieux. As he was leaving, he asked the Archbishop for his blessing. He received a blessing and was taken by surprise by Derek's remark to him as he went out of the door: 'When we meet again', he said 'we will be truly one.' The commitment to ecumenism, the mind of the reconciler, was still alive and well. Returning from France some days later, Nick Frayling was a little surprised to be told that the Archbishop was still alive and would see him. He took with him to the hospital a picture of St Thérèse, which from then on had pride of place in the room, although the Archbishop remarked, with the dry wit characteristic of him, 'Not a very good likeness actually, she was with me at Mass yesterday!'

Grace Sheppard recalls the difference she and David noticed after Derek's 'reconciliation week'.

> He got in touch with a number of people he had been out of sorts with, to see if he could make amends. When we came back from holiday he was a different man, softer, more relaxed and looked better. He told us the results of his attempts to get in touch with various people and for us it was a spiritual education, just to see the effect of unresolved relationships and then the difference when reconciliation takes place.

Sometimes ill at ease in female company unless he knew the person well, Derek now had to accept whatever help was needed from the nurses. Privately he would complain to others how humiliating he found this. He had been self-reliant but was now helplessly in the hands of others. The need to accept the help of others, for even the simplest tasks, spelt out for him the loss of his cherished independence. When one of the male nurses was assigned to the ward he seemed to settle better.

Each day saw a visit by the physiotherapist who tried to help him to walk. Aware of the frustration he was experiencing over this, the suggestion was made by the staff that he might take a trip out in the car. Deciding whether or not to do so was a matter of major debate but he was eventually persuaded to venture out. The process was a gradual one, at first no more than sitting outside in a wheelchair – another symbol of helplessness in his opinion. From this he progressed to walking the length of the hospital corridor and from there to a daily excursion in the car. It was as if a new-found world which he had not expected to see had opened up before him. Local places he had known well took on a new interest; he saw them in a new light, and every moment of his freedom, away from the hospital routine, was precious. Each visit began and ended with a short visit to the hospital chapel where he would pray intensely to God for strength. There were times when the simplest invocation, 'Jesus – help me', seemed to say it all. In his recently rediscovered prayer life, his motto was a saying of Clement Attlee: 'Why speak many words when one will do, why speak one word when silence is enough.' He summoned up the strength to go and say good-bye to his cathedral and to see the Stations of the Cross which he had bequeathed. The visit coincided with the Feast of Christ the King, the crowning feast of the Church's year.

As the days went by, he enjoyed anything to do with the sea and the river; watching cargo boats sailing from the Mersey estuary at Blundellsands, sitting by the harbour or marina at the Albert Dock. The dock, which had come to represent so much of the regeneration of Liverpool and hope for the future, had long been important to him. The river, which he had regarded as the life-blood for the 'hole in the heart' city, now became a sort of life-blood for him too.

There he would sit for a long time, thinking. As the excursions became more like expeditions they required more planning. A whole collection of items had to be carefully gathered together and put in the car: a scarf, gloves, hat, coat, blanket (even on warm days), a flask of coffee, biscuits, sweets, *The Times* newspaper. In addition, he decided to add purpose to his journey by beginning to read, for the first time in many years, the three volumes of the diaries he had written during the Vatican Council. Thirty years on, the names of Cardinals, the content of speeches and the events behind the scenes all began to come alive again from the pages.

Aaron Kiely, an assistant in the Archdiocesan Finance Office, offered his services as a driver. His interest in music provided a further comfort and ensured that there was always some music played in the car. It had been a source of relaxation in the past, now it added to the sense of space and freedom. Music had played an important part in his life before the pressure of work had relegated it; the enjoyment was now re-awakened. What had become lost in the busy routine of his life was now re-discovered – the quiet of the countryside, the sights and sounds of the river, the colour of the trees.

One memorable day he decided to visit Speke Hall. As he passed the entrance kiosk the attendant demanded a £1 entrance fee, which he explained was required 'unless you are a member of the National Trust'. The Archbishop, nonplussed by this, replied 'Do you know I am a Freeman of the City of Liverpool?' The attendant looked astonished and said 'In that case I'll only charge your driver'. Two minutes later the even more astonished attendant saw the car quickly disappearing again out of the gate; the Archbishop had felt unwell and had been able to do no more than make a rapid visit to the toilet and beat a hasty retreat. An expensive comfort stop.

Yet the welcome antidote which all this provided could not last much longer. The fresh air had helped but the symptoms of his illness remained. He was plagued by tummy troubles, aching legs and shoulders, sleeplessness, listlessness and anxiety. He gradually came to accept with a better grace the inevitability of being confined to bed. There was a general loss of appetite and food had to be liquidized to prevent choking. Hospital staff did everything to make him comfortable but there were times when nothing would satisfy. The wonderful nursing care became more intense as the illness took a stronger grip, and the end of the long plateau experience seemed to be approaching. In the evenings tension would mount as the time for the doctor's visit approached. The anxiety became acute and nothing would persuade him to relax until Brian Walker's footsteps were heard on the corridor and he walked into the room. The ward had an operating theatre and catered for patients requiring emergency treatment, which meant that the problems which the staff had to handle on a busy day or a traumatic night meant that sometimes he did not get the attention he craved – a cause of more frustration as his condition worsened.

Again he attempted to shake off the 'doom and gloom'. He tried hard to rediscover the purpose, the structure and spirituality of his life. He was helped in this by having Mass celebrated daily in his room, and a pattern of morning and night prayer from the Breviary. His faith had never failed and to everyone's surprise he found new reserves of energy, joking with the nurses, giving everyone nicknames such as 'Bossy Boots', 'Queen and Princess', 'The Sergeant Major', according to his approval or disapproval. The women who came in each day to clean his room were dubbed the 'Green Goddesses' because of the colour of their uniforms. No offence was intended or taken in any of this, it was seen to be his mechanism for coping with the situation, relieving tension and trying, in the days of declining life, to relate to those around him.

The stream of visitors had slowly given way to the small group of professionals. The harmless banter increased as the two great interests of his life, reading and writing, were increasingly denied to him.

His failing eyesight meant that books had to be read to him, television programmes explained. The radio became his stand-by. The spoken word was the only thing left, the last enjoyment, though concentration became difficult too. The benefits of modern technology did nothing for him now, and despite his life-long fascination with gadgets of all kinds, he had endless problems with the video recorder, the heating system in his room, even the simple act of opening the curtains.

The punctilious way in which he had approached most of his work in the past now found expression in an obsession about tablets and medication. He knew that he was having to relinquish control of this and began to be concerned that he had been given the wrong tablets or the wrong dosage. He needed to have continual bulletins on the weather or the room temperature and a hundred other things that assumed great importance in his mind.

He would wake very early in hospital, usually at about 3.00 a.m., and endure the long wait till breakfast. Night time was the most difficult of all. It was then that his fears and anxieties increased. The mornings unfolded slowly, beginning with prayers.

The days of autumn and winter drew on but there were some surprises in store. On 8 September word came through that the Pope would be making a telephone call that evening. The agony of anticipation and waiting was almost unbearable. Several times he asked that the Vatican be rung up to find out the exact time at which the call might be expected. At last it came, at 5.00 in the evening. There followed an emotional but deeply consoling conversation between two brother priests, two long-standing friends. It was a strengthening moment as the Holy Father thanked him for his perseverance, his work for the Laity Council in Rome. He assured him that he was praying for him. The call meant a great deal as it endorsed the friendship and the loyalty of all the years.

At the end of October he received an Honorary Degree from the University of Southampton. The Catholic La Sainte Union College affiliated to the university wanted to recognize his contribution and it was arranged that several friends and hospital staff should join the university and college representatives who had travelled up to Liverpool for the occasion of the presentation. It was a gratifying moment, adding to the degrees and awards he had received in recognition of his service to the Church and to the community over many years, not least in the Portsmouth diocese.

Soon afterwards there was to be another extraordinary honour bestowed on him. In early December he received a letter from the then Prime Minister, John Major, informing him that he was to be made a Companion of Honour in the 1996 New Year Honours List. It was an award of singular importance and merit which gave him a lot of pleasure since he saw it not only as a mark of personal achievement but also as a recognition of the Catholic Church's role in society. He had always struggled for equality and respect for the Catholic community. The days leading up to the announcement of the award were fraught with difficulty, however. How would he receive the honour, would he live to see it?

Christmas Day was approaching. He normally loved Christmas but this year, 1995, it was not to be an easy time for him. He felt very unwell on the morning of Christmas Day, though he ventured out for his car trip to the river and at lunch had something very vaguely resembling Christmas dinner – liquidized turkey and a small glass of white wine. The wine tasted good – it was the first wine he had tasted for over two years – but he could manage little else and was very much on edge, shaky and in low spirits all day.

He felt cheered by the arrival of David and Grace Sheppard, who were about to set off for Sussex to visit relatives for Christmas. Throughout the day a number of other friends came and went, and he made a phone call to his sister, Patricia, and brother-in-law, Paul. In the afternoon things were a little brighter and he made another phone call, this time to the Leader of the City Council, Harry Rimmer. He knew, amidst his own problems, that Harry Rimmer had had a difficult year and had been under a lot of pressure. The Labour members of the Council had just gained majority control on the Council and Derek wanted to register his approval, offer support. The affairs of the City Council had been close to his heart during the long years as Archbishop of Liverpool and were even now not forgotten.

Five days after Christmas he astounded the nurses by announcing that he would go out to St Joseph's, Upholland, taking up the invitation he had received to start off the annual CAFOD Family Fun-Run. It was not just a matter of attending a race, it was to him a symbolic gesture. He was showing his commitment to the work of CAFOD and the Church's missionary work which it represented. Even in those last weeks that were left to him he was clear about his priorities. Although he was very weak 'in wind and limb', as he put it, he gave the runners their starting orders. They did not hear him at first, and so the rasping voice tried again: 'Ready, steady, go!' The race was under way and his task was done. He then found just enough voice to record a few words on tape for local radio, expressing what the New Year Honour meant to him.

With remarkable resilience he set out for Upholland yet again, a week later. It was to be his last trip. He spoke briefly to the seminarians who had gathered for their annual reunion at the college. He seemed absolutely determined not to miss the chance, the final chance, to give a word of encouragement to those who would one day continue the sacred ministry of priesthood he himself had so faithfully exercised. Besides, he was still the Archbishop, still 'the boss' and as long as there was breath in him he would continue to be around. He knew that his resignation, proffered the previous May, had not been officially ratified, only accepted 'nunc pro tunc' – accepted now for implementation at a later date.

His mind was still planning. How could the good work of the Church be best carried on? If the Cardinal continued to lead the Church into the next millennium that would be a security and he would feel happier. He made this known to several of those who came to see him at the end. But any pretence about his own continuing role was now fast disappearing. One of those to whom he made his views known was Bishop Vincent Nichols. Vin recalls a conversation they had four or five days before Derek's death, when Derek told him about his concern that the Cardinal should stay to see in the year 2000. 'He was still thinking about the Church and was not afraid to let go, but he was saying that these are crucial years.'

His ever busy mind then turned to planning the trip to the Palace for that important award. He had decided to take two nurses with him (to look after him at night), two doctors, and his chaplain. He would accept the Cardinal's kind offer to stay at Westminster overnight, and transport by air-ambulance was discussed. He was trying desperately hard to be his old self, organizing everything to the last detail. Sadly, it was to be in vain.

At the beginning of February he was noticeably weaker, sleeping much more, and far less communicative. The cancer in the brain had obviously taken a firmer hold and in moments of semi-delirium he called the name of Peter, his brother. Perhaps he sensed he was closer now to his family, his parents, that he would soon be reunited with them and those he loved. His 'cloud of heavenly witnesses' was near.

He was conscious for a time on Sunday 4 February – his seventy-sixth birthday, and received Communion during Mass which was said in his room that day, as it had been every day. But on this occasion David and Grace Sheppard were present. He did not stir for much of the Mass but at the sign of peace he greeted his great friend David with all the energy he could muster – a moment neither David or Grace will ever forget. He lapsed again until Communion was given in the form of a tiny piece of the Host. Again he summoned up all his remaining strength to receive the Lord.

He was too weak to take more than a little water from a small syringe; the nurse administered doses of morphine during the day, cooling his face with a cold flannel whilst a vigil of prayer continued at his bedside. Those who came to his room from that time on knew that he was dying and words of prayer were the best and only form of words to be said; the Office for the Dying and the rosary were recited.

Everyone involved felt very close to him and saddened at his impending death, long expected and welcome release though it was. Somehow it was unthinkable too. Someone who had seemed so indestructible – so 'uncrushable', to use his word – was now to be taken away. In the hospital Sister Teresa came to keep vigil at his side, and Grace Sheppard also sat with him for many hours. By then he was scarcely conscious and could only receive water through a syringe.

On Wednesday 7 February at 8 o'clock in the evening, his pulse became erratic, his breathing noisy and irregular. Family and friends were informed that the end was imminent. But he settled again and appeared to rally. Prayers were being said continuously, a rosary was placed round his fingers and his hands folded. If he was aware of the support and love that surrounded him it would not have been surprising because it was real and tangible. Though unable to speak he could perhaps hear the prayers and sense the sustaining presence of so many friends around his bedside. The Sampsons were there, Aaron Kiely, Sister Rosalie and Father Gillespie from Warrington, the hospital chaplain, Father Brian Crane and the Matron, Sister Sheila, the local parish priest, Canon Peter Wilkinson. Con Gallagher and his wife arrived to say farewell to their long-standing patient and friend. It was not just in that room but in so many homes and churches everywhere that the Church was praying for him.

It was several hours later, just before dawn the next day, that he passed gently away, surrounded by the love and care he had always hoped would be there for him at the end. It was at 5.30 a.m. that this long and faithful Christian life came to an end, just as a new day was beginning. The long struggle was over, the laboured breathing, so painful to witness, was stilled. The desperation of those final hours was hushed and calmed. God had given him a time of suffering but now he had taken him peacefully to himself. At last he could rest in peace. His favourite white vestment, bearing the three rings, symbol of the Trinity and emblem of St Edmund, was put on him and a single candle was burning near his bedside. Several nurses remarked afterwards that there was a fragrance in the room which no one could explain, except as a sign of a holy death and a life acceptable to God.

The words of a hymn – his special hymn – which were to be sung at the Requiem Mass, seemed an appropriate description of his life and ministry and of the precious gift of priesthood in which he had shared: these gifts, because they were prompted by the grace of God, were 'richer than gold . . . better than splendour and wealth', and more enduring too.

One of Derek Worlock's closest friends and former Chaplain, Nick France, remarked 'The Archbishop's death was as eloquent as his life. He spoke of total dedication to the last.' A fellow bishop, Crispian Hollis, said of him 'He lived and died with a vibrant hope of salvation but in his suffering was content to wait on the Lord with persevering confidence'. These tributes captured something of the esteem Derek Worlock had rightly won among all who had known him in his days of suffering as well as in the days of his health and strength.

On the day of the funeral, Thursday 15 February – the day he had been due to go to Buckingham Palace to receive the Companion of Honour from the Queen – Cardinal Hume, in his moving panegyric, said that instead of 'waiting in the ante-chamber of the Palace to see Her Majesty he was now in the ante-chamber of heaven preparing to meet the Majesty of God face to face'. He poignantly referred to a remark made by an ordinary parishioner outside the Cathedral before the Mass: 'He loved us', she said. 'Could any priest or bishop want a better epitaph than that?' Cardinal Hume asked.

Derek chose as his final resting place St Joseph's Chapel in his beloved Cathedral. With his life-long commitment to the YCW and St Joseph the patron saint of workers, his choice was appropriate. He also wanted his burial place to be somewhere visible where people would come and pray for him, instead of in the Cathedral crypt with his predecessors, where he had feared he would be forgotten.

His choice, however, initially caused some problems, not just because the Cathedral is a listed building, but because the car park is underneath the Cathedral. The lead-lined coffin could not be sunk into the floor; the only solution was to make a permanent tomb above ground.

And how did he wish to be remembered? Nick France says he asked Derek that question on his last visit and his answer was simple: 'I would like to be remembered for the death of clericalism.'

Archbishop Derek Worlock's own words from his last will and testament say more eloquently than we can what was his own good-bye, his final reflection on his personal journey in the sight of God. They are words written before the ravages of suffering had encroached, through an anticipation of what he longed for beyond the grave, whatever sort of death was ahead of him. For that reason they belong here.

> Finally, I thank God for all his goodness to me, especially the gift of priestly orders. I ask forgiveness of all those I may have offended in my life-time. I have always endeavoured to be a true son of the Church, keeping as a touchstone loyalty to the See of Peter. Post-conciliar renewal has not always been easy, especially where personalities have been involved. But I thank God for letting me be involved in this work in this way. I beg you above all to pray that God may forgive me all my shortcomings in my heavy responsibilities which I have never sought.

This long signing-off formed a fitting prelude to the 'long good-bye' he had been obliged to say over the many difficult months of his illness and with which he had finally come face to face.

A Reflection
John Furnival

A life-time burning in every moment.

(T. S. Eliot)

As co-author of this book, I felt it important to let the text speak
for itself, and to allow readers to judge the merits of Archbishop
Worlock's life. For this reason, I felt it would be preferable to high-
light my personal involvement in his story in the form of a reflection rather than by referring to 'I' in sections of the text itself. The
process of reflecting and evaluating the nineteen years spent with
the Archbishop in Liverpool is one that will go on inside me for a
very long time. It may be that I lack the objectivity at the moment
to do more than offer this biography as part of a wider study. I hope
that others will also reflect on the Archbishop's life and the legacy
he left.

In January 1976 speculation about who would succeed to the positions of Archbishop of Westminster and of Liverpool was running
high in the press. An article in the *Daily Telegraph* on 12 January that
year lined up the candidates and described the qualities of each. The
article quoted a friend of the Bishop of Portsmouth as saying
'externally he may look cold, but those of us who really know him
would die for him'. This summed up rather well the paradox that was
Derek Worlock. He had shown that he was capable of attracting
loyalty, of inspirational leadership; at the same time he was thought
of by some as distant and reserved.

Basil Hume went south from Ampleforth to Westminster and
Derek Worlock went north from Portsmouth to Liverpool, and so
began an unexpected yet most successful partnership in the Catholic
Church in England and at the head of the Bishops' Conference: they
were two men very different in temperament and background but

with the ability of leadership and the vision to take the Church of the late 1970s forward.

On the day of his installation as Archbishop the *Liverpool Echo* had an unintentional juxtaposition of headlines on its front page. 'A city welcomes its new Archbishop' was written above his photograph, and underneath 'Remember to put your clocks forward!' It was British Summer Time, not a reflection of the new Archbishop's political views or avant-garde stance on ecclesial issues! There were certainly many who feared, or alternatively welcomed, someone whom they believed to be 'a radical'.

It was Derek Worlock's summertime too. It was the beginning of a remarkable ministry in the life of the city of Liverpool and the north-west region. If he was regarded as a radical, it represented a change which had come over him during a period of many years, from the established and cautious cleric of the pre-Vatican II era in which he had been brought up, to the zealous reformer of the post-Vatican II Church.

Lord Longford in his book *The Bishops* expressed the opinion that Derek Worlock changed more during his lifetime than any other Catholic. In some ways it is the investigation of this statement which forms the essence of this biography, the nature of his unique journey through life. It is possible to interpret the assertion in different ways – he himself changed and developed greatly, he also changed structures and changed the lives of other people.

Yet his perspective and priorities in life remained the same, strong and definite from the beginning to the end. The desire to be a priest was deflected by nothing and obstacles in his path to the priesthood only made him more resolute. But there were clearly identifiable moments of change in his life, some planned, many unplanned, which resulted in his exercising that vocation in ways different from his original vision and intention. He disliked inconsistency in himself or in other people, he could not work well out of familiar surroundings, out of the context of support and affirmation. At such times he could feel threatened and appear defensive.

After the watershed of the Second Vatican Council the changes and developments became more rapid. He became absorbed in the new ideas and the new language which emerged, he endorsed whole-heartedly the new relationships and structures which followed the Council's decrees. There was a tendency to ignore or underestimate the sense of fear and threat which others felt in the face of the post-conciliar changes, often railroading things through, anxious to get ahead and to implement all that had been put forward. Even those who embraced the same vision and shared his ideals felt that he went at it all too quickly and so tended to alienate some good people who might otherwise have become allies.

People could not fail to admire his determination and his capacity for getting things done. They recognized that he loved the Church and that his intention to serve the People of God was sincere. Christian and non-Christian groups could appreciate this. Shyness often prevented him from being the outgoing leader but there were times when he could carry people with him on the wave of his enthusiasm. More often he won their more gradual support by his hard work and commitment. It was like his endeavours on the rugby field in his student days, when he impressed more by dint of hard slog and gritty, dogged perseverance than by a natural aptitude for the sport.

A great friend of his, Bishop Alan Clark, said of him 'He was a Petrine bishop and a Pauline priest'. Whilst his absolute loyalty to the Pope was evident for all to see – even from the age of nine – he was not hesitant in speaking out for changes in the rules affecting pastoral and personal needs of individuals who were trying to be obedient but finding their spiritual and Catholic lives in disarray. People will remember how he spoke eloquently at the 1983 Synod on 'The Family' in favour of a more lenient approach to divorced and separated Catholics in second marriages deprived of Holy Communion.

Compassion played a central part in his work. It came into greater focus in the Liverpool years when the experience of strife – sectarian, political and social – tempered the steel of a more law-centred approach. The experience of tragedy and the grief of a whole community also brought from him the right words of consolation and strength at key moments. For him, endorsing the benefits of technology and scientific progress could not be allowed to override the need for a more human attitude towards people.

He once had the distinction of seeing his views publicized on the back of a matchbox when the Bryant and May factory were carrying out a promotional exercise and invited well-known personalities and community leaders to say what makes Britain Great. His choice of text was revealing: 'The prosperity of any nation depends on its family life. If the microchip is to serve commerce and industry, statistics must become human persons once again.' Although there was no direct connection, his words became prophetic when Bryant and May closed its Liverpool factory soon afterwards. He was a master of the sound-bite, able to find speedily for the purposes of the media what phrase would hold the attention and sum up the truth of a situation.

The themes of renewal and reconciliation ran like a double refrain through his ministry as priest and bishop. They became the hall-marks of his service to the community and the Church wherever he was. The experience of Vatican II re-affirmed his understanding of the continuity, the fundamental consistency of the Church's role to be Christ in the world. It demonstrated, in a way that his Church History lessons at college had not done, the connection between the Councils of the Church over the centuries, in which context Vatican II was firmly set, showing anew how the Council of Jerusalem had been essentially about better service of the people by commissioning the first deacons. It was this basic understanding that kept his vision of the nature of the Church strong and clear.

Renewal had to go hand in hand with self-analysis and even more with humility. Recognition of faults and shortcomings was necessary before a new start could be made. He liked the definition of recon-ciliation as 'making friends again after an estrangement'. This was to find expression in ways he could not have predicted, in the ecume-nical relationships and structures which grew out of the British Council of Churches, in the hurt people of the city and community of Liverpool, and among those clergy and people he wanted to serve in the archdiocese.

Each Maundy Thursday in the Cathedral he asked for forgiveness from anyone he might have offended during the year. The Chrism Mass was for him the supreme example of the Church's mission and service, the 'ministry of the towel' as he called it. The need to be reconciled and at peace with others was a major preoccupation of his life.

Some would say that it was needed! A person in that position and of that temperament, with the responsibilities he carried and the overriding ambition to succeed in his chosen aims, was bound to attract opposition and resentment. There was a certain alienation and he was aware of it but not always able to redress it. Prolonged illness took a hand in this, yet he attempted to go on being a priest in the ways he thought best and with customary tenacity to the very end. The failing which perhaps irked people most was that of a tendency to mistrust. The collaboration he called for, and the desire to have a less clerical, more laity-centred Church, did not always square with his own dominant leadership from the front. His experience and knowledge, which could open doors and pave the way, were an obvious asset, but they sometimes stifled initiative and made people feel they were superfluous, not genuinely consulted or heeded. Getting the balance of this right was something he struggled for but did not entirely achieve.

Recent developments like the Broad Based Community programme (a community self-help organization originating in the USA and now successfully established in Britain) and Credit Unions drew his interest and approval but fitted uneasily into the models of leadership and Church with which he had become accustomed throughout his life. Nevertheless, clericalism did diminish, and this could be said to be part of the legacy which he and others left to the Church. To break down barriers and build bridges, both in the Church and in society, was his goal in life.

It was in the celebration of the liturgy that many of these themes, themes emerging in a fresh way from the Vatican Council, found their unity. The Council had given new impetus to the place of Scripture and the importance of participation in the liturgy of the sacraments, especially the Eucharist. It was appropriate therefore that I first met Archbishop Worlock at a celebration of Mass.

The summer of 1976 was unusually hot. I had returned from college in Rome where it had been raining, to a heat wave in England with drought measures in full force. Making my way to St Joseph's convent in Freshfield where I had arranged to meet Derek to discuss plans for my ordination later that summer, I slipped into the back of a crowded and humid chapel. Confirmation was about to begin and those to be confirmed were young people with physical and mental disabilities. It was chaotic and noisy as everybody waited for the Mass to start. When the Archbishop's slim, slightly stooped figure entered the chapel all became quiet and still. He was wearing sunglasses and this gave him a rather sinister appearance. Two elderly priests at the side of the sanctuary, wearing cassocks and cottas, were reading their breviaries. He made his way across to ask them to stop as the Mass was about to begin.

There was an impressive inner calm about him, and the benign, rather self-conscious smile on his face, as he surveyed the congregation, could not quite disguise a trace of apprehension. The moment of silence had gone but he had their attention. The discordant hymn singing and general hubbub throughout the Mass were clearly due not to irreverence but to an attempt on the part of everyone present to join in and he seemed to sense this and help it along. From time to time, as he reached a high point in the Mass he would ask for their special attention and explain what his actions meant. Within the unusual setting there was a dignity and a poignancy about the whole celebration. Afterwards he told me that such an occasion gave one a great sense of the Kingdom. I must have looked doubtful: I wasn't sure if I wanted the Kingdom to be quite like that.

He had showered and changed after the Mass and looked refreshed, although there were signs of tiredness in his eyes which betokened a hard-working man. Before we could get down to talking about my ordination he went through a long introduction, the gist of which was that he was missing the place he had come from; 'Everything seems a far cry from Pompey' were his words. There was an energy about him and a mood of optimism. A new horizon was opening up in his life and in the archdiocese. There was a lot to be done. He was anxious to get on with things. Explaining about the two elderly priests he said, firmly, that if we get the celebration of the liturgy right, other things, relationships and structures, will fit into place – that was the lesson of the Council, he said. Here was an example of what Dr John Newton said of Derek Worlock: 'He always thought strategically as well as pastorally.'

The attempt to evaluate his life is a difficult one. He was seen by many as an enigma. Certainly there were paradoxes which make him difficult to assess. From a comfortable, very English background and a family that had traditionally espoused the Church of England, he became one of the most prominent Catholic churchmen of the twentieth century. Born of parents whose careers revolved around the politics of the Conservative Party, he became widely known for his advocacy of socialist Labour policies. A reserved and private person by nature he was eventually regarded as an outspoken contributor to Church and community affairs, making wide use of the media and the pulpit to air his views. Conservative in outlook, he nevertheless spearheaded the implementation of change in light of the Second Vatican Council. Whilst still young, he had to reconcile in his own life the politically conservative background inherited from his family with the rapid social reforms enacted in post-war Britain. The result was his own brand of cautious socialism. Though shy at social occasions, he was very confident and forthright in his public ministry. As Bishop and later Archbishop no one doubted his ability to get up and say what he felt about the Church, or present a case on behalf of the voiceless and the powerless.

Whatever is said in years to come about his contribution to the life of the Churches and to the city of Liverpool, this cannot be properly understood without reference to his great friend, Bishop David Sheppard. Bishop Sheppard pointed out the tendency Derek had, towards the end of his life, to be more sceptical, less positive about life, because of his illness. Yet he attested to the bold and assertive manner his colleague and partner adopted in younger days whenever they made a joint approach to the Government or to the local authority in the city. Together they provided a voice for the unemployed, the unjustly treated, the homeless, those in trouble of any kind.

Derek did not disguise his liking for material comforts but he also clearly had an eye on more lasting things, on the next world as well as the present one. Happy to be in the company of other priests, he had also chosen the path of a solitary hard-working individual who felt irritated if someone checked his step or interrupted his work in which he became engrossed. This tended to cramp his style. Often it was clear that he felt he was wasting precious time if he was not working at his desk or out on an engagement.

He believed firmly in collaborative ministry but found it very difficult to delegate, and often wanted people to be accountable to him, in the end, for what they were doing. This made him an efficient but exacting chairman at meetings and there were times when he found it difficult to assimilate a change of policy or accept a change of mind suggested by others. At other moments he was willing to give people their head and let them prove themselves. In my own regard this was often a difficulty for he was unwilling to let me out of his sight sometimes, yet recognized that there were other things I could do. If his plans for the day were disrupted by some unforeseen demand, he could be snappy and irritable about it. All this was partly a form of insecurity; he wanted constant affirmation for his own work and ideas, he needed to be able to call on someone at any time, for reassurance and support. Cardinal Hume has observed that there was an anomaly in such vulnerability and sensitivity being found in one so gifted, able and confident, but that this was reassuring to others. These various paradoxes will remain, but the underlying thread of his life, strengthened by prayer and fidelity to his calling from God, gave a unity which brought many of these things together.

His experience of the Vatican Council and the friendships he made in Rome and elsewhere with many of the leading figures in the Church were special features of his life. The friendship with Pope John Paul II, from the days of the Council onwards, was real. It was something he prided himself on. Those he worked with at the Council, the Council for the Laity and the Synod of Bishops, were cognizant of his special abilities as a determined taker of minutes and drafter of documents, capable of working long hours and seeing a task through. His advice and expertise were sought by many, especially those who saw the practical English approach that was so often needed in a stodgy debate. The work with Karol Wojtyła also enabled him to continue his interest in the work for the Polish community at home. The Catholic Council for Polish Welfare enjoyed his support and advice from the days when Cardinal Griffin made it one of his particular concerns.

People were mistaken in thinking that he never relaxed. His means of relaxation included reading novels and biographies, watching sport and comedy on television. In more energetic days he had loved gardening, was interested in photography and walking, and, as we have seen, had been a keen rugby player and spectator. He had even been known to go fishing. But it is true that in later years, when he allowed the cares of office and the pressure of demands to dominate, he found less pleasure in things outside his work.

The prodigious output of sermons, letters, talks and lectures, all carefully prepared and produced in type, show how a large proportion of his time was spent writing. That was the occupation in which I most readily envisage him: labouring over a text, seated at his desk, head on one side, absorbed in the task before him. Writing was his joy, but it was an increasing frustration to him that he never had time 'just to write what I really want to write'. Only on holiday did such brief opportunities come.

He retained a love of Ireland all his life, and made a visit nearly every year to Cornwall or to Hampshire. These were the places that had meant most to him through association with earlier times. The experiences of childhood or of his early priesthood could be relived there. The recollections of those who had been a force in his life, an influence in his formation, were time and time again renewed in a setting away from work and free from pressure. People mattered more than places but often the two things merged and a nostalgic turn of mind ensured that he never forgot the times, good and not so good, he had shared with friends and family.

For the first nine years of his life he lived in London, a city he always used to refer to as 'The Big Smoke', long after the dense smog and 'pea-soupers', vividly remembered from his youth, had disappeared. The first years were unsettled by many family changes and moves. There were recollections of the worst days of the Blitz, the doodle-bugs and barrage balloons, and the countless times he was called as a very young priest to attend the dying in the streets. In spite of the painful memories, London remained in his blood. It took a long time to shake off the sensation of 'returning home' each time he went back to London in later years. Once, leaving Euston station, he went off to telephone the Sisters at Archbishop's House in Liverpool to say he was on his way home but rang Westminster instead. Each time we drove into London through St John's Wood he would not fail to point out the flat in Grove End Road where he was born and the church in which he first went to Mass. London was home to him.

The short time he spent as parish priest in Stepney was memorable, his 'happiest time of all'. It did not last long enough to give him the insight into the life of people or the role of the Church there, yet the seeds of future ministry, and the priorities he wanted to follow, were rooted in that experience. It was a sort of prelude to the experience of urban ministry which was to become his special interest later, in Liverpool.

The ten years in Portsmouth, far from being 'an interlude', gave him the opportunity he needed to put into practice all the ideas of Vatican II – even if it courted unpopularity sometimes – and to take the Church, local and national, onto a different level, into a new consciousness of what it was to 'be Church'. They must have been exciting days for him in the area of his upbringing. Action for social development, the promotion of family life and the principles of ecumenism were built up and became the main aspects of his work in the years that followed. He gave himself completely to the place where he found himself at any given time, and although he thought a lot about the past, he did not let regrets obstruct him from living for the present moment.

The view has been expressed that he saw Christian Unity as a means to conformity with the Catholic Church. I think his understanding of the nature of the Church led him in two directions. He believed the Catholic Church to be the Church founded by Christ, and the Pope as the guarantee of an adherence to Truth: 'Follow Peter' was his principle. But he also saw the Catholic Church as a means to a far greater end, the promise and hope of salvation of all God's people, whose role was to aid all pilgrims on the road to the fulfilment of that promise.

Was he, in the end, a disappointed man? It is not my understanding of him. There were undoubtedly disappointments along the way. Failing to get to university, leaving Stepney and leaving Portsmouth would have been difficult times of transition, times when he might reasonably have expected his life to go another way. Not a few people in Liverpool felt he should have been made a Cardinal in recognition of his great contribution to the work of the Church. That may have been deserved but might not have added significantly to what he was trying to achieve. There were many other forms of recognition, civil and ecclesiastical, during his life-time, and no precedent, apart from Cardinal Newman, existed for having two Cardinals in England. It might have also seemed like a sort of 'consolation prize'. More important to him was that by 1996, after twenty years as Archbishop, he had made his home and found his family in the archdiocese of Liverpool, among the priests and people he loved.

On his seventy-fifth birthday, 4 February 1995, he delivered the Paul VI Memorial Lecture, sponsored by CAFOD, the Catholic Agency for Overseas Development. He had been reluctant about the choice of date, because he felt it highlighted his approaching retirement and retirement was not really in his vocabulary. But the work of CAFOD had been of special importance to him, he had been one of its founders and had always seen it as one of the ways the Church's mission to the world could be exemplified. He agreed to give the lecture, in Liverpool, in the grandiose – in some ways incongruous – setting of St George's Hall. On the night the hall was full. The address was to be something of a swan song. People recognized this and sensed the occasion was out of the ordinary. People had come in great numbers, on a cold night, to hear him perhaps for the last time. It was a *tour de force*, summarizing the long span of his ministry as a bishop.

The words of T. S. Eliot's poem *Four Quartets* with which I opened this reflection provided him with the inspiration for his text that night and seemed to contain the distilled wisdom of all the long years that had gone by. They were words which, on that significant night in Liverpool, said so much about the way he had chosen to give his life to God and to the people, because it seems to me that in him there was indeed 'a life-time burning in every moment'.

Epilogue
The Rt Rev. David Sheppard

I write nearly a year on from Derek Worlock's death; I find I'm still hurting from the loss of a friend, with whom I had worked in close partnership for almost twenty years. John Furnival and Ann Knowles have told the story of a pilgrimage: he remained a disciple all his life, learning from the faith once delivered, reflecting on events, listening to people.

I miss the phone calls, Derek ringing to discuss Liverpool's latest saga, or the press report of fresh Church developments. I feel the gap, where there were long discussions, seeking to tease out the Christian response to complex issues of the modern world, sometimes with diverging views listened to with respect.

I rejoice that we're building a new partnership with Patrick Kelly and a new generation of Church leaders, but inevitably and properly it is different. The steady rudder to Derek's pilgrimage was always the devotion and discipline of a loyal Catholic priest. Vatican II meant a deep and lasting renewal for him. From it flowed his insistence on the proper calling of lay people to be in the front line of Christian witness. There was always the heart of a pastor; his eyes would light up as he told me of a parish visit, or of going over to Ushaw to meet his seminarians, or of spending a day with a group of priests. And I would see the pain in his eyes, when he told me of a young priest who was dying, or of another who was in trouble.

I have been given hospitality quite often at Archbishop's House, Westminster, staying in what was 'Derek's room' for the years when he was secretary there. It gave me some insight into the world of the immensely competent young priest serving his archbishop; I could imagine his dealings with the national press, feeling at times the need for the Roman Catholic community to fight for a proper place in the sun.

In our many travels together he took me to his old stamping ground in Portsmouth and to the religious house in Devon where he took Cardinal Griffin when he was a sick man, caring for him as John Furnival was to care so faithfully for him. His generosity of spirit towards other Christians was based on secure conviction of his own faith as a Catholic and on the weight he gave to our common baptism.

After his death 'a senior Anglican source' was quoted as suspecting that 'at the end of the day ecumenism for Derek meant Anglicans becoming Roman Catholics'. I doubt if that Anglican source would have known his mind as closely as I did, and he got it wrong. Derek repeatedly said in meetings, as in private, that ecumenism was not about 'an ecclesiastical take-over'; the goal, he would say, was 'not uniformity, but legitimate diversity'.

The last of our three joint books was *With Hope in our Hearts*. We described the appointment of a Free Church Moderator for Merseyside, making up the Liverpool Three rather than the Two; we went on, 'In one sense that has been the most significant development of all'. Friends sometimes thought they could do some source criticism of our joint writings, and decide who was the author of particular sentences: Derek took a mischievous pleasure in proving them wrong. Those words about the significance for Christian Unity of the Free Church presence in Merseyside were written by Derek Worlock.

In my folder, where I have kept cuttings following Derek's death, there is one from *The Big Issue*, the paper sold by unemployed people on the streets. It's not many Church leaders who receive a tribute in *The Big Issue*. Derek cared very particularly for those who suffered exclusion from good housing, jobs, schools or health care. If we were accused of playing politics, he would often respond that love of neighbour insisted that he should not turn his back on those who experienced these human needs.

He loved Liverpool, wanted the well-being of the whole community, rejoiced to see its sectarian divisions breaking down. He worked also to help break down other divisions such as were caused by racial prejudice or economic exclusion. It was a regular commitment for both of us to meet with senior managers in private and public sector, to think about the regeneration of Merseyside.

He carried a prodigious work-load; though he would grumble at this, he loved it. He could not bear the thought of retirement.

Beneath the public face of this immensely skilled and devoted bishop, lay a sensitive and vulnerable person. It was a privilege for Grace and me to have known him closely; through moments in Liverpool when the heat in the kitchen was quite intense, on shared pilgrimages with young people, working through differences to an agreed statement, walking beside him through the valley of the shadow of death, I rejoice that we were 'pilgrims together on the way to God's Kingdom'.

Bibliography

Walter M. Abbott SJ (ed.), *The Documents of Vatican II* (Geoffrey Chapman, 1966).

Bishop's Brew: An Anthology of Clerical Humour (Churchman Publishing, 1989).

R. A. Butler, *The Art of the Possible: Memoirs of Lord Butler* (Hamish Hamilton, 1971).

John Campbell, *Nye Bevan* (Hodder & Stoughton, 1987).

Maurice Cowling, *Religion and Public Doctrine in Modern England* (Cambridge University Press, 1985).

Michael de la Bedoyère, *Bernard Griffin* (1955).

Michael Hare Duke, *Praying for Peace* (Collins, 1991).

Daphne Du Maurier, *Frenchman's Creek* (Victor Gollancz, 1942).

Gerard Dwyer, *Diocese of Portsmouth: Past and Present* (Portsmouth Centenary Committee, 1981).

The Ethics of the Fathers (Mesorah Publications, 1994).

Monica Furlong, *Story of a Soul: Thérèse of Lisieux* (Virago, 1987).

W. T. Gribben, *St Edmund's College Bicentenary Book (1793–1993)* (The Old Hall Press, 1993).

Bernard Griffin, *Seek Ye First* (Sheed and Ward, 1949).

Ian Hargraves, *The Liverpool Connection* (Countrywise Ltd, 1992).

Adrian Hastings, *A History of English Christianity, 1920–1985* (Collins, 1986).

Adrian Hastings (ed.), *Modern Catholicism: Vatican II and After* (SPCK, 1991).

J. A. Hilton, *Catholic Lancashire* (Phillimore, 1994).

Bede Jarrett OP, *A History of Europe* (Sheed and Ward, 1929).

Lord Longford, *Diary of a Year* (Weidenfeld and Nicolson, 1982).

Lord Longford, *The Bishops* (Sidgwick and Jackson, 1986).

Robert O'Neil MHM, *Cardinal Vaughan* (Burns and Oates, 1995).

Matthew Paris, *The Life of Saint Edmund*, trans. H. Lawrence (Alan Sutton Publishing, 1996).

George Scott, *The RCs* (1967).

Alberic Stacpoole OSB (ed.), *Vatican Two by Those Who Were There* (Geoffrey Chapman, 1986).

Gordon Wheeler, *In Truth and Love* (Gowland and Co., 1990).

Derek Worlock, *Take One at Bedtime: An Anthology* (Sheed and Ward, 1962).

Derek Worlock (ed.), *English Bishops at the Council* (Burns and Oates, 1965).

Derek Worlock, *Turn and Turn Again: An Anthology* (Sheed and Ward, 1971).

Derek Worlock, *Parish Councils: In or Out?* (Catholic Truth Society, 1974).

Derek Worlock, *Give Me Your Hand* (St Paul Publications, 1977).

Derek Worlock, *Bread Upon the Waters* (St Paul Publications, 1991).

Derek Worlock and David Sheppard, *Better Together* (Hodder & Stoughton, 1988).

Derek Worlock and David Sheppard, *With Christ in the Wilderness* (Bible Reading Fellowship, 1990).

Derek Worlock and David Sheppard, *With Hope in our Hearts* (Hodder & Stoughton, 1994).